Developing Good Practice
in Children's Services

of related interest

Developing Good Practice in Community Care
Partnership and Participation
Edited by Vicky White and John Harris
ISBN 1 85302 890 8

Social Work with Children and Families
Getting into Practice
Second Edition
Ian Butler and Gwenda Roberts
ISBN 1 85302 365 5

Child Protection Work
Beyond the Rhetoric
Helen Buckley
ISBN 1 84310 075 4

Assessing Children's Needs
The Impact of the Assessment Framework
Hedy Cleaver and Steve Walker
with Pamela Meadows
ISBN 1 84310 159

Supporting Parents
Messages from Research
David Quinton
ISBN 1 84310 210 2

The Child's World
Assessing Children in Need
Edited by Jan Horwath
ISBN 1 85302 957 2

Approaches to Needs Assessment in Children's Services
Edited by Harriet Ward and Wendy Rose
ISBN 1 85302 780 4

Developing Good Practice in Children's Services

Edited by Vicky White and John Harris

Jessica Kingsley Publishers
London and Philadelphia

First published in 2004
by Jessica Kingsley Publishers
116 Pentonville Road
London N1 9JB, UK
and
400 Market Street, Suite 400
Philadelphia, PA 19106, USA

www.jkp.com

Copyright © Jessica Kingsley Publishers 2004

Library of Congress Cataloging in Publication Data
Developing good practice in children's services / [edited by] Vicky White and John Harris.
p. cm.
Includes bibliographical references and index.
ISBN 1-84310-150-5 (pbk.)
1. Children—Services for—Great Britain. 2. Child welfare—Great Britain. 3. Social work with children—Great Britain. I. White, Vicky, 1959- II. Harris, John, 1952-
HV751.A6D48 2004
362.7'068—dc22

2004007503

British Library Cataloguing in Publication Data
A CIP catalogue record for this book is available from the British Library

ISBN 1 84310 150 5

Printed and Bound in Great Britain by
Athenaeum Press, Gateshead, Tyne and Wear

Contents

Chapter One

Changing Children's Services

Vicky White and John Harris

Introduction

There is a painting by Turner (*Snowstorm – Steamboat off a Harbour's Mouth* [1842]) that depicts a paddle steamer in the middle of a storm. Nothing can be seen completely clearly because the sky, the sea and the smoke from the boat's funnel all swirl into a sensation of movement. Social workers and managers in children's services have lived through an era of change that has sometimes felt like the swirling storm in Turner's painting. Report after report has scrutinised their performance and exhorted them to greater efforts in rising to new challenges. Criticisms, not least as a result of periodic press onslaughts, have added to the potential for uncertainty and insecurity. This book arises out of their experiences of steering courses through these choppy seas.

It is concerned with 'changing children's services' in three senses. First, 'changing children's services' is simply a statement of fact. Children's services have been, and are, changing rapidly. All of the contributors to the book have been caught up in the impact of the changes taking place. Second, 'changing children's services' is not only a statement of fact, but also has become an increasingly urgent imperative for social workers and managers who have been handed the responsibility of seeing through a complex change agenda emerging from the wider social and political context within which they work (see, for example, Department of Health 1998a, 1998b). Third, 'changing children's services' suggests that children's services can be changed at the initiative of social workers and managers themselves.

This opening chapter sets in context the experience and discussion of changing children's services (in all three senses) in the following chapters. It begins by considering the place of children's services in mediating between the state and the family. It moves on to consider the increasing emphasis on the rights of children and parents, before identifying a shift in the direction of policy. It concludes by identifying some of the responses that social workers and managers might make to these developments.

The state and the family

The origins of children's services were swathed in the political and professional consensus that welcomed the Children Act (1948) as a radical break with the punitive traditions of the Poor Law (Jones 2002, p.103), as a component in the construction of the post-war welfare state and as a tangible demonstration of the value the state attached to children, following the privations they had suffered during the Second World War (Holman 1996). This wave of optimism and goodwill extended to the location of children's services within the social services departments established by the Local Authority Social Services Act (1970), in the wake of the Seebohm Report (1968).[1] In these newly established departments, the emphasis was on family-oriented approaches, which were generously funded. (For example, there was a 63.4% increase in funding between 1970/1 and 1974/5 [Ferlie and Judge 1981, cited in Parton 1999, p.13].) However, this 'golden age' was short-lived. By the mid-1970s, children's services had already become a contested arena, in which politics, policy and practice were intertwined. The conventional marker used to indicate the shift into this less comfortable positioning of children's services is the report into the death of Maria Colwell (Department of Health and Social Security 1974). The report ushered in an era characterised by a succession of inquiries into cases of child abuse (Department of Health 1991a), which made headline news (Aldridge 1994) and which became the rallying ground for those wishing to engage in wider criticisms of services to children and their families and of social work more generally.

The era of child abuse inquiries resulted in a significant swing on what is often referred to as the 'damned if they do/damned if they don't' pendulum. On this pendulum, the social workers in children's services have been depicted variously as fools and wimps/villains and bullies (Franklin and Parton 1991). The inquiry reports categorised them largely as misguided versions of the former, criticised them for not intervening assertively enough in households and argued that children were being seriously or fatally abused as a consequence (Corby, Doig and Roberts 1998; Department of Health 1991a). Demands for more assertive intervention on the part of social workers accorded with the then Thatcherite emphasis on the need to remoralise recalcitrant 'underclass' families, as part of the reconfiguration of the welfare state (Deakin 1994). The pendulum swung dramatically in the other direction as a result of the events in Cleveland in the late 1980s, when large numbers of children were removed from their families on suspicion that they had been sexually abused. Despite occasional dissenting voices (see, for example, Campbell 1988), the emphasis shifted, with social workers depicted as lacking sensitivity, being over-zealous and too interventionist in their approaches to families (Department of Health 1988b). In other words, by the late 1980s, children's services were oscillating between imperatives to intervene more and to intervene less in families:

> Concerns about *both* the child care agents of the state doing too much, too coercively, *and* about them doing too little, too ineffectually, resulted in a wish for legislation and policy to attempt to proceed in two directions at once – both towards better protection of the child and better protection of the parent. (Fox Harding 1991, p.230, original emphasis)

Fox Harding refers to the attempt to reconcile these imperatives through the adoption of a 'bi-directional policy', made manifest in the Children Act (1989).[2] She argues that this bi-directional policy can be represented in terms of conflict or balance. On the one hand, the imperatives can be seen as in conflict and as being incapable of simultaneous resolution. From this perspective, if social workers are given more power in relation to children, parents lose some of their power and the Children Act (1989) side-stepped the dilemmas involved by denying that this conflict exists. The other perspective sees the Children Act (1989) as a balancing act, with conflicting objectives but seeking 'a genuinely more effective balance correcting tendencies both to over- and under-react, while helping parents and children as a unit where it is appropriate to do so' (Fox Harding 1991, p.231). There is general agreement that these imperatives pose a continuing dilemma, regardless of the perspective taken towards the Children Act (1989):

> the challenge of respecting parental rights whilst safeguarding the best interests of children is not new, since these were the twin concerns of previous child care legislation, but the 1989 Act gives added emphasis to both, thus sharpening the dilemma. (Packman and Hall 1998, p.262)

At the heart of the dilemma, at a macro level, is the relationship between the state and the family (Corby 2002), given that the family is a site for state intervention (Donzelot 1979). This relationship is complex and, at the micro level of everyday practice in children's services, it results in tensions and contradictions. In the years following the implementation of the Children Act (1989), social workers and managers have doubtless sometimes regarded themselves as having been left to handle an unresolved conflict and sometimes thought that the Act did achieve a successful balance between the powers that they needed to intervene on behalf of children and the rights that parents (and children themselves) ought to be able to exercise.

The shift towards rights

Rights – of parents and children – have grown in prominence (Space and Polity 2003; White and Harris 1999). Following the passing of the Children Act (1989), international influences have been increasingly significant in reinforcing a domestic agenda that promotes the rights of children. The landmark development in this respect was the United Nations Convention on the Rights of the Child (1989). Article 12 of the Convention states:

1. States Parties shall assure to the child who is capable of forming his or her own views the right to express those views freely in all matters affecting the child, the views of the child being given due weight in accordance with the age and maturity of the child.

2. For this purpose, the child shall in particular be provided the opportunity to be heard in any judicial and administrative proceedings affecting the child, either directly, or through a representative or an appropriate body, in a manner consistent with the procedural rules of national law.

(United Nations 1989)

The Children Act (1989) was consistent with Article 12 of the UN Convention in instituting a statutory requirement to ascertain the wishes and feelings of children and to take them into account when making decisions. The Act was seen as a positive achievement by the United Nations Committee on the Rights of the Child, when it reported on the actions of the UK government in relation to the Convention (United Nations 1995, cited in Sinclair 1996, p.93). Referring to the international standards laid down in the Convention has been seen as one of the ways in which advocates of children's rights can keep the issue on the domestic political agenda (McKechnie 2002, p.43). However, delivering children's rights in practice is far from straightforward (Morris 2000). For example, Harding points to a tension between protectionist and liberationist understandings of children's rights (Harding 1999). A protectionist perspective regards children as dependent and in need of special treatment, with adults as protectors of their rights. In contrast, a liberationist perspective holds that children are competent and emphasises the need to empower them in their own right, freeing them from what are seen as arbitrary age-based restrictions. Harding's summary of the standing of these two perspectives implies that, once again, practitioners and managers are left with tensions and dilemmas:

> Current debates seem to revolve around the claims and competence of children and their similarity to adults, the meaning of a rights-based discourse in relation to children, and whether differential treatment is equivalent to unjust discrimination. The coming to prominence of rights-based discourses in relation to children should be noted, with the attenuation of some

adult-child distinctions (a trend which is not necessarily in children's interests). Alongside all this, older protectionist discourses continue, and in addition there is a degree of hostile or negative 'adultisation' of children. (Harding 1999, p.75)

In an attempt to cut through the tensions and dilemmas raised by espousing children's rights, Sinclair argues that:

> it is very important to distinguish between consulting with children and abdicating to them the sole right (and with it, the responsibility) to make decisions … Giving children and young people the right to express an opinion and to have their views taken into account is not the same as giving them the final say when important decisions are made, especially when those decisions affect others. Judgements will still need to be reached but these should be based upon an accurate reflection of the child's wishes and feelings about the matter. (1996, p.92)

This statement of the position probably encapsulates the mainstream approach to children's rights in social services, but still leaves a great deal of discretion that has to be negotiated in day-to-day practice with regard to what, for example, having 'the right to have their views taken into account' actually means in particular sets of circumstances. After considering ways of communicating with children, Thomas provides five key points for practice in involving them in decision-making:

- Accept that all children have the right to be included.

- Look actively for children's competence.

- Use methods of communication that children find helpful or enjoyable.

- Give children time to express their views in their own way.

- Treat children and their views with respect.

(Adapted from Thomas 2001)

Whilst the later chapters in the book have no ready-made answers to the tensions and dilemmas raised by promoting children's rights, Tuck (see Chapter Three), for example, identifies the need to explore the value and effectiveness of his model of risk assessment with children and Seal (see Chapter Seven) takes the applicability of the United Nations Convention on the Rights of the Child (1989) to preventive education in the UK as her starting point. Evidence from other parts of the world is reviewed and the key messages from research into preventive education are distilled as a precursor to analysing the experience of a preventive education project in which she is involved.

In parallel with the increasing concern about children's rights, the rights of parents have figured prominently. As we saw earlier, parents' rights were one of the main drivers in debates about the extent to which children's services should intervene in families and, hard on the heels of the Cleveland Inquiry (Department of Health 1988b), the Children Act (1989) and the associated child protection guidelines (Department of Health 1991b) addressed the rights of parents (Hill and Aldgate 1996, p.4), particularly in relation to their being properly informed of action to be taken, being more fully involved in decision-making processes and being able to make legal challenges against key decisions (Corby 2002, p.142). The emphasis was on partnership with parents, as much as it was on their rights, and the White Paper that led up to the Children Act (1989) prefigured much of what was to follow (Department of Health and Social Security 1987). The Department of Health later tied working in partnership with parents together with their rights as the route towards a more effective service that promoted children's welfare. Families were seen as having strengths, as well as difficulties. Members of families were represented as having rights as citizens both to hear what was said about them and to be able to have their own say when decisions were being made. If these aspirations for partnership could be realised, parents were regarded as likely to function more competently (Department of Health and Social Services Inspectorate 1995). However, these laudable aspirations have to be striven for by hard-pressed managers and practitioners in their day-to-day work. Again, whilst the book has no instant solutions to the issues raised by seeking to work in partnership with parents, Tuck (see Chapter Three), for example, indicates the importance of parents' evaluation of his model of risk assessment.

Changing the direction of policy

With greater recognition of the rights of children and parents, the dominant policy and practice direction came under increasing scrutiny (Aldgate 2002). Under the pressure exerted by streams of circulars of guidance from central government to social services departments (Hallett 1995), produced in response to the concerns raised by the child abuse inquiries, there had been a trend towards children's services focusing heavily on allegations of abuse, under Section 47 of the Children Act (1989), and towards detection and procedural monitoring. This focus on whether children were at risk of significant harm (Hardiker 1996) led to support for families of children in need, under Section 17, tending to recede from view (Aldgate and Tunstill 1995; Baldwin and Spencer 1993; Department of Health 1995), especially as social services departments were able to restrict services for 'children in need' to the most vulnerable and to define what 'in need' meant according to local circumstances. On the basis of their review of the research evidence, Hill and Aldgate concluded that access to services had become more confined to those families where a child was thought to be at risk:

> This is a crude method of targeting, given the inherent difficulties of discriminating between those who are at risk and those who are not. It excludes many other needs of children and their families. Narrow interpretations of the category 'in need' and resource constraints have evidently contributed to this more restricted access to family support than was hoped for by many who influenced the formulation of the Children Act. (1996, p.18)

Packman and Hall's detailed study of children's services in two social services departments confirmed that support was concentrated on child protection cases but questioned whether this meant that others in need of assistance were being excluded:

> an alternative conclusion might also be reached: since protection concerns were voiced about so many children in the cohort, had notions of risk come to dominate the professional discourse and were these concerns being exaggerated in order to gain access to scarce resources? If so, perhaps child protection cases were not being overlooked in the provision of support services, nor were they receiving the lion's share; rather it may be that risk arising from need was being emphasised, when need on its own might not have been enough to qualify for help. (Packman and Hall 1998, p.258)

The Audit Commission had already questioned the effect of this trend in undermining the intentions of the Children Act (Audit Commission 1994) and central government sought a shift towards emphasising the needs of children, with support to families seen as having a crucial role to play in addressing those needs (see, for example, Department of Health 2000a, 2000b, 2000c).

Johnson and Sawbridge (see Chapter Nine) highlight the issues underpinning this change in policy direction. They begin with family placement services as the starting point for exploring the use of a commissioning strategy for 'looked after' children. However, the initial focus on family placement is questioned as their research reveals the need for a broader approach to planning, commissioning and delivering services for all children in need, not just those who are looked after. During the course of their research, it became clear that efforts could not be limited to improving services for 'looked after' children. To have the greatest impact on children's lives, a range of services is seen as necessary in order to support children in need before they enter public care and, they argue, that means moving away from the current position of directing resources at the highest level of need, without paying attention to the potential benefits of early intervention. The introduction of *Quality Protects* (Department of Health 1998a) sought to incorporate this emphasis in a wide-ranging initiative, whilst the *Framework for the Assessment of Children in Need and their Families* (Department of Health, Department for Education and

Employment and Home Office 2000) was intended to address the issue specifically through the use of a standardised assessment tool in initially assessing all children in need, under Section 17 of the Children Act (1989). In Chapter Four, Quiggin considers some of the benefits and constraints involved in using the framework and identifies the need to mesh elements of its approach with the strengths evident in previous social work perspectives.

Making responses

Children's services have had to respond to the issues we have identified (i.e. mediating the relationship between the state and families, enhancing the rights of children and parents, re-focusing services on the needs of children and identifying the support required by families if they are to meet those needs) in the context of wide-scale changes in organisational structures and cultures. The Children Act (1989) was part of a broader reconfiguration of social services, which was, in turn, a component in the wholesale Thatcherite reshaping of the welfare state, using the twin forces of marketisation and managerialism (Harris 2003, chs.3 and 4). The Act, as we have seen, was not an unambiguous product of Thatcherism, given its emphasis on rights and partnership, and key aspects of its formulation and implementation set it apart from dominant trends in social services in that era, particularly the degree of responsiveness to professional agendas (Hallett 1991). Nevertheless, it was implemented against the backcloth of root-and-branch changes in the *modus operandi* of social services departments and children's services were deeply affected by them. The election of New Labour, from 1997 onwards, brought no respite in the pace of organisational and cultural change. If anything it intensified the stress on audit, standards, performance management, regulation and inspection (Harris 2003, ch.5). Stevenson concludes:

> paraphernalia such as proliferation of forms and 'paperwork' [have become dominant]. As anxiety has mounted (especially in the child protection sphere), as rationing of resources (with consequent 'prioritisation') has become sharper, as the influence of managerialism from the world of industry penetrated local government, so the opportunities for creative justice, for flexible, creative response within local government to unique individuals in difficulty, have diminished. (1999, p.91)

Although Stevenson may be right that these opportunities have diminished, they have not disappeared. Set against the pressures that she identifies are countervailing tendencies which open up possibilities. We consider four of these tendencies.

First, there has been the re-emergence of what we might broadly describe as a community development agenda. In the late 1960s, there was an interest in the way that community development might contribute to making the state work better and this was reflected in its official recognition as part of social work in the Seebohm Report (1968) (Tucker 2001, p.112). Stevenson notes that, subsequently, the increased emphasis on legal responsibilities in children's services made informal, voluntary relationships with the community seem unrealistic (Stevenson 1999, p.88). However, the shifts in policy from the late 1990s onwards have brought such relationships within reach again. The Social Exclusion Unit's brief, for example, has been to promote an understanding of the key characteristics of social exclusion, to generate solutions, encourage cooperation, disseminate best practice and make recommendations for practical interventions to overcome the bureaucratic constraints and limited horizons of departments by promoting 'joined-up' solutions.

In Chapter Six, Hill shows how this agenda can be used. He outlines the origins of multi-agency children's services development groups, placing this in the context of the re-emergence of community development. He considers how initiatives can be linked to this resurgence in community development and how collaboration initiatives can widen the service provision available. (The example provided by Seal in Chapter Seven, of a project concerned with children's safety, sprang from the developments Hill discusses.) Hill's approach illustrates how community development can be a strategy for working towards empowering local communities through analysis of local needs, local resource development and an increased level of partnership between local communities and the statutory and voluntary sectors (Tucker 2001, pp. 112–14).

At a more strategic level, Lord (see Chapter Two) reflects similar concerns (see also Department of Health and Department for Education and Employment 1996, p.3). He argues for the importance of strategic planning, particularly in relation to the government's modernisation agenda. He identifies key themes from that agenda and explores them in relation to Warwickshire Social Services Department's organisational structure and culture. The work he describes is indicative of the importance of social workers and managers engaging with the change agenda they face, reflectively and proactively, taking part in the construction of that agenda, rather than being simply passive recipients of its outcomes.

Second, sexual abuse has received increasing recognition (Corby 2002, pp.141–2), which has included the role of children as abusers (Erooga and Masson 1999). Developments in this area of work have opened up the possibility of challenging conventional gender relations and the marginalisation of other sexualities, which have dominated approaches to sex education (Haydon and Scraton 2002). In approaching sexually inappropriate behaviour amongst young people, Durham (see Chapter Five) rejects mainstream conventional assumptions about sexuality as his starting point and indicates, *inter alia*, how the preparation of young men for sexual relationships, called for by Corby (2002, p.149), might be approached. He discusses the practice framework used by the Sexualised Inappropriate Behaviours Service (SIBS), a county-wide resource in Warwickshire, that provides direct services, resources, research, consultation and training for therapeutic work with children and young people who have sexual behaviour difficulties, or who have difficulties arising from the sexual behaviour of others. This practice framework is concerned with meeting the therapeutic needs of children and young people, highlighting the importance of the social context of their experiences as central to an understanding of how and why particular behaviours take place. The chapter provides an outline of a therapeutic schedule used by SIBS and considers the application of the SIBS practice framework to the process of engagement and to the provision of sex and sexuality education, looking at issues of masculinity and peer pressure. The chapter concludes by using the framework to draw together a matrix of the potential influences on a young person's inappropriate sexual behaviours.

Third, there has been increasing awareness of child poverty and the impact of social divisions and diversity on children's lives (Jones 2002; Jones and Novak 1999; Novak 2002). For example, the links between social and economic deprivation and children being accommodated in social services care have long been established (Bebbington and Miles 1989), as has the disproportionate number of Black children in that situation (Barn 1993). In 1999, central government committed itself to the abolition of child poverty within 20 years (Department of Health 1999a; Fimister 2001). There is potential in this recognition of children's lives in the round to move beyond the individual pathology approach that has dominated the field of child protection and focused practice on the investigation of incidents and events, with case conferences for the most part homing in on the specifics of abusive occurrences (Department of Health 1995) and little attention paid to wider factors (Corby 2002, p.147) involved in the causation of abuse or the responses made to it. This approach has been regarded as 'inadequate for purposes of assessment and consequently for planning and intervention' (Stevenson 1999, p.89). Tuck (see Chapter Three) is keen to open up wider factors through use of a model for risk assessment and analysis that he devised and introduced in Warwickshire. He discusses the historical, legal and procedural context within which this initiative was developed and how it links with the wider child protection system. He suggests why this model is effective in assessing risk and identifies the professional skills necessary for sound practice in risk assessment that is thoughtful, systematic and holistic.

Similarly holistic concerns underpin the account by de Waal and Shergill (see Chapter Eight) of a project geared to ensuring that children from minority ethnic backgrounds have their cultural needs assessed, met and monitored by social services. At the core of the project is the drive to make a difference to the lives of children from minority ethnic backgrounds; to improve their life chances; to help them combat racism; to help them make and maintain links with their communities; to help them to enjoy and be proud of their heritage;

and to give them the skills, the information and the confidence to celebrate difference and diversity.

Fourth, there has been growing recognition and expansion of the contribution of fostering to children's lives. Berridge captures the wide scope of what is now covered by fostering:

- Physical nurturing and care through a positive experience of family life, dependable relationships and adult role models.

- Responding to children's experience of separation, together with possible feelings of rejection and guilt.

- Being alert to the temporary nature of fostering as a form of substitute parenting.

- Facilitating a return home or other more permanent arrangements.

- Liaising with birth families, encouraging contact and visits.

- Dealing with a range of emotional and behavioural problems, which might include low self-esteem, sullen withdrawal, poor social skills and possibly violent or other forms of challenging behaviour.

- Liaising with the social worker to implement the care plan.

- Reinforcing a child's ethnic identity.

- Promoting children's educational experiences.

(adapted from Berridge 2001, pp.171–2)

These developments, and the national standards associated with them (UK Joint Working Party on Foster Care 1999), have placed 'considerable burdens upon the lives of foster carers operating at the sharp end of child care practice' (Sellick 1996, p.165) and in carrying out effectively the varied and complex tasks that are now required, foster carers need to have access to avenues for developing their skills. In Chapter Ten, Vickers takes as her starting point the assumption that competent and confident foster carers improve the quality of care for vulnerable children and young people. She provides an account of Warwickshire Social Services Department's introduction of NVQ qualifications for foster carers, as an attempt to 'professionalise' the Foster Care Service and as part of the department's 'retention of carers' strategy. Her chapter considers the main policy documents that have brought NVQs and professionalisation of foster care into prominence and describes the development of the Foster Care NVQ Assessment Centre, as part of an overall NVQ strategy for foster carers. User feedback is provided and outcomes are analysed.

Concluding comment

The swirling storm of change in children's services, referred to at the outset of the chapter, shows no sign of having blown itself out. Change – not least the continuing trend towards delivering services through new organisational forms (Garrett 2003, chs 4 and 8) – looks set to remain on the agenda, as Hallett makes clear in Chapter Eleven. Packman and Hall reject a monolithic view of a straightforwardly imposed change agenda and suggest that organisational features, departmental traditions and culture influence service attitudes and outcomes (Packman and Hall 1998, pp.268–9). The contributors to the book indicate in the following chapters some of the ways in which they have tackled change in their particular organisation. Drawing on lessons from their past experience, they provide glimpses of how practice might develop in the future. In different ways, each of the chapters identifies the potential contribution social work can continue to make in children's services, a contribution that will impact upon children's lives and those of other members of their families. The chapters indicate that children's services will continue to be a challenging and demanding setting in which to work but they also suggest some of the ways in which those challenges and demands can be faced.

Notes

1 Whilst recognising that the policy and service developments have followed different trajectories in the other countries of the UK, this book focuses on the situation in England because the following chapters draw on material from an English social services department.

2 Given that the material in the remainder of the book is drawn from an English context, the emphasis here is on the Children Act (1989), as the key legislation.

Chapter Two

Strategic Development
Managing the Vision
Simon Lord

Introduction

The notion of strategy can be slippery and it is all too easy to slide into preoccupation with different ways of defining exactly what strategy is or into disentanglement of its component parts of planning, development and management. In this vein, much time could be spent ruminating on the respective notions of strategy, policy and tactics, the points at which they overlap and the boundaries between them. However, from the substantial literature on strategic development, the definitions given by Hussey are most relevant to the concerns of this chapter:

> *Strategy* is taken to be the means by which an organisation achieves the attainment of its long-term aims or vision.

> *Strategic planning* refers to the detailed specification of both the long-term aims or vision and the strategy for achieving those aims.

> *Strategic management* is the process by which the long-term aims or vision, the strategy and its implementation are managed.

> (Hussey 2000, p.1)

Hussey argues that these three concepts are inextricably bound together and:

> that strategic planning is more than just writing down the strategy: it should give consideration to the culture, structure and system in the organisation, so that every element of the organisation can be mobilised. Strategic management encompasses both strategy and strategic planning, but means something more: it is the way in which strategy becomes the driving force of the organisation. (Hussey 2000, p.1)

From this perspective, a strategy is a large-scale plan geared to achieving an organisational vision of how things should be. A strategic manager develops

19

and implements the strategic plan or, to put it another way, manages the vision. The remainder of the chapter considers strategic development along these lines. It begins by considering the emergence of strategic planning, before considering strategy in the public sector. The chapter then moves on to the modernisation agenda, and its implications for social services, followed by a discussion of three approaches to strategic planning. Key themes are then identified from the literature and from the government's policy agenda and explored in relation to experiences in Warwickshire Social Services Department. The chapter concludes with thoughts about the future of strategic development in social services.

The emergence of strategic planning

There is little literature about corporate planning and strategy before the mid-1960s, the era in which the contemporary personal social services originated. The body of literature on strategic planning that has emerged since that era presents a central argument. Whilst the development of a performance management culture in social services in the UK – a trend given added impetus by New Labour's 'modernisation agenda' for public services – has witnessed an increasingly strong orientation towards strategic planning, the literature suggests that the trend in this direction has been consolidated over a much longer period. Its origins are considered to lie in global trends in the world economy and in different strands of thinking about business and public sector strategy and management that have been developed by management gurus and government reformers around the world over the last three decades (Eppink and de Waal 2000).

As far as business is concerned, perspectives on strategic planning stress the imperative to operate effectively in a climate of continuous change and emphasise that strategic thinking is central to managing this challenge (Hussey 2000). In this rapidly moving context, the impact of political, economic, social and technological influences (Eppink and de Waal 2001) has been as significant in the public sector, as it has been in relation to business. The trends highlighted by Eppink and de Waal – towards deregulation and privatisation, the liberalisation of world trade and globalisation of the economy – have not only changed industrial and social structures but also public sector management. Demographic change, the free movement of people, goods, capital and services have created fresh challenges with which the public sector is expected to deal. Moreover, as Eppink and de Waal have also argued, developments in the medical field, telecommunications and advances in information technology (including the Internet), all mean that strategic planning has come to be seen as essential in enabling public sector organisations, including those with social services responsibilities, better to prepare for a future dramatically different from the past.

The general trend towards a more high-tech society where knowledge workers play a dominant role seems to be at odds with observations that in many developed countries the level of 'virtual illiteracy' is alarmingly high. *The Economist* of 31 July 1999 stated that in the USA and UK this is slightly above 20%. If this trend continues, the danger of an underclass is far from imaginary. Clearly, it is an enormous challenge for society and particularly for the public sector (education, social work organisations) to prevent this disaster scenario from becoming reality. (Eppink and de Waal 2001, pp.45–6)

However, while the cumulative impact of these global trends is now being felt more keenly than ever before, neither they nor the responses developed to manage them are new. Alford (2001), for example, sets out the belief held by government reformers that the introduction of more business-like management and market discipline into the public sector would improve the efficiency and effectiveness of public services, a belief which has included the fostering of strategic management techniques. New Labour's initiatives in recent years have built upon and extended these concepts and practices, rather than breaking with them. It might be argued that New Labour in government has sought to blunt the edges of some of the previous Conservative governments' approach to public services, as evidenced in the contrast between *Compulsory Competitive Tendering* and *Best Value* (Department of the Environment, Transport and the Regions 1998). The former was ostensibly a drive towards deregulation and privatisation of public services, while the latter purports to achieve the best balance between cost and quality, with less emphasis placed on whether the service is delivered by a private or public provider. Despite this difference in emphasis, New Labour has been as wedded, if not more wedded, to the introduction and extension of strategic planning and management in the public sector as its predecessors were.

Strategy and the public sector

Many of the developments in utilising the concept of strategy have come from the business world. As Alford (2001) indicates, the desirability of applying such developments wholesale to the public sector has been questioned, on the basis that the private and public sectors are different and call for correspondingly different management approaches. Critics highlight the distinctive political, ethical and organisational dimensions of the public sector and query whether concepts useful for business can also be valid in central government and local government (Frederickson 1997; Hood 1991; Pollitt 1990). There are undeniable differences between the private and public sectors. Collier, Fishwick and Johnson (2001) stress first, how the public sector is still required to conform to statutory and other formal regulations, to a greater degree than the private sector. Second, managers are responsible to different stakeholders. Third, there remains a greater emphasis on net public welfare – promoting the common good – and this means that there are different core objectives. Fourth, public sector managers regard political processes as more significant. This is likely to be the result of a number of characteristics of public sector organisations, not least the need for explicit bargaining between senior managers in the public sector and central government in order to obtain resources and inter-departmental bargaining for the allocation of those resources.

The counter-argument to the proponents of public sector distinctiveness is that the public and private sectors are not two distinct and internally homogeneous domains:

> Very few organisations are purely public or purely private – most sit somewhere on a continuum between these two extremes. Indeed...governmental reforms have been designed to install private sector mechanisms into agencies precisely in order to mitigate their public service orientation. (Alford 2001, p.2)

One example of this is the way in which public sector organisations have been made more accountable for the achievement of 'best value' performance, as we have already seen, often within a more market-focused milieu (Collier *et al.* 2001, p.31). In these circumstances, there is likely to be a greater role in strategic direction for senior managers – 'the command role' (2001, p.31). In occupying the command role, senior managers face the challenge of managing strategic change *within* their organisations, in response to external developments, and hence the need to understand, implement and cope with cultural change, as will become clear when we turn later to the implications of New Labour's modernisation agenda for the personal social services.

In this debate about strategy and the public sector, only one type of strategic management has tended to come under consideration: rational planning towards clearly defined coherent goals (Alford 2001). In Alford's view, this approach has informed government prescriptions and enabling legislation that have underpinned the reforms of the public sector. However, as Johnson and Scholes (1999) have demonstrated, there are many strands of strategic management theory. They can be divided into two main groupings. Some are about the *content* of strategy; they are concerned with *what* an organisation is to do. Others focus on the *strategy process*; on *how* strategies are formulated and implemented. Social services managers are likely to draw upon both.

Social services and the modernisation agenda

Coulshed and Mullender (2001) have charted the 'modernisation' project in social services, which they see as characterised by regulations and standards set by central government that are designed to secure continuous improvement and are externally monitored. One mechanism for this was the process of Joint

Review undertaken by the Social Services Inspectorate and the Audit Commission (Department of Health, Social Services Inspectorate and Audit Commission 1998). This monitoring function was itself modernised with the introduction of the Commission for Social Care Inspection, which has responsibility for inspecting independent and public sector social services in England.[1] The ultimate sanction for serious or persistent failure to meet these standards is government intervention under the Local Government Act (1999), when responsibility for running a social services department may be handed over, for example, to a neighbouring local authority.

The framework established by central government means that managers are less often involved in setting standards from scratch, except in relation to particular quality or change management initiatives, and are more often concerned with measuring continuous improvement against externally determined criteria (Coulshed and Mullender 2001). The Quality Protects Programme (Department of Health 1998a) is one such example, based on published national objectives that local authorities are required to meet, with more detailed sub-objectives and exhaustive performance indicators to measure outcomes for children. The performance assessment framework (Department of Health 1999a) also established strategic objectives for children's services covering costs and efficiency, effectiveness of service delivery, and quality of and access to services. The approach is further embedded in the development of the *National Service Framework for Children, Young People and Maternity Services* (Department of Health 2001), with similar NSF initiatives for older people, people with learning disabilities and those with mental health problems. The introduction of league tables for social services departments and the award of one, two or three stars according to performance, as measured by the various monitoring mechanisms set in place by central government, adds another dimension (Department of Health and Social Services Inspectorate 2003). The recipients of the maximum three stars are accorded privileges such as greater freedom in how they spend their budgets and less inspection.

This momentum towards increased strategic planning in social services has been given added impetus by government guidance on the formation of Children and Young People's Strategic Partnerships in local areas (Department of Health 2001a). Local authorities are expected to work with partner agencies in the voluntary and community sectors in developing a Children and Young People's Strategic Plan that is responsive to the needs of all children. They must involve children, young people and their families in the process. The aim is to plan services through one coordinated exercise, bringing together all agencies to achieve this. All of these initiatives are located within an overarching national agenda that is concerned with what 'good enough' means in terms of service provision (Coulshed and Mullender 2001). This concern underpins the 'Best Value' criteria applied by local authorities in operating their own services and in assessing their quality, with quality being a key concept in the 'Best

Value' agenda. The legislative framework for 'Best Value' requires: an overall statement of what a local authority intends to achieve; an agreed programme of performance reviews over a 4- to 5-year cycle, beginning with the weakest areas; targets for improved performance and efficiency, published with annual reports on progress in local performance plans; and independent audit; with the possibility of intervention by the appropriate Secretary of State in the case of serious or persistent failure (Department of the Environment, Transport and the Regions 1998).

Many local authorities have sought to assist their own processes of strategic planning and management by adopting the Business Excellence Model (BEM), developed by the European Foundation for Quality Management (EFQM). This model for the public sector assesses areas of strength across the organisation and requires the development of annual improvement plans (see Appendix One). Most social services departments have chosen to apply one or more model or set of standards (Darvill 1998). The Charter Mark Scheme[2] has also been adopted as a means of measuring public satisfaction with services, emphasising the quest for quality in the delivery of public services. These trends confirm social services', and other local authority departments', recognition that continuous improvement 'can only be looked at within a broader approach to the whole culture of the organisation and its overall mission' (Coulshed and Mullender 2001, p.50). It is important to stress that underpinning these cultural shifts is increasing recognition that the ultimate test of quality is what service users – referred to, of course, as 'customers' in the business world, and sometimes in the public sector (Harris 2003, ch.7) – think of the services provided. The need to seek out their views and consult with them in planning and delivering services has become a fundamental element in the strategic planning of social services, a point confirmed by the earlier reference to Children and Young People's Strategic Partnerships.

Three approaches to strategic planning

From the wide range of thinking about strategic planning and management, three approaches have been selected for their particular resonance with children's social services:

- strategic choice
- mega-planning
- benchmarking.

Strategic choice

Strategic choice (Friend and Hickling 1997) is based upon a conception of planning as a continuous process, that is, a process of choosing in a strategic *way* rather than at a strategic *level*. Choosing at a strategic level implies a prior view of some hierarchy of levels of importance in decision-making. The concept of strategic choice is concerned with the *connectedness* of one decision with another, rather than with the level of importance to be attached to one decision relative to others. Friend and Hickling's approach to strategic choice is, therefore, not only about making decisions at what is usually thought of as *the* strategic level:

> It goes beyond this in addressing the making of *any* decisions, whether they be at a broader policy level or a more specific action level, whether they be more immediate or longer term in their horizons, and no matter who may be responsible for them. (Friend and Hickling 1997, p.2, original emphasis)

This notion has an immediate applicability for those working in the social services field because, as Coulshed and Mullender (2001, ch.1) have argued, we are all managers. Many practitioner skills in social work are also managerial ones and all social workers increasingly work to managerialist agendas (Harris 2003, chs 3–5). For their part, those who are formally designated as managers of service provision and of people need to demonstrate skills essential to good practice: the ability to write and speak clearly and to engage in purposeful interpersonal relationships:

> Engaging with and relating to people, helping others to achieve their goals, supervising their efforts, maintaining morale, consulting a wide range of sources prior to making decisions, problem solving, and introducing and managing the crisis of change are just some of the tasks common to the practitioner and their manager. (Coulshed and Mullender 2001, p.13)

Mega-planning

Mega-planning (Kaufman 2000) focuses on the practical tasks for strategic planning and management, which Kaufman suggests need to be underpinned by three models:

- the organisational elements model
- the six-step problem-solving model
- the six critical success factors.

THE ORGANISATIONAL ELEMENTS MODEL

This model defines and links what any organisation uses, does, produces and delivers with external clients and 'societal value added', that is adding value for external clients and society, thereby achieving positive societal results. Successful planning links and relates all of the organisational elements, which are: outcomes, outputs, products, processes and inputs. This links with the Business

Excellence Model referred to earlier (see Appendix One) and, as we noted, this model has been adopted by many local authorities as a tool for strategic planning. In emphasising a focus on outcomes for the community and promoting social benefits, the model addresses the question of 'adding value', a phrase heard increasingly in public sector management circles.

THE SIX-STEP PROBLEM-SOLVING MODEL

This model defines a process for strategic management:

- identifying problems based on needs
- determining detailed solution requirements and identifying solution alternatives
- selecting solutions from among alternatives
- implementation
- evaluation
- continuous improvement.

Again, these components in the model, and the language used to describe the process, will be familiar in social services departments, grappling with the range of government initiatives outlined previously.

THE SIX CRITICAL SUCCESS FACTORS

These factors focus upon a process for identifying and resolving problems and identifying opportunities. The goal is to determine and promote effectiveness and efficiency:

- Use new and wider boundaries for thinking, planning, doing, and evaluating/continuously improving: move out of today's comfort zones.
- Differentiate between ends and means – focus on 'what' (mega/outcomes, macro/outputs, micro/products) before 'how'.
- Prepare objectives – including ideal vision and mission objectives – that have measures of how you will know when you have arrived (mission statement plus success criteria).
- Define 'need' as a gap in results (not as insufficient levels of resources, means, or methods).
- Use an ideal vision as the underlying basis for planning (don't be limited to your organisation).

Benchmarking

Wisniewski (2001) describes continuous planning as a key element in performance management, as exemplified by the Best Value framework. As we have seen, local authorities must demonstrate a commitment to identifying and introducing improvements to services in a significant and meaningful way. A critical part of such a commitment is ensuring that managers are constantly searching for better practice in other organisations – both private and public. One way that they can do this is through 'benchmarking':

> Benchmarking is best thought of as structured and focused approach to comparing with others how you provide services and the performance levels you have achieved. The purpose of such comparison is to enable you to identify where and how you can do better. Benchmarking is concerned with finding and implementing better performance wherever it is found. (Wisniewski 2001, p.85)

Advocates of benchmarking contend that it is not about copying what other organisations are doing. Rather the focus should be on what makes one organisation better in terms of service delivery, with the aim of enabling an organisation to assess how it might improve its own performance. Some have seen benchmarking as an integral part of promoting Best Value. Keady (1998) cites examples of its application to social services, leisure services, road maintenance, cleansing and refuse collection.

Key themes

A number of key themes can be identified in the literature and the government's policy agenda. These will be considered in the light of experiences in Warwickshire Social Services Department. The themes are:

- Foundations: strategic planning and management is not a phenomenon created by New Labour in the past few years but rather has a much longer history in public service.

- Continuous change: the history of strategic planning and management is characterised by searching for continuous change in the organisation as it seeks to fulfil its fundamental aims.

- Systematic approach: effective strategic management and planning requires the capability to capture and use information through systematic processes that inform continuous change.

- Connectedness: internal coherence of effort seeks to ensure that all parts of the organisation are contributing optimally to achievement of the organisation's main aims.

- Partnership: an extension of connectedness but broader and more outward-looking based on the premise that other stakeholders are needed to assist in achievement of the organisation's aims.

Foundations

In considering how an organisation's aims and objectives, its vision, appear, it is vital to determine *what* the organisation is seeking to achieve, but there is another and higher level of understanding to be attained by asking *why* does this vision matter? The question 'why?' is likely to take us into the realm of values, notions in our minds about what is important and gives meaning to our lives. Although values change over time they are much more enduring than any strategy or, indeed, any organisation. They are a foundation upon which to build and develop an organisation and its strategies.

What then are the key values underpinning Warwickshire's children's services, what significance have they had over time and how have they fared?

FAMILY LIFE IS BEST

This value has been a particularly strong and enduring feature of the culture of the social services department in Warwickshire. It is a belief that children should, wherever possible, be brought up in a warm loving family setting, and is based on the conviction that growing up in such a setting affords the child the best prospects of developing into a well-rounded adult citizen. Children are thought to need stable long-term everyday relationships with a small number of people who care about them in order to learn, develop emotionally and become self-confident. Children are also thought to need to be part of a wider local community, to have friends and be known in a locality, and to attend a school consistently. Families, located in communities, are considered well placed to meet these needs.

It is not suggested that the valuing of family life as best is unique to Warwickshire, nor is the potential destructiveness of families denied. What is contended is that the value has been strong and explicit within Warwickshire for a long time, and most importantly it has strongly informed strategic development, service configuration and outcomes for children. Thus, for example, Warwickshire was the first local authority to close all its children's homes in 1986 heralding its so-called 'non-residential' strategy. (Actually this is a misnomer because Warwickshire has always placed a small number of children in external residential provision where their specific needs can only be met in such a provision.) Another outcome has been a twenty-year history of strategic development and investment in Warwickshire's internal foster care service, which has withstood rapid market development and the emergence of a private and independent sector that has presented major difficulties for many local authorities. (The development of Warwickshire's internal fostering service is described more fully in Chapter Ten.) The effect of this fundamental value finds its way through to the high proportion of its 'looked after' children who are fostered. For example, in the March 2003 statistical returns to the Department of Health, Warwickshire reported that 98.5% of its 'looked after' children under 10 years old are placed in foster homes or placed for adoption. (For this, the Department of Health awarded Warwickshire a top performance rating.)

SOCIAL WORK WORKS

Back in the pre-Thatcherite era a champion of professional social work came to Warwickshire in 1978. Bob Bessell, the then Director of Social Services, believed passionately that if excellence in social services provision was the goal, excellence in the workforce was a key means of achieving it. The workforce had to be valued and had to be seen as requiring investment. Bessell created a vision of excellence for public social services for and with the councillors in Warwickshire. A key feature of this vision was to have a social work workforce that was 100% professionally qualified, not only in field social work but also in residential homes, where the special skills of the professional social worker were most needed in prolonged face-to-face contact with troubled youngsters. This was radical in that era, very expensive and a ringing endorsement of valuing people. The fundamental belief that social work works was combined with that of family life is best. There was a strong belief that highly competent social workers could and would work with troubled children and families, providing support to enable families to surmount their difficulties so that children could remain within their families and continue to be part of their local communities. This again gave added impetus towards Warwickshire closing its children's homes in 1986. Fewer children were going into them, and most of those already there were able eventually to return to their natural or substitute families with extensive skilled support provided particularly by staff in residential homes working out from those homes into the community.

This theme of valuing the workforce has endured, although it has waxed and waned in the hands of different managerial regimes. It has also managed to flourish better in Children's Services than Adult Services, which have been subjected to devaluing of professional social work to a greater extent through implementation of the NHS and Community Care Act (1990) (White and Harris 2001, ch.1). The publication of *Messages from Research* (Department of Health 1995) was a helpful and timely reinforcement of the effectiveness of social work in children's services. The theme of valuing people will be elaborated further in due course, with regard to how human resources strategy can be developed, but for now the simple message is that if you have valued, excellent and motivated staff they will innovate and develop good practice for you.

A HISTORY OF STRATEGIC DEVELOPMENT

Along with the emphases placed on family life and on the value of social work, another part of the foundations in Warwickshire is that strategic management has a long history in its own right. Since the late 1970s, with the exception of a three-year period in the early 1990s when the social services department dabbled with a purchaser/provider split approach to its organisational structure, strategic lead responsibility has always been firmly allocated to a single senior manager, currently called Head of Children's Services, who also has direct operational responsibility. This has been of critical importance. Currently, it means that whoever is responsible for strategic development has personal accountability for implementation of the strategy in all of the geographical districts of Warwickshire. Strategy and operations are, therefore, firmly linked and interdependent. There have been no remote departmental strategy units drawing up wonderful but unrealisable strategy and nor does strategy consist of short-sighted pragmatism driven solely by day-to-day operational exigencies and pressures.

The strategic lead senior manager is seen as the champion for her or his allocated service area, children's services in this instance. She or he is expected to provide high-profile operational management leadership for children's services and most of the director's powers are delegated to her or him. She or he will chair key operational bodies such as the Children's Services Group (consisting of all children's senior managers), the Adoption Panel and the Area Child Protection Committee. In terms of very difficult and high-profile cases, the buck eventually stops with that person. The strategic lead manager is also expected to be very knowledgeable about contemporary regional and national developments and policies, and to blend such knowledge into a regularly reviewed strategy for the service, department and the local authority as a whole. Needless to say, this is a demanding role, which requires the post-holder to have highly developed personal skills in leadership.

Although the departmental strategic lead senior manager has a very demanding role, she or he is not expected to undertake it alone. There are three ways, evolved over the past twenty years, in which the lead position is supported. The first, and most important, involves sharing and delegating responsibility widely throughout the operational workforce. This is an extension of the principle whereby the director delegates to the senior strategic manager and it results in a continuation of the linkage between strategy and operations. As Warwickshire has always been a low spender on social services, particularly in relation to children's services, there has been a 'needs-must' factor in this emphasis on linking strategy and operations. In this context of scarce resources, spend on infrastructure through the creation of policy units and the like has been modest, and an expectation developed that all staff should have an opportunity to influence the formation of strategy. In other words, a virtue has been made of a necessity and the resultant structure and culture have endured over the years.

Two notable features that have emerged from this structure and culture are the use of 'champions' from the workforce and the creation of 'lateral groups' of staff by whom specific strategic development issues might be addressed. An early example of use of lateral groups concerns the department's development of a county-wide Intermediate Treatment (IT) strategy to meet the needs of the 1982 Criminal Justice Act. The deputy director at that time, Peter Smallridge, asked the four district-based IT managers to produce such a strategy together and particularly to provide an alternative to custody service available to all courts consistently across Warwickshire. The strategy was duly produced via county-wide workshops including all IT staff and key stakeholders. A rolling programme of specialist intensive groupwork designed to reduce offending was established and offered in courts as a realistic and effective alternative to custody. Within a year, custodial sentencing was reduced by half and expertise developed that led to specialist Youth Justice Teams in the early 1990s and through to today's highly successful multi-disciplinary Warwickshire Youth Offending Team.

The devolution of strategic development has become more formalised over the years. For example, a departmental reorganisation in 1995, from the purchaser-provider split model to a geographical five-district structure, was used as an opportunity to strengthen the department-wide Children's Services Group. Part of the strengthening involved redrafting the job descriptions of service managers, reporting to the head of Children's Services, so that they had responsibility for strategy in defined areas. Team managers (reporting to service managers) were also allocated contributory strategy roles and this was further formalised in 2001 through up-rated job profiles and remuneration.

The second source of assistance has been a steadily increasing, though still modest, use of a project officer role, as resources have allowed. Project officers work to assistant heads of Children's Services, assisting them to discharge their delegated strategic lead portfolios: Child Protection; Children in Need; Health and Disability; 'Looked After' Children; Leaving Care. Typically, project officers are seasoned operational managers, seconded to these roles.

The third source of assistance to the strategic management system has comprised the evolution of a highly effective Children's Planning Team. This unit is relatively lean and has developed its role from its user-focused intelligence, derived from chairing case conferences and 'looked after' children reviews. This unit now provides information and intelligence to inform effective strategic planning, with a quality assurance function to monitor implementation. Further consideration will be given to its significance later, in connection with the importance of a systematic approach.

Continuous change

The foundations discussed in the previous section are counterpoised by a willingness to innovate and take risks. In this respect, the government's modernisation agenda for social services in general and children's services in particular, outlined earlier, has been challenging and at times uncomfortable. Nevertheless, the agenda's aspirations and intentions have been seen as laudable and in line with what has been long-striven for in Warwickshire – better outcomes for vulnerable children. Thus for example *Quality Protects*[3] has been embraced enthusiastically and its additional resources have been used effectively to improve key services and outcomes. *Quality Protects* performance indicators have become integral working components in each team's unit plan. Performance across the range of services has been improved continuously so that performance overall is now within the top quartile nationally. Former areas of underperformance, for example placement moves for 'looked after' children, have been raised to top level (five star) performance rating.

Best Value reviews are a key feature of the modernisation agenda, and they have been grasped with alacrity as vehicles for change. Children's Services have put forward large and vital parts of the service for review, including assessment and care planning, fostering, adoption and services for disabled children. The reviews have been challenging, rigorous, subject to external inspection and used to effect major change. The adoption service, for example, was restructured, re-invested and also nominated to, and accepted by central government for, a Public Service Agreement.[4] Performance improvement has been spectacular and actually ahead of the step-change target agreed with the Department of Health. This means that many more children are being found permanent parents and the local authority is likely to receive a 'reward' of £750,000 for further investment.

Warwickshire's willingness to change is illustrated by its having completely restructured its social services three times in the past ten years. Each time it has done so to obtain optimal benefit from its own resource base within the wider operational and political environment. The current shape, a functional county-wide arrangement of separate children's and adults' services, with a local district base, is serving the present and emerging environment well. There have, however, been mistakes.

The imposition of a purchaser/provider split structure in 1991 was a hasty response to wholesale Thatcherite reforms of social policy following the Griffiths Report (1988) and the National Health Care Service and Community Care Act (1990) (Harris 2003, ch.3). They were principally aimed at community care services for adults driven by the failure of the earlier Thatcher governments to shape social services policy through financial control (White and Harris 2001, ch.1). A particular driver was the escalating costs of social security payments for people in private sector residential and nursing homes (Harris

1998). The purchaser/provider split organisational model was unsuccessful because it was hastily conceived and implemented with scant regard to the foundations of the organisation. It took little account of differences and subtleties in the public sector mentioned earlier (see, for example, Frederickson 1997; Hood 1991; Pollitt 1990). It did not accord with the values and culture of its workforce or indeed those of the political administration, a Conservative one in a county with, at that time, nearly a century of unbroken Conservative administration. In children's services the purchaser/provider split was particularly anathema and inherently inappropriate given the nature of the service, the limited applicability of the model and the very immature state of the market.

A more successful and enduring example of Warwickshire's willingness to change and take risks is that of the so-called 'non-residential' policy referred to earlier. A key feature of this change was its being the logical culmination of a six-year process of implementing a strategy to promote effective professional social work, dedicated to sustaining children in family settings. At the time it was seen by many outside Warwickshire as radical, risky and unworkable. It endures to this day, and many authorities have followed suit.

Systematic approach

As well as sound foundations and a disposition towards continuous change, a systematic approach has been needed to generate the intelligence that informs such change. The previously described interweaving of strategic and operational responsibility ensures that reality prevails and that 'soft' wisdom and intelligence inform strategy. In addition, rigour is required in order to add objectivity and a firm evidence base. This entails having some dedicated capacity to generate that evidence base and the tools to do the job.

The most important dedicated capacity in Warwickshire's Children's Service is the Children's Planning Section. This highly effective unit was established in 1993 for the purpose of providing a rigorous and consistent reviewing and case conferencing service across the department. Hitherto, this service had been commissioned from and provided by a large voluntary organisation. Interestingly, at a time when the trend within social services was generally towards marketisation and contracting out, Warwickshire made this unusual decision to contract in, a decision that was vindicated thereafter. The original purpose of the unit was planning, in the sense of individual care planning, and comprised a small central team of independent reviewing officers drawn from within the operational service and led by a similarly experienced team manager.

The Children's Planning Section proved very successful in its main purpose but also created valuable intelligence about the quality of service being provided, which was useful to all those charged with leading strategic development. Thus it was contributing to planning in the sense of developing large-scale plans or strategies. Appreciation of this contribution, together with

New Labour's burgeoning requirements for formal large-scale plans (Children's Services Plan, *Quality Protects*, Strategic Plan for Vulnerable Children), has resulted in the Children's Planning Section growing in importance and achieving its current status as a highly effective unit for information processing, intelligence supply, quality assurance, strategic development support and production of plans. It is still relatively small, mostly populated and led by experienced operational staff but now includes a number of specialist planning, development and contracting posts, some of which are joint funded by other departments and agencies. Although it is a central unit, it has its feet well on the ground, provides information and support directly to front-line teams and is valued by operational staff. It is line-managed by the assistant head of Children's Services (Quality). An example of the Children's Planning Section's work, and its contribution to strategic development can be found in Chapter Nine.

Another piece of capacity, though for the social services department as a whole, is its information systems. The department has been prudent and prescient in giving early priority to development of and investment in its information strategy. Despite the department's perpetually lean resource base it has consistently invested heavily in information and computer technology. An Information Strategy Team was established in 1991 which ensured that Warwickshire was at the forefront of developing and implementing a computerised client record management system (CRMS) jointly with OLM, a commercial company that is now a market leader. CRMS has now been superseded by a new system, Care First, and again Warwickshire is well advanced in implementing and developing the system. Although implementation of information and computer technology has not been without criticism over the years, and practitioners have been burdened with some irritating and onerous shortcomings, the department is now capable of producing high-quality information for a number of purposes. These include case management, management information for team, service, departmental and national/governmental purposes, linkage of financial and activity data and benchmarking.

Benchmarking is a tool which has been in regular use in Warwickshire for a number of years and this is dependent upon being able to produce the information, year-on-year, for trend analysis and continuous planning purposes. The department is a member of the West Midlands Benchmarking Club and has used benchmarking techniques routinely during the process of its Best Value reviews. Benchmarking and Best Value reviews have thus been particularly helpful in identifying strategically which areas of service require particular improvement and how that might be brought about. They are also helpful in levering in additional resources as the example of the adoption Best Value review, mentioned earlier, illustrates.

The most comprehensive development tool in Warwickshire has been the European Foundation for Quality Management (EFQM) model. The Department adopted this model, then known as the Business Excellence Model (BEM), at an early stage in 1997 and has used it continuously since then. It is well embedded and used in a thoroughgoing way. The annual Departmental Service Plan is constructed according to the model and the Service Plan is then used in every team plan throughout the Children's Services. EFQM is now part of the fabric of the organisation, understood and used by staff at all levels. It exemplifies Friend and Hickling's concept of connectedness (addressed in the next section), with strategic development and management being undertaken at all levels in the organisation. A particularly noteworthy example of how the BEM model has helped is that the department's understanding and use of 'processes', one of the most significant 'enabler' factors in the model, was relatively poorly developed (see Appendix One). This prompted engagement of an external expert consultant on process mapping and development who, together with a working group of practitioners and managers, has been streamlining and integrating the key processes for child protection, children in need and 'looked after' children. This in turn is linking in with the government's Children and Young Persons Unit's development of the 'Integrated Children's System', as well as current ongoing Best Value reviews for Assessment and Care Planning and Services to Disabled Children.

Connectedness

This theme is about internal coherence of effort, ensuring that all parts of the organisation are contributing optimally to achieving its main aims which, in the EFQM parlance, are Customer and Key Performance Results (see Appendix One). It is about putting the customer first, second and third when considering design and delivery of service, including the so-called support services. How are support services best configured and operated to enable excellence of service at the customer interface? The key support services are human resources, financial and information services and if any of these are misaligned or off-message it will have a seriously disabling effect upon the organisation's performance. This is not at all uncommon in a large and complex, publicly accountable service organisation such as a social services department. Information strategy has been addressed above in relation to the need for systematic approach so the concentration here will be on the contribution to connectedness of human resources and financial strategy.

Earlier in the discussion, the vision of excellence in the social work service for children of the late 1970s/early 1980s was coupled with a drive for an all-qualified workforce. The latter might not have been graced with the term 'strategy' at the time but it was a wise and necessary measure which did presage an era of determined human resources strategy development. In 1986 the then director, Peter Smallridge, determined that the hitherto lightweight training section should be much strengthened. Over the next five years a strong and effective Staff Development Unit was built up, having benefited from substantial departmental and governmental investment through the Training Support Programme. A training and staff development strategy was produced and updated through an Annual Training Plan. An impressive range of development programmes were available and were linked to individuals' development needs in relation to service objectives, formally and variously accredited by external bodies and academic institutions.

The appearance of NVQ was grasped by the Staff Development Unit, which became a pilot site and eventually an accredited awarding body. Partnerships with local universities were created to deliver professional social work training programmes, complete with a greatly expanded practice teaching capability in the social services department. The reorganisation of 1991 gave the opportunity for training and staff development to be merged with the personnel function to produce a new Human Resources Section. This new section was in a position to and capable of developing a more imaginative and holistic view of how the organisation should develop. Consequently in 1993 it produced the department's first comprehensive human resources strategy. This was an unusual and early achievement for a local authority service department and has been helpful to the county council in its ongoing development of a corporate human resources strategy. Unfortunately, after the 1995 reorganisation referred to earlier, this advanced and sophisticated human resources strategy fell into relative decline for a number of years but is now gathering momentum again in the new guise of Organisational Development. Recognition of this renaissance was achieved in 2000 with the award of 'Investor in People' status.

The significance of human resource strategy is not confined to departmental or authority-level organisations. It is also critical at national level, given a national crisis in staffing levels, recruitment and retention of social services workers of all kinds, particularly qualified social workers. Even in Warwickshire, the vacancy rate for social workers peaked at 17% during 2002 but this has now been reduced to 11% following a concerted campaign, with a range of measures to attract and retain. Many other authorities have had much greater problems. There are hopes that one of the constructive outcomes from Lord Laming's report on Victoria Climbié's tragic death (Department of Health 2003a) will be a realistic long-term national workforce investment and development strategy for social work.

In terms of finance and budgeting, the department has always been a sound performer. (There was a blip in 1994 when a projected overspend of £3 million had to be ruthlessly managed down to £0.9 million overspend at out-turn, but this was a national problem associated with implementation of community care legislation. This seriously dented the department's reputation for financial management competence for a number of years.) It has also always needed to be prudent and focused due to its perpetually challenging low resource base. Financial management and investment strategy has been led by and closely linked to the service strategies. This has been vital in achieving the outcomes of these service strategies and has entailed careful financial planning, innovative investment and the taking of calculated risks. One excellent example is that of Warwickshire's fee-based fostering scheme, where the desired results of retaining and developing foster carers and a reduction of placement moves have been achieved. This required a courageous invest-to-save financial strategy in the clear knowledge that it would inevitably have an adverse effect on one of the key performance indicators, unit costs, by which the Social Services Inspectorate assess the service.

A final positive and resonant feature of financial strategic development and implementation is the high level of involvement of and dependence on operational staff. The financial systems are highly devolved and delegated to the front-line managers, who take responsibility for spending and forecasting. Financial management is owned widely and the skills are spread throughout the workforce. This again has required linkage of information, human resources and service strategy development.

Partnership

Partnership is another of the five 'enablers' of the Business Excellence Model and thus an important factor in any organisation's success (see Appendix One). It is especially important for Children's Services. Long before the government declared it *de rigueur*, Warwickshire Children's Services had established a thoroughgoing *modus operandi* of working in partnership with key stakeholders, be they stakeholder agencies or service user groups. This tradition has grown out of an abiding realism and appreciation that the children's social work service, whilst proudly skilled and committed, is small and on its own does not have the resources and range of expertise to bring about major improvements in the lives of very troubled youngsters and their families. This means that potentially life-changing forces around individual youngsters and families need to be levered in, coordinated and influenced, whilst continuing to work with those individuals directly in a skilful interpersonal way, which both challenges and supports in effecting change.

The world of education is a massively significant feature in any child's life, particularly for one beset by difficulties in other aspects of her or his life. Developing joint strategy in a partnership between education and social services is challenging, largely because the remits of the two services are fundamentally different. Education is essentially a universal service provided to all children, while social services is a targeted service for a few, very needy children. There is thus a built-in tension. For example, should the unhappy disruptive child be tolerated and helped within a mainstream school or should she or he be excluded in the interests of harmony and the academic progress of their classmates? Unfortunately, even now government guidance on this one issue vacillates and practice varies hugely between schools, which themselves have considerable autonomy. Once again though, Warwickshire made progress early on, when in 1995 a Children and Young Persons' Sub-committee (of the then powerful Policy Committee) was established, as a joint councillor and officer initiative. The primary purpose of the Sub-committee was to generate strategy and initiatives that 'cross-cut' departments. Amongst its major successes was a strategy called TELAC (The Education of Looked After Children), an information system which ensured that the educational needs of 'looked after' children and their attainments were a focus of attention in both departments. As a result, by the time the government's Quality Protects programme was introduced in 1998, which included a focus on educational attainment of 'looked after' children, Warwickshire was already performing comparatively well (though nowhere near well enough), giving a platform from which to benefit from Quality Protects and to build further. In November 2002, further joint strategic proposals were agreed by both departments and included establishing a new team of specialist teachers to boost the achievement of 'looked after' children within mainstream educational settings.

Youth Justice is another partnership success story, building upon sound early foundations. From 1981 onwards, when the department anticipated and then rose to the challenge of the Crime and Disorder Act (1982) to reduce offending and provide credible alternatives to custody, there has been highly effective collaborative work between social services, probation, police, magistrates and Clerks to the Court. Offending Reduction Groups were run on a multi-agency basis and offered to the courts as a sentencing option. All Social Enquiry Reports were submitted to a gate-keeping panel to assure quality and consistency of recommendation, before submission to court. Consequently, in the early 1980s the custodial sentence rates for juveniles plummeted as they were dealt with effectively in the community to the benefit of taxpayer and young offender alike. When the incoming Labour government published its plans for multi-agency Youth Offending Teams (YOTs) in 1997, Warwickshire quickly and willingly set one up and was the second department in the country to appoint its Youth Offending Team Manager. In terms of results, Warwickshire has one of the lowest rates of juvenile crime in England. The national Youth Justice Board regards Warwickshire YOT as an exemplar of good practice and the team was visited by the then Home Secretary, Jack Straw, in 2000.

Warwickshire's most impressive example of partnership and strategic development is in child protection. The Department of Health has consistently described multi-agency arrangements, led through the Area Child Protection Committee (ACPC), as 'excellent' in its regular annual review of the service. The Joint Review of Warwickshire's Social Services in 2003 also described the multi-agency ACPC, led by Social Services, as an area of strength. For Social Services itself, performance against its child protection indicators has been consistently sound. ACPC's success is founded on consistent informed leadership over a number of years, together with a sophisticated infrastructure of sub-committees, which include a wide range of managers and practitioners from the full range of agencies. Strategy is, again, developed and owned by those who have to implement it. Vision and expertise is enhanced by multi-agency employment of an ACPC Development Officer. (See Chapter Three, which describes the development of a risk assessment tool to promote good practice in child protection.)

Involvement of service users in partnership arrangements for developing strategy might seem like a self-evidently good idea. After all, they know what services feel like and change is much more likely to be brought about if they are on board with it. However, such service user involvement is notoriously difficult to achieve in practice and it is tempting to slip back into a more easily managed benevolent paternalism. Nevertheless, the involvement of service users is worth striving for. For example, Warwickshire's track record of working successfully in a culturally sensitive way was recognised by the Social Services Inspectorate in 1998 when it was chosen to be a national exemplar demonstration project for Black and minority children and their families. Two pieces of research were commissioned, one from a university concerning the experience of Black children in care, and one from an independent voluntary organisation concerning the experiences of disabled Black children and their families. The findings were considered by a councillor and multi-agency officer steering group. Strategy was drafted, shared with and endorsed by the user groups, and new service provision was set in place. Implementation plans were drawn up and executed and a range of measures are in operation. One of these, 'REACCH' (Recognising and Celebrating Children's Cultural Heritage) comprises a specialist worker, a tool kit and an advisory panel to assist practitioners in working in a culturally sensitive and appropriate way with all Black and minority ethnic group service users. (The 'REACCH' project is described fully in Chapter Eight.)

Linked to working in partnership with service users is the notion of doing likewise with the wider community on whose behalf, at the end of the day, services are provided. This can also be difficult because much of what social services do is highly contentious (for example, removing or not removing children from abusive situations, see Chapter One) and requires sophisticated professional judgement in emotionally charged arenas. Social work generally gets a bad press precisely because of this and because responsibilities are being undertaken that often have been abrogated by the wider society. Nevertheless, it is worth robustly and proactively engaging with the community and the media because the job can be done so much better if people in the community have a better idea of what the job involves and assist in doing it. In this vein, and on the advice of the editor of the 'Society' section in *The Guardian*, Warwickshire Area Child Protection Committee developed a media and communication strategy. As part of this, a carefully prepared workshop was arranged for all publications and radio stations covering Warwickshire. The journalists participated in real but anonymised case simulations and were provided with information and statistics about child abuse in their local areas. The following week, every newspaper carried extensive and positive reportage of child protection work, mostly on the front page, and a number of radio interviews were given.

A further example, involving direct work with the community, is provided in Chapter Six. This initiative had its origins in a high-profile issue – protection of children in a locality in relation to resettlement of a registered sex offender – and involved trust and collaboration between parents, community, voluntary and statutory agencies.

The future of strategic planning in social services

It would be difficult to overstate the magnitude of the agenda for change introduced into UK social services since 1997. Consideration of the future scale and direction of this agenda, in so far as children's services are considered, must inevitably involve reflecting upon the implications of Lord Laming's report into the death of Victoria Climbié (Department of Health 2003a) and the impetus for strategic development in children's services is unlikely to slacken. On the contrary, Laming's unprecedented focus on the conduct and quality of senior management in the organisations involved in Victoria Climbié's case, and his subsequent emphasis on the need for major structural reform of the management of child protection services, will quicken the pace of change (Department of Health 2003a).

That some form of structural and organisational change in children's social services will happen may in part be a consequence of the perception, seemingly confirmed by the findings of the Laming Report, that while notions of strategic planning and management have been increasingly to the fore in the vocabulary used by social services managers, some social services departments have in practice remained relatively immune to these trends. More accurately, they have failed adequately to connect strategic development concepts to their operational activities. Making this connection on a consistent basis may now be the most important step for public sector organisations to take and it will probably be the most challenging. What is certain is that the lasting legacy of Laming's report, and the government's response to it, will be even more radical organisational change. The national and local tasks will be to manage that legacy strategically, so that maximum benefit is secured for children, using and building upon the existing reservoir of commitment and expertise of partners and staff. It is, after all, they who will deliver the future vision through the quality of their practice.

Notes

1 In Scotland, the regulation of Child Care Agencies is undertaken by the Care Commission and in Wales by the Care Standards Inspectorate for Wales. In Northern Ireland inspection is carried out by the registration and inspection units within the four health and social services boards, but this is planned to be superseded by a Northern Ireland Commission for Care Services.

2 The Charter Mark Scheme is a Cabinet Office initiative to promote the focus on improving customer service by public sector organisations. Such organisations would include local authorities, schools, and social services departments. It can also be applied to the independent sector and to sub-contractors. There is a strong focus on customer first and continuous change and improvement. Achieving the standard means that the prestigious Charter Mark logo can be displayed by the organisation.

3 Quality Protects is the government's vehicle to drive forward its modernisation agenda in relation to children's social services. It started in 1997 and comprises a set of objectives and performance indicators which all local authorities have had to incorporate into an annual Quality Protects Management Action Plan. Substantial additional resources have backed the initiative, and these will be mainstreamed into departmental budgets from 2004.

4 Public Service Agreements (PSAs) were introduced by Government in 2001. They involve piloting innovative ways of achieving step changes in performance of particular local government services. Local authorities volunteer exemplar schemes and commit to stretched performance targets. In recognition, they are permitted to streamline/short-circuit some regulations and receive financial reward for success. It is a form of deregulation and encouragement to innovate.

Chapter Three

Analysing Risk in Child Protection
A Model for Assessment

Vic Tuck

Introduction

This chapter describes how a model for risk assessment and analysis was devised and introduced in Warwickshire. It will commence with a discussion of the historical, legal and procedural context within which this initiative was developed, and its linkage with the wider child protection system. Having asserted that an explicit risk assessment and analysis must constitute a core element of interventions designed to safeguard children and promote their welfare, the chapter will then consider some of the obstacles professionals face in undertaking this work. This will make it possible to identify key strands which an effective model for risk assessment needs to weave together. The theoretical basis of the Warwickshire model will then be explained, followed by a description of the model itself. The chapter will go on to show how the model was tested, evaluated and implemented. Plans for further evaluation will be described. The discussion will continue with a brief account of the professional skills necessary for sound practice in risk assessment. The need to explore directly the value and effectiveness of the model with children and families will be the concluding point of the chapter.

The wider context

The child protection system in England and Wales is the product of decades of evolution of which the publication of the Laming Report into the death of Victoria Climbié was another landmark event (Department of Health 2003a). This system has been shaped by numerous other public inquiries, some of which, in common with Lord Laming's, have highlighted the failure of agencies adequately to protect children, while others, most notably the Cleveland Inquiry (Department of Health 1988b), have criticised professionals for intervening too swiftly in families, sometimes separating children and parents when there may have been no need for this.

The Children Act (1989), which provides the statutory framework for safeguarding children and promoting their welfare in England and Wales, and government guidance issued under its auspices (Department of Health 1999a) seek to encourage a balance between protecting children from significant harm and working in partnership with parents, ensuring families receive the help and support they may need. Whether this balance has been satisfactorily achieved has been questioned by researchers who have investigated the operation of the child protection system (Department of Health 1995). Their findings led to serious soul-searching by child care professionals as the Department of Health launched what came to be known as the 'refocusing debate' (Rose 1994). One of the outcomes of this debate was the publication of *The Framework for Assessment of Children in Need and their Families* (Department of Health, Department for Education and Employment and Home Office 2000), which is discussed more fully in Chapter Four.

The document has been welcomed because of its emphasis on the identification of holistic child needs and the avoidance of unnecessary inclusion in the child protection system. However, this enthusiasm has been tempered by a concern that its underlying view of abusing parents as essentially well meaning but overstressed, may not be adequate in responding to those with more serious problems and who may pose a more severe threat to the health and safety of their children, particularly when these children are very young (Dale, Green and Fellows 2002). Moreover, it has been pointed out that while the government may have redefined 'risk' as 'need' in the Assessment Framework document, this is not convincing when there is: 'repeated back-tracking from needs-led assessment to a reminder that the child's safety is the primary objective of professional intervention' (Calder 2003). There is evidence of this in the government's response to the Climbié Inquiry report, where the emphasis has been on ensuring that basic child protection practices and systems are in place in social services (Social Services Inspectorate 2003). Health trusts (Commission for Health Improvement 2003) and the police have also been required to review and audit local child protection arrangements.

The reality is that, as has always been the case, professionals operating in this field continue to tread a fine line between protecting children, avoiding unnecessary intrusion into family life and, where this intrusion is unavoidable, framing interventions which balance safeguarding children with supporting their families. However, *Working Together to Safeguard Children* (Department of Health 1999b) does define a sound process for intervening to safeguard children, which multi-agency Area Child Protection Committees (ACPCs) are required to translate into inter-agency child protection procedures, for use by professionals in their locality. The guidance sets out the action to be taken at the point at which concerns are first identified about a child; the referral to social services as the lead agency in child protection; the initial assessment, which determines whether an investigation under Section 47 of the Children Act 1989 is necessary; the planning and conduct of this investigation, involving the police and social services; the decision to take the case to a multi-agency child protection conference; the placing of the child on a child protection register; the construction of a child protection plan; and the subsequent management, monitoring and review of the case. (One of the most important outcomes of the Laming Report is that Working Together and the Assessment Framework document are likely to be simplified and integrated, so clarifying their currently poorly defined relationship to one another. This work appears to have commenced with the publication of a practice guidance document for Children's Services [Department of Health 2003b])

A report by government inspectors into arrangements for safeguarding children (Department of Health 2002) seems to confirm the effectiveness of Working Together, concluding that although the priority given to child protection has not been reflected firmly, coherently or consistently enough in service planning and resource allocation nationally or locally across agencies (a point confirmed by the Laming Report):

> In the vast majority of individual cases that we examined, the children were protected from the risks of further harm. In all authorities [in which the inspectors scrutinised work], children on the child protection registers were allocated to social work staff, who were working well with professionals from other agencies. (*ibid.*, p.3)

This is an important distinction to keep in mind when considering the case of Victoria Climbié, because the failure to carry out basic procedures and adhere to good practice meant that she never actually entered the child protection system. However, both the Children's Safeguards and Laming reports (Department of Health 1999b, 2003a) have highlighted inadequacies in the assessment of vulnerable children, even though this remains the key to good quality decision-making and planning. The *Framework for Assessment of Children in Need and their Families* seeks to rectify this deficiency by providing professionals with a systematic approach to the collection and appraisal of information in circumstances where children and their families are facing difficulties.

However, even when properly applied, the Assessment Framework may not go far enough in equipping professionals properly to assess the level of risk to a child's health and safety. This may partly be a conceptual problem arising from the reclassification of 'risk' as 'need', as observed earlier. There are those who have even argued that 'risk' has been effectively deleted from the vocabulary of child protection, as expressed in the Assessment Framework (Calder 2003), and in support of this contention, one would be hard-pressed to find reference to the 'r' word within it.

It is more likely, though, that what is required is even more sophisticated analytical tools than the Assessment Framework currently provides for practitioners. In particular, those tools which assist them in judgement forming, enabling them to complete what Hollows (2003) has described as the judgement task. While the Assessment Framework provides some limited, explicit guidance on undertaking analysis of information, it arguably does less to assist workers in this regard than it does in guiding the collection of information. Arising from this perceived deficit, and also feedback and observations from practitioners, managers and reviewing officers (who chair child protection conferences in Warwickshire) about the need better to support professionals in this area of work, the local ACPC set about developing a model for risk assessment and analysis. The primary aim of this model was not only to help identify risks to the health, safety and welfare of children (though the need for greater precision in this lay at the heart of many of the concerns expressed by the individuals described above), but also to enhance the ability of professionals to arrive at judgements about the significance for the child of those risks and the action that would subsequently need to be taken to help change the situation. This was to be done by seeking to define a pathway that would help lead workers to a position where they could form and express their judgements about a child and her or his family, particularly in the context of child protection conferences where the key decisions about children at risk are made.

Why is risk assessment necessary?

Before moving into a brief consideration of some of the very real obstacles that have been encountered in constructing risk assessment models, it is important to retrace our steps and reflect a little more on why risk analysis in child protection work is necessary. It has been suggested, as we have seen, that in the desire to focus much more on the needs of vulnerable children, the notion of risk has been downplayed, even eliminated from discourses on safeguarding children. In reality, as professionals operating in this field will confirm, need and risk have to be defined in terms of each other (Munroe 2002). They are two sides of the same coin. Where the emphasis contained in this chapter differs from, for example, that which appears to underpin the Assessment Framework, is in contending that no genuinely holistic conception of 'need' can afford to fail to encompass unambiguously consideration of possible threats to a child's safety and the source(s) of those threats.

This may not be a popular view. Seden (2001), in summarising studies that inform the Assessment Framework, focuses upon what she describes as 'the preoccupation with risk assessment' and summarises literature that highlights problems with risk assessment models. However, *Working Together to Safeguard Children* (Department of Health 1999b) places risk assessment and analysis at the centre of sound decision-making and planning in cases where children may be at risk of harm. Professionals are required to determine if a child is at continuing risk of significant harm, whether as a consequence they need or continue to need a child protection plan and, by implication, whether their name needs to be placed upon a child protection register. The need for professionals and agencies to engage in risk analysis is emphasised by criteria that were applied by the Audit Commission and Social Services Inspectorate in joint reviews of social services departments. Social services departments were asked:

- What risk assessment procedures do you have in place across user groups?

- What evidence do you have available to ensure that there is a timely and assured response for those at highest risk?

- What response times do you operate to meet the needs of people with the highest level of risk?

(Adapted from Audit Commission, Social Services Inspectorate and National Assembly for Wales 2002)

Its seems unlikely that new arrangements for evaluating performance, by the Commission for Social Care Inspection, will ignore such considerations, particularly in the aftermath of the Victoria Climbié Inquiry. In short, there is a clear procedural, professional and organisational responsibility to undertake risk assessments of children. The key issue seems to be how we build on best practice by promoting a systematic, logical approach to risk assessment, located within a strong theoretical framework. The aim should be to establish a consistent standard of risk analysis, the value of which can be seen by all those involved in the child protection process, particularly those whom it is intended to serve – children and families.

Sound risk assessment helps practitioners to explore more explicitly with families what needs to change if children are to be kept safe and healthy, and no longer to require a child protection plan. It makes it possible to be clear with parents and carers what is expected of them and it enables professionals and family to identify more precisely the help and services needed to support the required changes and fulfil these expectations. In explicitly and clearly addressing both sides of the assessment coin, we should all be better placed to build upon a family's strengths, but act decisively should this not prove possible within an acceptable timescale for the child, always keeping in mind that the child's welfare is defined within the Children Act (1989) as the paramount consideration.

Obstacles to risk assessment and analysis

It is important to acknowledge some of the very real problems that exist in undertaking risk assessment in child protection cases. Seden (2001) has argued that risk assessment procedures are likely to vary on a number of dimensions and are complex to compare against each other. She concludes that:

> despite increasing sophistication in the design and evaluation of risk assessment tools, the variables for assessing children in the contexts of their families are so complex that professional judgement underpinned by theory and research still remains the cornerstone of best practice. (*ibid.*, p.12)

Confirming these complexities, Munroe (2002) provides a valuable appraisal of two competing models of risk assessment: clinical and actuarial. She cites the definitions offered by Grove and Meehl to explain the distinction. An actuarial assessment 'involves a formal, algorithmic, objective procedure (e.g. equation) to reach the decision' (Grove and Meehl 1996, p.293). A clinical assessment 'relies on an informal, "in the head", impressionistic, subjective conclusion reached (somehow) by a human clinical judge' (*ibid.*, p.294). Put another way, an actuarial risk assessment provides a statistical formula for working out the final risk assessment, whereas a clinical risk assessment relies on the intuitive expertise of the professional, though this can be based on a more or less structured guide to collecting the relevant information (Munroe 2002).

In terms of child protection, Munroe concludes that there are good reasons for supposing that an actuarial risk instrument will be more useful than leaving difficult judgements to intuitive appraisal alone, though she in no way denies the importance of this as part of the repertoire of social work skills. However, at best an actuarial instrument will help in making a judgement about the level of risk to a child at a particular time. This approach does not take into account that risk assessment is an ongoing process not a 'once-in-a-lifetime matter': 'Families and their circumstances change and their dangerousness alters' (*ibid.*, p.82). Assessing immediate harm can skew practice so that longer-term risks are ignored or undervalued. Moreover: 'It would appear that the overwhelming message from the discussion of difficulties of accurate risk assessment is that child protection workers should be very cautious in their claims to be able to predict abuse' (*ibid.*, p.82).

Sinclair and Bullock (2002) agree that the assessment of harm will always be problematic given the lack of any theory of causation of harm. They summarise research that highlights the difficulties in predicting which children are likely to experience harm and the virtual impossibility of identifying those who are likely to be murdered or suffer serious injury. However, in reviewing situations which have been the subject of Serious Case Reviews under Chapter 8 of Working Together, they contend that 'practice can be enhanced to bring greater consistency to decision-making among professionals, both within and across agencies' (*ibid.*, p.29). They go on to conclude that 'the fashioning and research-testing of practice tools designed to improve decision-making are…likely to have beneficial effects on vulnerable children' (*ibid.*, p.63).

An effective model for risk assessment in child protection therefore needs to be able to weave together a number of important strands if these obstacles are to be overcome. At the heart of its construction there has to be a recognition of the difficulties and dangers in seeking to predict child abuse or 'future harm', and consequently the importance of viewing risk assessment as an ongoing process. As such, the model needs to be one which defines a dynamic structure for judgement-forming and decision-making: judgements and decisions have to be revisited by professionals in accordance with the reviewing mechanisms and timescales defined in *Working Together*. (These stipulate that a multi-agency 'Child Protection Review Conference' must take place three months after the 'Initial Child Protection Conference', which first considered the concerns about the child. Subsequent review conferences, which continue to consider the child's status as a child in need of a child protection plan, must take place at intervals of no greater than six months.)

Upon these foundations, there is a need to construct and test practice tools that enhance planning and decision-making for children who have or who are likely to experience significant harm. These tools need to be underpinned by good professional judgement, grounded in an evidence-based approach to practice. Such an approach involves the professional bringing relevant research findings to bear when weighing up the significance of different factors in a child's situation.

The Warwickshire response

With these considerations in mind, in my capacity as Warwickshire ACPC's Development Officer, I began the task of constructing a model for risk assessment. I then sought to translate this model, and the theoretical concepts on which it rested, into practical tools. This was done by working with colleagues, most notably the manager of our conference reviewing officers, on developing templates for compiling reports for child protection conferences that contain risk analyses. The need to promote an inter-agency approach, by developing templates that could be adapted to fit the requirements of different professionals, was seen as being fundamental to the success of the enterprise.

Before outlining the theoretical basis of the Warwickshire model, it is important to describe another local development that gave impetus to this work. The need to better equip practitioners for the task of risk assessment and analysis was further highlighted in the county by an audit commissioned by the ACPC of the small number of cases where children had been on the child protection register for a very lengthy period. These tended to be cases of chronic neglect or emotional abuse and the drift that was evident could be attributed to the lack of risk assessment at the outset or a failure to re-evaluate the original analysis. As a consequence, there was little basis for coherent planning and decision-making, even though there might be a good deal of professional activity. This audit coincided with the decision to proceed with the task of constructing a risk assessment model and served to confirm the course of action we had decided to embark upon.

Theoretical basis of the model

Two strands were woven together to construct the Warwickshire model. The first of these was derived from my research into links between social deprivation and harm to children (Tuck 1995, 2000a, 2000b). The second emerged from an appraisal of literature in the field of forensic psychology, which has considered processes and components in risk assessment (Moore 1996; Towl and Crighton 1996).

To take the first strand, I have used my own research, and the study on which it was based, to construct an integrative model of harm to children. Put simply, this seeks to blend insights derived from theories developed in the fields of sociology and psychology in order to produce an interpretive framework, which explains the harm of children in terms of the complex interplay between the personal characteristics and histories of individuals and the social environments in which they and their families have to function. It therefore sees harm to children as deriving from a variety of sources and integrates a number of perspectives to account for this, rather than attributing causation to a limited number of factors.

Underpinning this model is a social constructionist perspective, which attaches great significance to the meanings which people attach to their experiences (Bluner 1990; Gergen 1982, 1985; Plummer 1983). How individuals perceive their lives and themselves has an enormous bearing on their coping capacities, including the care they are able to provide for their children. A social constructionist perspective is a key component of a risk assessment model in child protection because an understanding of parents' perceptions of the harm experienced by their child, and the care they are providing, gives professionals an insight into the functioning of the family, parental motivation and, as a consequence, the prospects for change and improvement in the child's circumstances. I shall endeavour to unpack this integrative model a little more.

In my study, in which I asked parents living in a neighbourhood characterised by high levels of social deprivation and high rates of child protection referrals to relate their experiences of caring for children, I concluded that social deprivation constitutes both a primary and secondary source of harm to children. By impacting adversely on the health and development of children, and hindering the ability of socially disadvantaged parents to care for their children as they may wish due to the presence of multiple adversities, poverty and social deprivation contributes to a general prevalence of harm in the UK. It is a primary source of harm. However, the experience of chronic material and psychological depletion may be so acute for some parents that they may find themselves locked into a downward spiral of inability to cope, despair and helplessness, compounded by negative perceptions they hold of themselves and perceive others to have of them. In some circumstances, this may manifest itself in harmful responses to their children – a secondary source of harm.

The reality is that in coping with a range of adversities, most poor parents demonstrate huge resourcefulness and care for their children adequately. Moreover, while my study confirmed that there is a correlation between high rates of child protection referrals and neighbourhoods experiencing high scores on indices of social disadvantage, the abuse of children also occurs in more affluent homes. It is therefore necessary to see the impact of social deprivation as one of a constellation of factors that influences causal pathways and outcomes for children. Among these factors, which influence whether a parent is able to maintain a safe balance between social support and coping capacity on the one hand and psychosocial stress on the other, are: the personal history and characteristics of the individual; their perception of themselves and the meanings they attribute to their experiences; their coping capacities and the confidence they have in these; the stock of successful adaptive strategies on which they can draw; and the levels of social support at their disposal. Moreover, adverse outcomes may manifest themselves in all sorts of ways, not just in damaging behaviours and reactions to children. For example, adults may experience physical illness, mental health problems, misuse substances and/or behave in a criminal way. Of course, if these adults are also parents then these outcomes may come to have a deleterious impact on their children's development, particularly if they occur in combination (Cleaver, Unell and Aldgate 1999).

The key consideration is likely to be the impact of an accumulation of stressors or risk factors, and the way in which these interact over time with each other, and also with protective factors that may be present in the child's world. Where a number of risk factors are present, then their impact is likely to be accentuated. In becoming more than the sum of their parts they acquire greater force and impact. As a consequence, they are more difficult to manage.

An understanding of theories of psychosocial development and the acquisition of resilience, as expounded by Rutter and others, is therefore a foundation stone of this integrative model of harm, which in turn informs the Warwickshire model of risk assessment (Rutter 1981, 1985, 1988; Wadsworth 1988). This also means that an ecological perspective of harm to children – one that considers the impact of all the factors within the child's environment and their interplay (Garbarino 1981) – lies at the heart of my integrative model of harm to children and the Warwickshire risk assessment model. As such, while I have previously highlighted the limitations of the *Framework for Assessment of Children in Need and their Families*, the Warwickshire model is firmly embedded in it, in so far as any analysis of risk needs to derive from information collected under the three domains that constitute the *Framework*:

- the child's developmental needs
- parenting capacity
- family and environmental factors.

Constructing the model

To construct the model, I completed a functional analysis of risk assessment in child protection work. Using the integrative model of harm I have described, I spelt out, step by step, what I believed a risk assessment model in child protection should look like. I first identified the constituent parts. Having unravelled the components of the model, I was then able to determine the order in which they should be tackled, in other words the process of the risk assessment. The test here is: how does each stage build incrementally upon the one before it, in terms of constructing a picture of the child, their situation and the risks they face? This picture will enable the practitioner to reach a judgement about the risks to the child and what should be done to safeguard them and promote their welfare.

Having identified both the content and process of the model, I was able to translate this into a flowchart. This left me with a visual image of the seven stages of the risk assessment which I had identified. Where necessary, I broke down some of these stages into a number of parts, the completion of which, by the person undertaking the assessment, would enable the stage to be fully completed. Later, for ease of reference I converted the flowchart into a circular diagram. This also served to emphasise the need for the risk assessment to be dynamic and ongoing, as highlighted by Munroe (2002). The outcome of all this work appears as Figure 3.1.

I referred previously to the fact that I drew not only on my own previous work in constructing this model but also on material from forensic psychology. Towl and Crighton (1996) have identified a generic model for risk assessment, and this proved very valuable in piecing together the Warwickshire risk assessment model. It was necessary to discard some aspects and elaborate on other aspects of the Towl and Crighton model in order to ensure it was made fit for the purpose of assessing and analysing risk in child protection. However, reference to their work made it possible to appraise the coherence of the emerging Warwickshire model. A further invaluable source for completing this work was Moore (1996), whose insight into the area of risk assessment was to prove particularly useful in compiling practice guidance notes that we later devised for professionals completing the documentation for child protection conferences.

What follows below is a brief description of each of the seven steps and where necessary the constituent parts of each.

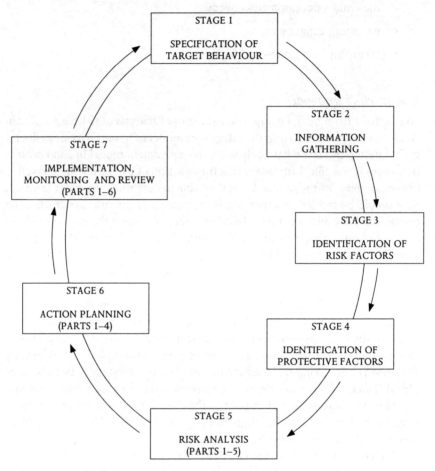

Figure 3.1 Seven stages in assessing risk in child protection

STAGE 1 – SPECIFICATION OF TARGET BEHAVIOUR

Towl and Crighton define risk as 'a combination of an estimate of the probability of a target behaviour occurring with a consideration of the consequences of such occurrences' (1996, p.55). This definition is fundamental to the model because it invites us to define how the child is being harmed or is likely to be harmed: precisely what are we trying to prevent from occurring or recurring in terms of parental behaviour and what is the likelihood of the child experiencing future harm? We are linking this to an appraisal of the impact future harm will have on the child's safety, health and development. From the outset the question is posed: 'What is it we are seeking to change in order to make this situation safer and healthier for the child?' If we are talking about changing harmful behaviour, this is likely to mean we need to explore and effect change in the values, attitudes and feelings of the parent or carer which underpin the problematic behaviour.

STAGE 2 – INFORMATION GATHERING

Information on the child and their family is gathered using the three domains of the Assessment Framework:

- child's developmental needs
- parenting capacity
- family and environmental factors.

STAGE 3 – IDENTIFICATION OF RISK FACTORS

From information gathered at the previous stage, we identify risk factors. A risk factor can be defined as any agent, whatever its source, that poses a threat to the child's health and safety, and which is likely to increase the likelihood of harm occurring/recurring.

STAGE 4 – IDENTIFICATION OF PROTECTIVE FACTORS

The same information is used to identify those factors in the child's world that contain a protective component for the child. As such, they are likely to counteract the impact of the identified risk factors and diminish the risk of harm occurring/recurring. Among these will be the strengths of the parents and extended family, the adaptive strategies they are able to deploy and the support networks on which they can draw.

STAGE 5 – THE RISK ANALYSIS

There are five stages in the risk analysis:

- Assessment of the balance and relative strength of the risk and protective factors in the child's world: are protective factors outweighed by risk factors? If so, how? To what extent?
- Estimation of the level of risk present for the child and the probability of future harm.
- Assessment of the likely outcomes of any future harm for the child – the likely impact on their safety, health and development.
- Assessment of the acceptability of the estimated risk given the likely outcomes for the child of future harm.
- Using the above components to compile a risk assessment report for the child protection conference.

STAGE 6 – ACTION PLANNING

There are four parts in the action planning stage:

- Using the risk assessment report to specify those actions, resources and services needed to boost the strength and range of identified protective factors.

- Using the report to specify the actions, resources and services needed to diminish the identified risk factors.

- Using the report to specify what needs to change if the child is to be kept safe and healthy and not to require or no longer to need a child protection plan.

- Incorporating these specifications into the proposed child protection plan to be presented to the child protection conference.

STAGE 7 – IMPLEMENTATION, MONITORING AND REVIEW

There are six parts in this stage:

- Specification of arrangements for implementing, monitoring and reviewing the child protection plan.

- Continuous assessment of the balance of risk and protective factors in the child's world and what needs to change for the child to be kept safe and well.

- Monitoring of shifts in this balance and interaction, and the pace and extent of necessary change.

- Assessment of the consequences/outcomes for the child of such shifts, including possible future harm.

- Assessment of the consequences/outcomes for the child if necessary change is not being achieved.

- Specification of the contingency plan – the actions to be taken in the event of the child protection plan failing to work, i.e. in circumstances where it is not proving possible to maintain a safe balance between risk and protective factors and necessary change is not being achieved.

As already commented, the circular nature of the seven stages of assessing risk, depicted in Figure 3.1, demonstrates that the process of risk assessment is dynamic, requiring practitioners to re-evaluate and update their analyses, and subsequent planning.

Implementing the model

The model laid the foundation for significant consolidation and development of best local practice. However, we needed to translate it into formats that could be used easily by practitioners and which defined a clear pathway to forming judgements about a child and her or his circumstances. Working with the manager of conference reviewing officers in Warwickshire, templates for initial and review child protection conferences were developed. We also constructed a format for the outline child protection plan agreed at the initial conference: one for the first core group meeting when the detailed plan is agreed; one for subsequent core group meetings, which would assist the group in monitoring the implementation of the plan and measuring progress. The ultimate aim was to devise a collection of templates that would facilitate a coherent flow of information and analysis, when linked together; the intention being to provide the basis for sound planning and decision-making throughout the duration of the case.

The Social Worker Report for Initial Child Protection Conference addresses the need for risk analysis as follows: having requested basic information on the child and family, the worker compiling the report is asked to provide summaries of information gathered so far under the three domains of the Assessment Framework. From this, they identify risk and protective factors, recording these on a grid. This device is already in use in some parts of Warwickshire and it provides an accessible format for viewing those factors that pose a threat to the health and safety of the child and those likely to have a positive influence. Following completion of the grid, the worker is then taken through a series of questions, derived from the model described earlier in this chapter, each building on the one before it. The questions are:

- Which of these factors are likely to be most significant for the child in terms of reducing or increasing the probability of future harm?

- Estimation of the level of risk that therefore appears to be present for the child and the probability of future harm.

- What are the likely outcomes of this for the child?

- What needs to change if this level of risk is to be reduced?

The first of these questions is crucial. Having identified risk and protective factors in what approximates to a balance sheet of indicators, the worker needs to appraise the relative strength of these factors and assign weight and meaning to them. How influential and powerful are these factors? It may be that superficially our grid indicates one set of factors outweighing the other. We may, for example, have a longer list of protective factors. However, this may be deceptive because, when considering these factors in more depth, we may find that the strength of a smaller number of risk factors has more impact. As described earlier, my study of links between social deprivation and harm to children indicates that we need always to give consideration to the interaction of different factors and their cumulative effects on the child and family. Support for this is provided by the Assessment Framework:

> In weighing up the impact that various factors have on the child, it has to be borne in mind that not all factors will have equal significance and the cumulative effects of some relatively minor factors may be considerable. Thus the analysis of a child's needs [and the possible threats to their health and safety] is a complex activity drawing on knowledge from research and practice combined with an understanding of the child's needs within his or her family [and the possible risks they may face]. (Department of Health *et al.*, 2000, p.55)

In other words, central to the whole process of risk assessment and analysis, and the identification of need, is an evidence-based approach to practice. In Warwickshire, we have sought to firm up this approach by making available to practitioners, through the medium of the ACPC website, a database of research summaries, including for example, the work of Cleaver *et al.* (1999). This pulls together knowledge on the impact on children's development of parental mental illness, problem alcohol and drug use, and domestic violence, factors likely to loom large in the lives of many children who may need to enter the child protection system. An understanding of the problems these issues may generate for children and knowledge of those factors likely to offset their impact is clearly important. We plan to consolidate the availability of this material by launching a series of multi-agency research seminars across the county.

Having compiled her or his analysis, the worker is then able to complete the document by giving a view of whether the criteria for child protection registration are met. She or he is invited to present a proposal of what they believe the outline child protection plan should contain, should the conference agree that one is needed. The outline plan covers four areas:

- Change required: what needs to change if the child is to be kept safe and no longer require a child protection plan? (The areas of change are listed.)

- Management of risk: what actions, resources and services are needed to diminish the identified risk factors and boost protective factors? (The action to be taken, by whom and when is set out.)

- Monitoring arrangements: how will the plan be implemented, monitored and reviewed? By whom? When?

- The contingency plan: what actions will be taken in the event of the plan failing to work? (Circumstances where a safe balance between risk and protective factors is not maintained and necessary change is not being achieved.) By whom? When?

The first core group meeting will use the agreed outline plan as the basis for the detailed plan it will devise and enter this on a template designed for this purpose. Core groups comprise the key professionals involved in the implementation of the child protection plan, and wherever possible the child's parents. They meet ten days after the initial child protection conference to agree the detailed plan, and thereafter on a regular basis to review and monitor the plan.

Three months after the initial child protection conference, the worker compiling the Review Report for the Child Protection Review Conference uses a template that enables her or him to update the risk analysis. Having systematically presented information about the progress that has been achieved in each aspect of the child protection plan, and provided completed summaries of the three domains of the Assessment Framework, she or he is able to address these questions:

- How and to what extent have the risk factors identified at the last conference diminished/increased?

- How and to what extent have the protective factors identified at the last conference diminished/increased?

- How has the level of risk present for the child and the probability of future harm altered since the last conference?

- What are the likely outcomes for this child now?

- What does the above information and the progress of the current child protection plan indicate about the likelihood of sustained change within the family?

These questions enable the worker and their core group colleagues to measure the progress of a child and her or his family, against the objectives set out in the child protection plan. The template for recording second and subsequent core group meetings supports this work, with the inclusion of grids that assist in measuring change and analysing whether the situation has become safer or less safe for the child. Being able, as a consequence, to make stronger judgements about the family's propensity for change provides a firmer basis for future planning, including ultimately a consideration of whether the current care arrangements are viable. This, in turn, reduces the risk of cases drifting. The process is further assisted by inclusion in the templates of a requirement that consideration is given throughout to the timescales within which necessary change will need to be demonstrated. Practitioners should be looking for evidence of progress and necessary change within the periods of time between child protection conferences stipulated in *Working Together*, and adapting their plans accordingly.

The pilot project

These tools and templates were tested by means of a pilot project. Two child care social work teams undertook to use the formats and provide feedback. We were also able to assess the overall impact on practice by scrutinising the reports compiled for conferences using the formats and by obtaining the observations of reviewing officers, who chair child protection conferences in Warwickshire. Both social work teams found that the templates incorporating the risk assessment model were valuable for a number of reasons.

First, they appeared to assist in the compilation and evaluation of information collected in relation to the children and their families. This was confirmed by reviewing officers, who commented that the conference process was assisted by conference reports that now contained sharper analyses of risk (though this is not to say that this was absent before – one of the teams in the pilot project had been using risk assessment material for some time, and the new formats helped to consolidate their practice). Reviewing officers found that conferences were able to spend more time on the part of the meeting concerned with analysing risks to a child – making sense of information presented to the conference – and less on the actual information sharing, which previously dominated proceedings. As a result it seemed to be less difficult and less time-consuming to reach an informed view about the risks faced by a child.

Second, workers believed that the new formats contributed to a more focused and systematic assessment of risk, which made it possible to assert more confidently whether there was likely to be a continuing risk of significant harm and the likely impact of this upon the child. It was felt that thought processes and judgement-forming were assisted by the structure supplied by the questions posed. Comment was made that this made it easier to make judgements about continuing registration or de-registration (i.e. whether the child still required a child protection plan and whether as a consequence they needed to remain on the child protection register).

Third, an area where some variability in practice was observed by reviewing officers concerned the appraisal of identified risk and protective factors and the attribution of meaning and significance to them. In some cases this aspect of the risk analysis was very detailed, in others it was relatively sparse. Surprisingly perhaps, this did not always appear to prevent the worker from reaching what appeared to be a reasonable and confident estimate of the probability of future harm, suggesting that in some situations analysis was taking place even if it was not clearly set down in the report. However, it confirmed the need to explore and develop media through which research evidence can be made available to practitioners to assist professional judgements, such as through the locality-based seminars and ACPC website described earlier.

Fourth, although the quality of risk analysis seemed to have improved, this was not necessarily reflected in the outline child protection plan. Reviewing officers often still found themselves having to encourage workers to make the connections between the nature of the risk they had identified, what needed to change, and the implications of this for the content of the plan. This was identified as another area for future training in the application of the model.

Fifth, earlier in the chapter, it was made clear we were seeking to develop a multi-agency risk assessment model. Health trusts in the county have been keen to adopt the templates, for use by health professionals preparing reports to child protection conferences. It has been possible to speak to groups of these staff with a view to their using a version of the templates. The Education Service in Warwickshire has also incorporated a consideration of risk and protective factors in its pro-forma, for use by teachers in compiling reports for conferences. An independent reviewing officer, whose specialism is undertaking reviews of children in residential schools, has taken forward this work by developing a more detailed set of questions, which apply the risk assessment to the specific issue of the educational development of the child (Jones 2003). It is too early to say if our objective of a genuinely multi-agency risk assessment model has been achieved, but what has already been described gives cause for some encouragement. However, one possible area of difficulty is that the submission of a particularly thorough report by one professional (for example the social worker) may contribute to other professionals concurring too readily with their findings and conclusions, rather than asserting their own unique contribution and perspective and building a genuine composite picture. The skills of conference chairs in drawing out discussion have been tested in this regard.

Further evaluation

The plan is to evaluate the model further now that it has been launched across the county. The methods for this evaluation will be: a training audit (picking up on themes that practitioners would find useful to explore, as well as those already emerging); seeking further feedback from conference reviewing officers; directly observing a sample of child protection conferences; and the continued scrutiny of reports presented to conferences.

Other social work teams have already been approached about their experience of the model and the templates and their feedback is similar to that received during the pilot project. Managers have commented upon an apparent improvement in the quality of reports and the analysis contained within them. Practitioners have found the formats helpful in compiling reports, organising their thinking and arriving at judgements about which they can feel confident. There are more recent indications from conference reviewing officers that some professionals may need further encouragement in making comparisons between risk and protective factors originally identified and those present at the time of the review conference. Templates for review conferences have been modified to better facilitate this activity. However, the key question to address in this subsequent evaluation will be: how do we know if the model really does work? Will it lead to shorter periods for children on the child protection register? Will the possibility of drift, identified in the Warwickshire ACPC audit referred to earlier in this chapter, be reduced? Will outcomes for children at risk of significant harm be improved?

There is already evidence that the consequences of the model might be rather complex. Some parts of the county have seen a significant increase in the levels of registration since the risk assessment model has been implemented. Investigation has indicated that there are likely to be a number of complex factors at work, not entirely related to the model, for example, large sibling groups of children requiring a child protection plan, or the addition of a baby to the register alongside already registered siblings. When we are talking about quite small numbers of children on child protection registers, relative to the wider child population in a district, such factors can have a marked effect on levels of registration. However, it has also been suggested by front-line managers that the cumulative impact of our model and the Assessment Framework may have been to help identify more families where the children require a child protection plan, particularly in the notoriously difficult areas of neglect and emotional abuse. We have to be careful about describing as a trend an upward movement in a single set of figures, but it could be that the success of this model may, in part, have to be measured in terms of how far it has led to an initial increase in the numbers of children identified as experiencing harm.

What skills do professionals need to do this work?

Our experience in Warwickshire suggests that it is possible to construct practice tools designed to improve decision-making in relation to particularly vulnerable children and their families, even in an area as complex and uncertain as risk analysis. Such tools need to be grounded in a strong theoretical framework, translated into a model that makes them operationally viable and tested in practice. Making available succinct guidance notes on completing forms is likely to help. For example, to assist with estimating the probability of future harm, a series of questions developed by Moore (1996) was drawn to the attention of practitioners. The evidence is that, once convinced of their usefulness, practitioners are keen to take up such tools and contribute to their application and development.

However, an important qualification needs to be made to this. While the development of these sorts of practice tools is necessary and helpful, their effectiveness is ultimately dependent on the quality of analytical skills that practitioners bring with them. My previous experience, as director of an agency-based post-qualifying training programme in child protection, suggests that such practice models and tools seem to enhance the analytical skills of those workers who already possess them to a greater or lesser degree. However, they are unlikely to compensate in situations where individuals lack these basic, but absolutely essential, skills. We need, therefore, to look to the quality of entrants to the helping professions, to processes of selection, to the quality of qualifying training and the preparedness of these programmes of study to exclude those unable to demonstrate to a satisfactory standard the pre-requisite skills and knowledge. We need to assess whether educational and training frameworks, established to promote post-qualification development, are proving sufficiently robust in consolidating and developing skills, including those necessary to safeguard children.

Trotter (2002) has provided a useful account of the wider skills needed to undertake this work, which could be usefully incorporated into supervisory and post-qualifying training mechanisms, geared to ensuring that practitioners continue to practise safely and effectively. He contends that effective child protection workers have the following characteristics:

- They have skills in clarifying their role to children and parents.

- They have frequent, open and honest discussions about: the purpose of intervention; their dual role as an investigator and helper; the client's expectations of the worker; the nature of the worker's authority and how it can be used; what is negotiable and what is not; and the limits of confidentiality.

- They focus on helping the client to understand the nature of the child protection process.

- They make use of collaborative problem-solving processes (sometimes referred to as working in partnership).

- They help clients to identify personal, social and environmental issues which are of concern to them.

- They then help them to develop goals and strategies to address these issues.

- Effective workers tend to work with the client's definitions of problems and deal with a range of issues which are of concern to the parent and family.

- They take a holistic view and systemic approach and focus on the issues which have led to the abuse and neglect, rather than just the abuse itself.

- They balance collaborative or partnership approaches by skills involving the use of confrontation and the reinforcement of the individual's positive and 'pro-social' actions and comments – such as attending case-planning meetings, using non-physical means of discipline or reduced drug use.

- They encourage comments which acknowledge the harm that abuse can cause or comments which acknowledge the need for the individual to change.

- They focus on the positive things that the person is saying and doing but do not minimise the nature of the abuse or neglect which has occurred.

- They are viewed by their clients as fair, open, respectful, punctual and reliable.

- They have strong 'relationship skills' such as empathy, self-disclosure, humour and optimism.

To this it should be added that such skills are likely to be most effectively exercised when they are grounded in an understanding of the processes and components of change. Using the comprehensive model of change developed by Prochaska and DiClemente (1986) which is based upon core components of the change process identified in a review of eighteen major therapies, Horwath and Morrison (2000) have explored the applications of this to work with families where there are child protection concerns.

Conclusion

The ultimate challenge is to ensure that the tools described in this chapter are recognised as valuable by children and parents. I commented at the beginning that one of the benefits of sound risk assessment in child protection is that it helps professionals to explore with families our expectations of them, in a more explicit and focused way, and to consider what needs to change (and within what timescale), if the child is to be kept safe and well; in effect, for there to be no need for a child protection plan. It is no accident that a social constructionist approach – one that emphasises the importance of the meanings which individuals attribute to their experiences and their perceptions of themselves – underpins the theoretical framework which informs the Warwickshire model. Ascertaining and analysing the perceptions of parents about what has happened to their children, and the quality of care they believe they are providing, is central to sound risk assessment. Our templates allow for exploration of this dimension.

The success of this process is heavily dependent on practitioners being able to present and interpret risk assessment models of the sort implemented in

Warwickshire in terms that can be easily understood by parents. The rationale for the activity and the terminology used needs to make sense to them. We return to the quality and skills of workers involved in child protection. However, it also means that the formats used, the language employed within them and the sources of information which support these endeavours need to be kept under review. Their impact needs to be appraised by seeking feedback from families. The model and tools described in this chapter provide the platform for this further development.

Chapter Four

Assessment of Children in Need and their Families

Jude Quiggin

Introduction

The introduction of the *Framework for the Assessment of Children in Need and their Families* (Department of Health, Department for Education and Employment and Home Office 2000) was an attempt to rectify some of the weaknesses in social work practice concerned with identifying and assisting children in need. The Framework arose out of specific government objectives, was influenced by findings from research and emerged from a context shaped by the implementation of the Children Act (1989). These influences are discussed, before turning to the Assessment Framework itself and exploring an example of working with a family in the light of the Framework's guidance.

Influences on the Assessment Framework

The implementation of the Children Act (1989)

The Children Act (1989) emphasised local authorities' duty to safeguard and promote the welfare of children and the concept of a *child in need* was introduced (Part III Section 17[10]). Part III also outlined a range of family support services local authorities were encouraged to provide in order to assist parents in bringing up their children. Duties in relation to safeguarding children were detailed in Parts IV and V of the Act, which introduced the concept of *significant harm*. Under the Act, the local authority has the primary duty to investigate and protect children from harm (Section 47). This protection can be afforded by providing support services under Part III as well as via a compulsory order. Furthermore, after a court order has been made, children continue to be *in need* and can require support services for effective protection. Thus there is no dichotomy in the Act itself between safeguarding children and promoting their welfare. However, this was not how the Act came to be implemented in practice, as Horwath (2000) notes, drawing on evidence from a number of reports. For example, *The Children Act Report 1993* (Department of Health 1994) noted that Section 17 was not being implemented in full accordance with the spirit of the Act. Instead, the emphasis seemed to be on a reactive policing role, with services targeted at children at risk of significant harm.

The modernisation agenda

The Assessment Framework was not only influenced by the implementation of the Children Act (1989). It was also part of a wider government policy agenda and was launched as a component in the government's stated commitment of 'ending child poverty, tackling social exclusion and promoting the welfare of all children' (Department of Health *et al.* 2000). The guidance in the Framework was a key element in the support to local authorities implementing Quality Protects (Department of Health 1998a), the government's programme for improving the management and delivery of children's services. In addition, as part of its 'modernising agenda', the government published a set of objectives for children's services. The Assessment Framework was developed to supply guidance on the specific objective in relation to assessment: 'to ensure that referral and assessment processes discriminate effectively between different types and levels of need and produce a timely service response' (Department of Health 1999a, p.30). The guidance provided by the Framework was produced under Section VII of the Local Authority Social Services Act (1970), which requires social services departments to act under the general guidance of the Secretary of State. Whilst such guidance does not have the full force of statute, compliance is expected unless 'exceptional reasons' justify a variation. When there are child protection concerns, the Assessment Framework is also expected to be used in conjunction with *Working Together to Safeguard Children* (Department of Health 1999b; and see Chapter Three). As we have seen, in the period leading up to the publication of the Framework, there had been concern that the emphasis on child protection had been at the expense of service provision and this had been noted in a number of research projects conducted in the 1990s.

Findings from research and reports

In 1995, the Department of Health published a summary of the findings of twenty research studies on child protection. *Child Protection: Messages from Research* (Department of Health 1995) was very influential and confirmed the existence of a general trend towards child protection and Section 47 enquiries rather than supportive interventions. Gibbons, Conroy and Bell (1995) also found that investigations were focused on the details of abusive incidents and took little account of the context of abuse, which their research suggested was more significant in terms of having a lasting impact on children. Many families were also found to have received no services or support once they were filtered out of the child protection system (Gibbons *et al.* 1995). Other studies raised serious concerns about the quality of assessments with regard to disabled children (Morris 1995, 1998, 1999), who were often the subject of multiple assessments and were marginalised from mainstream services. Furthermore, an inconsistent response was noted in relation to children from minority ethnic groups. While children from Asian communities were under-represented on child protection registers and in local authority care, there was over-representation of African-Caribbean children both in local authority care (Luthera 1997) and on child protection registers.

There was also growing criticism of social work practice, which failed to address the impact of discrimination and racism on Black children and their families, while the MacPherson Report (MacPherson1999) pointed to the operation of institutional racism, from which children's services could not be excluded. Not surprisingly other research highlighted the lack of take-up of (largely white) family support services by Black families (Butt and Box 1998).

In parallel with research that indicated tendencies for services to be child protection-focused, inquisitorial, disablist and racist, the quality of assessments was being called into question by reports from the Social Services Inspectorate. A summary of its findings from child care inspections (1993 to 1997) concluded that assessments were of variable quality, lacked systematic approaches to information-gathering, failed to obtain children's views and did not appreciate the needs of Black and minority ethnic children. Inconsistencies of procedure and practice were also found across services and there was an absence of inter-agency protocols or frameworks for assessing children in need. Timescales for completion were variable and families were given inadequate initial responses when seeking help (Department of Health 2000d).

The 'Orange Book'

The use of *Protecting Children: A Guide for Social Workers Conducting a Comprehensive Assessment* (Department of Health 1988c), widely known as the 'Orange Book', was also coming under scrutiny. It had been intended as an assessment tool in situations involving child abuse and was not adequate for assessments of children in need. O'Hagan and Dillenburger (1995) argued that the questions it posed were intrusive, repetitive and sometimes irrelevant, with equal weight being given to each question and too little emphasis placed on the use of discretion. In his critique, Katz (1997) noted that some practitioners used the 'Orange Book' as a checklist. This led to mechanistic assessments, which alienated families because they were not sufficiently included in this approach to assessment as an 'event', rather than a process. In addition, services were withheld from families awaiting the completion of assessments. The lessons from inspections and the findings from research heavily influenced the principles enshrined in the Assessment Framework.

The Assessment Framework

The Assessment Framework consists of three interrelated domains, represented in the form of a triangle: the child's developmental needs, parenting capacity, and family and environmental factors. Each of these domains has a number of critical dimensions and it is the interaction between these critical dimensions that is assessed in order to understand how they affect the child or children in the family. The information is collected in a lengthy record book, which is age-related, and, as well as including sections on the three domains, the recording format also provides space for analysis, professional judgement, the views of parents and children and a detailed care plan. The Framework was issued with a plethora of other materials, including a set of scales and questionnaires, practice guidance, a training pack and a reader *The Child's World, Assessing Children in Need* (Horwath 2000). These materials were intended to inform practitioners about the findings from research and the implications for good practice.

The key features of the Framework are that it made available a consistent approach for assessing all children in need, introduced mandatory timescales for the completion of initial assessments (seven working days) and core assessments (35 working days) and emphasised an inter-agency approach to assessment and service provision. The principles underpinning the Assessment Framework are that assessments:

- are child-centred
- are rooted in child development
- are ecological in their approach
- ensure equality of opportunity
- involve working with children and families
- build on strengths as well as identify difficulties
- are inter-agency in their approach (to both assessment and service provision)
- are a continuing process not a single event

- are carried out in parallel with other action and with providing services
- are grounded in evidence-based knowledge.

(Department of Health *et al.* 2000, p.10)

These general principles reflect core social work values and the introduction of the Assessment Framework represented significant progress in promoting their consistent application in practice. Whether some of the more specific content of the *Framework* facilitated this progress will be discussed later.

Assessment in practice

Is it possible to preserve some of the strengths of practice that predated the introduction of the Assessment Framework and combine them with the new format and the use of research findings? This question is now pursued through a case study[1] in the hope that the issues raised, difficulties experienced and solutions pursued will prove useful to social workers who are seeking to incorporate the *Framework* into their practice.

Background

Alex was 6 months old when I began working with the family. He is the son of Roger, a 45-year-old English former manager, and Anna, a 40-year-old doctor, who was an illegal immigrant. The couple had met over the Internet and, after a brief introduction in Anna's country of origin, they had married. The couple had entered the UK illegally because Anna had been unable to get a visa. They had rented a property in a village and hoped to start a new life. Problems quickly developed as Anna felt isolated from her family, had no links with anyone from her country of origin and felt alienated in a foreign culture. There were also difficulties stemming from their significant emotional problems. Roger had sustained short-term memory loss following a suicide attempt using carbon monoxide gas, after his second marriage had broken down some years previously. This had been a major turning point in his life as he had lost the high status associated with his managerial career. Anna had long-standing problems with alcohol misuse and had been facing prosecution in her country of origin for a drink driving offence in which someone had been seriously injured.

Concerns began emerging about Alex failing to thrive, the police being called to a number of domestic violence incidents and evidence of Anna's drinking coming to light. A case conference was called. Anna presented reasoned responses to the concerns raised as she (via an interpreter) broke down each piece of 'evidence' presented by social workers and the police and argued effectively that there was no real risk to Alex and that his failure to thrive had not been diagnosed as non-organic or emotional and therefore could not be linked to any potential emotional trauma resulting from turbulent parenting. Alex's name was not placed on the child protection register. However, the Assessment Framework stipulated that a core assessment be undertaken following Section 47 (Children Act 1989) inquiries. The couple were quite resistant to the process, given that they would probably have assumed that social services would disappear out of their lives following the decision at the case conference not to place Alex on the child protection register. An additional difficulty was the cultural and linguistic chasm between Anna and myself, which could have made a fair and accurate assessment of her parenting problematic.

The core assessment

My concerns proved fairly accurate during my first visit, which was marked by Anna's complete incomprehension of the rationale for and process of the assessment, outlined with the assistance of an English interpreter. Unfortunately, her knowledge of Anna's language proved to be insufficient to translate the nuances of meaning required. She referred frequently to her dictionary and told me she was unable to translate many of my questions or explanations. In addition, there was clearly an element of cultural dissonance in that I was emphasising an 'exchange model' of assessment (Smale et al. 1993), while Anna's previous experience of 'the authorities' appeared to be one of totalitarian control, to which the best response was deceit or manipulation. She was very mistrusting of an approach which valued people gaining insight into their behaviour and taking personal responsibility for change. I had also not anticipated the length of time the process would take and found that the first session was completely taken up with discussing the purpose of the assessment and acquiring the couple's consent to contact their doctors for their medical history.

I ensured that I was more prepared for further sessions by requesting an interpreter from Anna's country of origin, who was able to share cultural nuances. I met with the interpreter before the next session to explain my function and clarify the aims of the overall assessment, as well as going over particular questions, which I asked to be translated in full. I was aware from previous training on using interpreters that abbreviations were often used that could change the tone and even meaning of questions. I also asked for everything Anna said to be translated, even asides, as I have often found throwaway comments more revealing than prepared answers. I allowed longer for the sessions and encouraged the interpreter to inform me if I was being culturally insensitive or if certain questions made little sense within Anna's cultural context. During the course of the assessment, Anna's English also improved (another social worker had organised English lessons) and she would often interrupt the interpreter to talk directly to me. The timescale of 35 days, stipulated by the Department of Health, proved to be inadequate for the purpose of completing a thorough assessment and I had to agree with Anna's complaint that 'four sessions are not enough to sum up my life'. However, I was able to complete an assessment that served as a baseline from which to plan interventions and assess change and developments. This necessitated extended involvement, which allowed me to form a much closer working relationship with the couple and resulted in a more rounded assessment. The key development was that the level of alcohol misuse and violence in the relationship had led to a change of social work plan as Alex was accommodated and care proceedings initiated. I was then asked to expand my assessment to include an analysis of risk and parental capacity to change.

Extending the assessment process

In order to ensure that my assessment was evidence based, I drew information from a number of sources in addition to the parents' accounts. This included social work files and discussions with other professionals: the sessional worker who observed contact, the childminder, the foster carer and the police who attended the home during incidents. I observed Alex with the foster carer and during contact with each parent separately and together on a number of occasions and in different settings. I also referred to relevant research (see below). The wider environmental factors (in this case dominated by Roger's loss of employment and Anna's status as an illegal immigrant, her social isolation and financial dependency on her husband) will be discussed later.

An essential component of any assessment is to explore each parent's background, to seek to identify the origins of the behaviour identified by professionals as problematic. My sessions with the parents were based on practice I have developed over the years, derived from my family therapy training, using tools such as genograms and circular questioning to elicit more dynamic information about individual parent's family backgrounds, relationship patterns, myths and scripts. I also used some of Maine's questions about adult attachment from the 'Orange Book' (Department of Health 1988c, p.52), with the proviso that I explored the meaning of, and insight into, past difficult relationships and traumatic events, rather than assuming a negative impact. My analysis of risk was also influenced by Adcock (2000), Bentovim (1991), Milner and O'Byrne (2002), Morrison (1991), Reder, Duncan and Gray (1993) and, particularly by Moore (1996).

Moore (1996) outlines a cognitive behavioural approach to risk assessment. The initial tasks are to:

- identify the harmful behaviour, establish its frequency, severity and contexts

- determine influences from past learning and experiences

- identify conditions and triggers and any potentially deviant drive or mental illness (which I would always refer on for a specialist assessment).

The next steps are to analyse controls and disinhibitors, such as:

- people's moral code and the congruence of their behaviour with their self-image
- the level of empathy or cognitive distortion in relation to understanding the effect of the behaviour
- the general degree of impulsivity and strength of individual needs which may override their ability to meet a child's needs
- the impact of any substance misuse.

The wider emotional and social environment also needs to be addressed to determine whether the couple's relationship is supportive or not, as well as whether the housing or financial situation adds to or detracts from stress. The Assessment Framework reintroduces an ecological element to assessments and emphasises the role of supportive and unsupportive factors in people's environment (Jack 2000). This was particularly pertinent in Anna's case as she expressed considerable distress about her separation from her family and culture and her lack of 'true friends'.

In order to avoid too much descriptive content, I have summarised conclusions I derived from sessions on the parents' background and relationship. My goal within this process is to help people gain insight into the influences on their personality and behaviour that may help with the change process. I use their language in reports as much as possible in order that they feel heard and can relate to the analyses. Sometimes (as in this case) I offer a list of descriptive words (with the same number of strengths and weaknesses) for people to choose from, if they struggle with finding words to describe themselves or their partners. I always ask people to offer anecdotes to explain their choice of words, to ensure a common understanding and to gather qualitative information about past behaviour. In future sessions, I can use their descriptions to jointly identify weaknesses to work on. If change is not possible, I document the way in which parents have responded to past intervention and attempts within the assessment to address change.

ROGER

Roger described himself as warm, generous, impulsive and hot-tempered. He prized material success and wealth and said he had had 'balls of brass', as he described ruthless business techniques. He had been married twice, had had many affairs and felt remorse about them when his second marriage ended, which triggered his suicide attempts. There was considerable evidence of Roger behaving impulsively without thinking of the consequences. For example, he had been determined to get Anna to the UK, using what he described as 'technically illegal methods'. I established that his mental health difficulties, which he minimised, were still very apparent. He saw himself as a shadow of his former self and was desperate and ashamed about his circumstances, describing his home as a 'hovel'. He acknowledged feeling depressed but said he responded to stress by 'pretending it's not happening'. He felt that mental health professionals were of little assistance and his strong family script of self-sufficiency made it difficult for him to receive help with the debt the couple was amassing, which added greatly to his stress. His short-term memory loss was incapacitating and made it difficult for him to gain employment. However, he was also immobilised by his inability to come to terms with the loss of his previous life and could not benefit from help offered or adapt his employment goals to be more realistic. He did not perceive professional concerns regarding Alex as valid and did not accept that he could be negatively affected by incidents of domestic violence or Anna's alcohol misuse, both of which he minimised.

ANNA

Anna described herself as intelligent, hardworking, passionate, impulsive, worldly-wise and controlling. In describing events that had occurred in her past, I ascertained that she was a very determined person who had a strong survival instinct. Both her parents had been at the top of their professions and she had had a relatively privileged lifestyle. She was an outgoing child who was challenging to her parents. Her father, who she had seen as a 'god', had been very strict and she felt he had kept her under control. However, he had died when she was in her 20s and after this time she said there was no one to influence her behaviour. She had had a daughter at an early age, who had virtually been brought up by Anna's mother, while Anna continued her studies. Her experience of parenting had been somewhat at arm's-length as a result and she described herself as having a sibling-like relationship with her daughter. She showed little empathy towards her past partners or her current partner and commented that she would leave when she 'got fed up of seeing the same face every day'. She described life in her country of origin as very primitive and had escaped what she considered to be a very harsh existence and possibly imprisonment (although she never acknowledged this). However, she had underestimated the emotional cost of emigrating, as she had always relied heavily on her family for support. She found living in an English village extremely isolating, as she had been used to living in small flats with her extended family.

AS A COUPLE

The couple had also underestimated the difficulties of successfully negotiating a new relationship, particularly a cross-cultural one. Each had assumed that their relationship would meet their unmet needs, Anna for an affluent lifestyle and Roger for an undemanding and passive wife. When these expectations were not met, the relationship began to deteriorate and Anna returned to old coping mechanisms, using alcohol to escape from her isolation and the loss of her family and country. Conflict was exacerbated by Anna's extensive use of Roger's credit card, based on her belief that he was as wealthy as he had implied when they first met. This would infuriate Roger who became increasingly exasperated. He tolerated Anna's contempt for what she felt was his ineffectual failure to address his problems and get an ordinary job until (in his own words) he 'blew', allowing his anger to explode in outbursts of violence. This pattern became very apparent, as I was able to observe some of the conflict at first hand. As intervention is an important element of assessment, I discussed my observations with the couple, being careful not to blame either of them for the conflict, while being clear that violence was unacceptable. This proved difficult as Roger continued to bury his head in the sand and answered 'pass' to any questions focusing on resolving conflict. Anna became increasingly frustrated with his pessimism and passive approach to life.

RELATIONSHIP WITH ALEX

As well as discussing the couple's backgrounds, relationship and individual problems, I also observed their relationship with their son and discussed their feelings towards him. Reder and Duncan suggest that it is important to explore the meaning of a child to his or her parents, as children can acquire an unconscious 'script' derived from their parents' unresolved conflicts and past influences:

> The meaning of the child includes overt and covert motivations for wanting and having a child, as well as conscious and unconscious determinants of the parent's attitudes, feelings and relationship with the particular child. (1995, p.42)

Anna had decided to get pregnant early on in her relationship with Roger and had had a previous miscarriage before giving birth to Alex. She was aware that having a child strengthened her immigration case. Her isolation and lack of role had also motivated her wish to have a child to care for. Anna spoke of her love for Alex but tended not to see him as a separate person and described him as 'a present to me'. She also described his personality as 'serious and quiet like me'. Her parenting style reflected an inability to allow Alex to develop autonomy and she was observed to be reluctant to allow Alex to feed himself or explore his environment fully.

Roger tended to see his children as his partner's responsibility and his older children of 17 and 15 seemed to offer him support (including financial assistance), rather than his assuming a supportive and stable parenting role. During my visits he was always preoccupied with his fight to regain his business career and was more animated when discussing the cars he had owned, than when talking about Alex. Alex also appeared to represent a fantasy of recreating the family life he had lost, while there was an element of his using Alex to maintain his relationship with Anna, when she left him after a violent outburst.

ALEX

As well as exploring the origins and severity of parental difficulties, a central task in any assessment is to define the nature and severity of the harm the child has suffered and to identify the links between the two. In Alex's case, he was failing to thrive which was, after some months, linked to foetal alcohol syndrome. In addition, there was considerable evidence of his being an unresponsive, immobile baby at six months. For example the police officers who had attended a number of the domestic violence incidents had frequently found him lying silent but awake in the cot. Furthermore, his childminder reported that at six months he lay on the floor still and silent for long periods of time.

Babies need close confident and caring physical and emotional contact with a parent in order to grow well. While Adcock (2000) recognises Milner and O'Byrne's (1998) point that attachment theory has been overemphasised in the UK, Adcock refocuses attention on Fahlberg's argument that attachment influences a child's physical, intellectual and psychological development: 'The child's earliest attachments become the prototype for subsequent interpersonal development' (Adcock 2000, p.69). I was struck by the apparent absence of attachment behaviour, which is usually common in children of Alex's age, either in the foster home or during contact. He was by this stage 9 months old and smiled in response to anyone smiling at him but showed no reaction when separated from his main carers. At his age, attachment theory suggests that he should have developed a strong attachment to his parents and if separated would be expected to become temporarily distressed (Howe 1995).

Alex's lack of response, which Anna presented as evidence of his being a 'good baby', could suggest that his early demands were not responded to consistently so that he gave up. My observation of contact between Alex and his parents also confirmed that he did not distinguish his parents from other adults and was neither excited at their arrival nor distressed at their departure. As I had observed this lack of response during earlier home visits, before Alex was taken into care, I felt his behaviour could not be explained by the effect of separation and phases of protest, withdrawal and detachment (Howe 1995). I had noticed during these visits that Alex was usually in his cot or buggy, and when his parents did hold him, he was generally facing outwards with no eye contact or communication. Roger did seem warmer with Alex and would cuddle him closely, whereas Anna was more functional in her care and held to rigid routines saying that before the age of 1, babies need little more than food and sleep.

It was important that I did not stereotype Anna's child care practices and assume that mothers in her country of origin were less warm and affectionate. I was also careful not to impose western values, which favour practices like demand feeding, and I distinguished cultural differences that are not necessarily harmful from parenting which is by any standards neglectful. For example, I was supportive of Anna's practice of prioritising sleep in a quiet unstimulating environment, in between feeds. However from discussions with Roger about the content of the couple's rows, I learned that Anna tended to put Alex to bed early in the evening or late afternoon so that she could continue drinking without disturbance, a practice that would be deemed unacceptable by professionals in any culture.

Both parents clearly had considerable emotional difficulties and I concluded that the combination of alcohol misuse and domestic violence was likely to have resulted in their being emotionally unavailable to Alex at a crucial stage in his early life. The work of Cleaver, Unell and Aldgate (1999) on factors affecting parenting capacity was particularly relevant and many of the findings relating to alcohol misuse and domestic violence were applicable. Cleaver *et al.* suggest that parental depression or inebriation can lead to missed health appointments and Alex's medical history reflected this. Also, Anna was discovered to have been drinking alcohol from a water bottle during one of her contacts. When this was discovered, and Anna's behaviour was clearly seen to be distressing Alex, the contact was stopped, but I was able to reflect on the behaviour I had observed.

My observations confirmed the research findings that impaired concentration resulting from excessive alcohol use leads to parents being less attentive and responding less frequently to their baby's cues (Cleaver *et al.* 1999). When they do respond, it was found that they are more likely to do so in a controlling rather than facilitative manner. I noted that Anna continued to try to feed Alex when he was giving clear signals that he had had enough. She also insisted on putting Alex in the cot for a nap when he was obviously not tired and protested vociferously. Alex appeared to be familiar with his mother's approach and had established coping mechanisms of avoidance, pushing her away or crying. In addition, there were safety issues surrounding the parents' difficulties, as Anna had been found on one occasion carrying Alex down the middle of a road at night following a drinking bout and an incident of domestic violence. It was also apparent that Roger's violence put Alex at direct risk, as shown by an observed contact when the child was caught on the shoulder by a food bowl Roger had thrown at Anna during a row. Apart from leading to immediate action to secure Alex's safety, these incidents provided information that assisted in the assessment of the level of risk.

I incorporated into my assessment findings from research that suggest children can cope with one adversity but the combination of adversities, such as alcohol misuse and domestic violence, can have a cumulative effect (Kaplan 1999). It was clear that Alex had had to endure a range of adverse experiences, which given his vulnerable age were more likely to have had a greater impact (Cleaver *et al.* 1999). There was tangible evidence that he had already been negatively affected, from his failure to thrive, diagnosis of foetal alcohol syndrome and delays in both his general development and his ability to develop trusting attachments.

Intervention

As the case took some time to progress through court, complicated by the additional proceedings in relation to Anna's immigration status, I was heavily involved in intervention as well as assessment, which is vital if parents are to be given the opportunity of reflecting on their behaviour and contemplating change. My recent practice has been influenced by Jenkins' approach to the interpretation of denial as a function of social 'restraints' rather than evidence of an inability to change (1990). Jenkins developed a working model for engagement with abusive and violent men, which 'invited' them to address their violence by recognising the factors that stopped them from contributing to a more equal respectful sensitive and caring relationship. Such restraints may include an exaggerated sense of entitlement in relation to others, a socio-cultural belief in female submissiveness, a reliance on others to take social and emotional responsibility in relationships and a tendency to blame abusive behaviour on other people, events or factors beyond their control. A key role of the worker is to interrupt the man's attempts to avoid responsibility and praise any evidence of acceptance of responsibility even if it is merely for his attendance at the sessions.

Jenkins' 'invitations' to abusive men to take responsibility for their behaviour is a less confrontational and judgemental model than a common social work approach, which tends to pathologise denial. Accordingly, I fed back my assessment to the parents in order to elicit their views and 'invited' them to take responsibility for harmful behaviours. This session did not go well and Anna argued about much of the content of my assessment report and backtracked on much of what she had said. Roger took exception to a few minor points relating to his approach to seeking employment but did not comment on the central concerns. I agreed to rewrite some of the contentious elements of the report, but did not change the evidence relating to Alex's experiences and the analysis of risk. I also included the parents' opinions in my report. This helped me move forward with them and focus on behaviour that they were prepared to accept was potentially damaging to Alex and that they planned to address. The couple were able to accept that their relationship was problematic and although they did not recognise that Alex had been damaged by the violence they agreed that it could be damaging if it continued.

I worked closely with the key social worker, who made a referral to the Domestic Violence Support Service, and I encouraged the couple to approach Relate if they wanted to work at remaining together and resolving their disputes. Roger was also referred to the Council of Disabled People for an advocacy approach to his difficulties in dealing with finances and finding work. This was more acceptable to him than other assistance, which, he said, made him feel like a 'charity case'. Anna was referred to the Alcohol Advisory Service to address her problematic drinking, which she acknowledged had damaged Alex following a confirmed diagnosis of foetal alcohol syndrome. Her isolation was also addressed by her being put in touch with other people from her country of origin and, as mentioned earlier, by assistance to take up English classes.

I also discussed at length my observation of Anna and Roger's inability to talk to, give eye contact or warmth or to play with Alex. Recognising that this was partly a result of lack of knowledge about his needs, I suggested intervention by an experienced family support worker to model interactive play and give advice about feeding. Anna was initially resistant to this, saying that as a doctor she did not need this input. She was mollified however by the knowledge that the worker was an expert in her field and Anna chose to interpret this as having some medical training. This input proved the most successful and there was evidence of the couple learning to engage with Alex in a more age-appropriate manner and with more open expressions of warmth. Other difficulties proved more intransigent however.

The intervention process did not run smoothly and events tended to overtake the work as the couple lurched from crisis to crisis, separating and reuniting. I knew from my experience of working with domestic violence that women do not find it easy to leave violent men, given the way in which women's self-esteem is eroded by repeated physical, emotional and sexual abuse to the extent that they experience differing degrees of post-traumatic stress disorder. They need to be empowered by a believing and sensitive approach (Humphreys *et al.* 2000). Anna was a very strong and resourceful woman, but her relatively weak position was exacerbated by her dependency on Roger for accommodation and finance; her illegal status in the UK meaning that she was initially unable to work or access income support or housing benefit. I also discovered, during one of the couple's separations, that Anna could not be given a bed at any women's refuge, as they required her to be an asylum seeker to be able to apply for funding for her place. I was drawn into a supportive role as Roger had dropped Anna off at the Family Centre where I was based, with all her belongings in black plastic bags. After considerable consultation with the local authority's Legal Department, an Asylum Seeker Team and Anna's immigration solicitor, it was discovered that she could receive assistance in the form of a shared house and weekly vouchers from the Refugee Council in another location. In the event Anna chose to return to Roger rather than take up this option. She returned to what was familiar and in her perception 'safer', despite the ongoing risk of violence.

Decision-making

A decision had to be made about the likelihood of change within timescales that were acceptable given Alex's age and need for stability: 'Parental care should be competent enough, with the assistance of supports and services, to respond to the child's needs within a space of three to six months' (Adcock 2000, p.74). Ultimately neither Anna nor Roger was able to benefit from the services that were involved in change work. Anna struggled with the 'talking therapy' approach of the Alcohol Services and told me almost wistfully that in her country of origin she would have been put in a psychiatric hospital and injected with a drug, which would have killed her if she had used alcohol. She had gained benefit from the support of her domestic violence worker and had secured a job and alternative accommodation, which afforded her considerable independence and a potential future alone. She had shown considerable determination and resilience, important strengths that supported the change process. However, she was unable to realise this potential and returned to Roger who had not progressed at all.

He had not taken up support to assist him in gaining employment or receiving benefits and he was in severe debt with the threat of eviction looming. The couple had been to Relate once, asserted that they did not have any relationship difficulties and had not returned. There were ongoing reports from the police about continued violence, which the couple denied. I spoke to the attending police officer who gave me an account of one particular incident, detailing what the couple had said, but both Anna and Roger continued to deny they had had a dispute and suggested the police had misunderstood. The couple continued with the pattern of calling on support agencies to step in after a violent incident, following a drinking binge, and then retreating from these agencies after the crisis, when they reverted to the belief that they had no problems. I had to conclude from this that they had both slipped back in the cycle of change, from the stage of determination to change to denial and minimisation (Prochaska and DiClemente 1982) and were unlikely to make sufficient changes to be able to care for Alex safely. I wrote an addendum to my report detailing my analysis, based on research findings, and my understanding of the change model. In April 2002, a Freeing Order was granted in the County Court (Section 18 of the Adoption Act 1976) and Alex was placed with an adoptive family.

Conclusion

In Alex's case, I found the timescales that were laid down by the Assessment Framework were impractical for the purpose of conducting an assessment thorough enough to be a basis for deciding Alex's future, although the Court's timescales allowed me to continue assessing and intervening over a six-month period. This experience was symptomatic of the teething problems associated with staff initially feeling overwhelmed by the demands placed on them by the Assessment Framework. There were a number of meetings at which the difficulties of realising the requirements of the Framework within existing staffing resources were discussed. Some additional staffing had assisted with initial assessments but teams were struggling to cope with the detail required to complete the core assessment records. A departmental review confirmed difficulty in completing core assessments within the timescales. My experience and that of the remainder of the staff group in a Family Centre indicated the difficulty encountered in trying to complete assessments that were thorough and engaged the family positively, within 35 days.

Furthermore, completing the core assessment booklet produced a huge unwieldy document, which encouraged the amassing of sometimes repetitive and irrelevant information. Little space is devoted to the analysis of the material obtained and ultimately I wrote an additional report using the same headings but unconstrained by the recording format in the Assessment Framework. I was also able to draw on my past experience and materials to ensure that the process was more dynamic than completing the questionnaire format of the booklet.

The therapeutic relationship, valued so highly in conducting assessments, was being threatened by the need to complete all the questions in the core assessment record, which were not always relevant and were frequently repetitive. Workers were becoming overwhelmed with the amount of information they collected. Parents were also questioning the repetitive and intrusive nature of the questions and a social worker reported that one mother had asked her, when the booklet had been completed, 'Have I passed?' This exposed a fundamental problem with the way in which the Assessment Framework involves using what is essentially a long prescriptive checklist. While the guidance recommends the Framework should be used in a 'guided conversation', the questions in the age-related records are too specific to allow this. Social workers have been given competing messages; on the one hand to ensure these records are completed and on the other to avoid being bogged down in detail and to produce succinct analyses.

Another problem with the Framework relates to the separation of the 'domains' of parenting capacity and children's needs. Although the guidance emphasises the interconnection between the domains, their separation into different headings focuses attention on static needs and functions and away from the dynamic relationships between parents and their children. Reder and Lucey emphasised that 'parenting is not a quality that someone does, or does not, possess, but a relationship that responds to fluctuations in other relationships' (1995, p.13). In addition to the failure to prioritise the interaction between parents and children, the use of the term 'parenting capacity' is potentially pejorative and alienating for many parents, who in my experience have either not understood what it meant or, worse, have felt insulted by it.

The Assessment Framework's emphasis on family and environmental factors, however, is a definite improvement in that it discourages social workers from adopting an individual pathology model and implies that the 'community' is a legitimate area of social work support. However, I feel this is unlikely to lead to a return to the community action model, given the current under-funding of social services departments, the national recruitment crisis and the renewed focus on child protection following the publication of the report into the death of Victoria Climbié (Department of Health 2003a).

Perhaps the most problematic aspect of the Framework, however, is ironically the emphasis on the assessment itself (and the timescales it is completed within) rather than the service that is provided. While assessment is a key social work task, the current use of the Assessment Framework's recording booklets runs the danger of fetishising this task at the expense of social work intervention. The assessment is in danger of becoming *the* service, as all energies are focused on presenting families with their core assessment record within 35 days and recording their level of satisfaction. It is unfortunate that valuable resources have been diverted into implementing and monitoring the assessment process and potentially diverted away from providing family support. It may be that social workers will continue to refine their use of the Framework over time and find ways to apply it, as its principles suggest, working with children and families to identify their strengths and linking assessment and intervention.

Note

1 The names and other identifying features have been changed to preserve anonymity.

Chapter Five

Children and Young People with Sexual Behaviour Difficulties

A Practice Framework for Holistic Interventions

Andrew Durham

Introduction

This chapter will discuss the analytical practice framework used by the Sexualised Inappropriate Behaviours Service (SIBS). SIBS is a county-wide social services resource in Warwickshire, which provides direct services, resources, research, consultation and training for therapeutic work with children and young people who have sexual behaviour difficulties, or who have difficulties arising from the sexual behaviour of others. The service was set up initially in 1994 as an exploratory project; it became a permanent resource in 1996. The practice framework allows a sensitive approach to meeting the therapeutic needs of children and young people with sexual behaviour difficulties, highlighting the importance of the social context of these children and young people's experiences as being pivotal to understanding how and why these behaviours take place (full details of applying the framework to therapeutic interventions with children and young people who have been sexually abused have been documented elsewhere [Durham 2003]). The framework emphasises the importance of an anti-oppressive and child-centred approach to the work, which overtly models an appropriate use of adult power and specifically challenges oppression based on age, 'race', class, gender, ability and sexuality.

The chapter will provide a brief outline of a therapeutic schedule used by SIBS and will consider the application of the SIBS practice framework to the process of engagement and to the provision of sex and sexuality education, looking at issues of masculinity and peer pressure. The chapter will conclude by using the framework to draw together a matrix of the potential influences on a young person's inappropriate sexual behaviours.

The social context of young people's sexual behaviours

The prevalence of children and young people with sexual behaviour difficulties is becoming widely known in the literature. Home Office criminal statistics for England and Wales 1996 show that 35% (700/2000) of people cautioned for sexual offences were between the ages of 10 and 17. Of 6500 people who were cautioned or found guilty of sexual offences, 23% were aged between 10 and 20 (Home Office 1997). The vast majority of these young people were male (Masson and Morrison 1999). Children and young people are generally being exposed to increasing amounts of sexual information at an increasingly earlier age (Gil and Johnson 1993) and are often confronted by complex sexual and social dilemmas before they have the intellectual and emotional maturity to cope (Gil 1996; Moore and Rosenthal 1994). It is therefore no surprise that many children and young people are showing increasingly sexualised behaviours and demonstrating, much earlier in their lives, an awareness of sexual matters.

The wide social availability of sexual information serves to emphasise the importance of talking to children and young people about sexual matters, as part of the responsibilities carried by parents and other adults entrusted with their emotional well-being and development (Johnson 1999; Moore and Rosenthal 1994). There is also evidence that it is beneficial for children and young people to be encouraged to talk to each other in a more formalised manner, through the use of structured peer support, particularly where there has been sexual abuse (Alaggi, Michalski and Vine 1999). Without this support, children and young people are left to cope with the many confusing and prejudiced messages propagated by the media, popular culture and the fashion industry. Throughout society, there is a powerful and oppressive social policing and shaping of sexuality and sexual desire (Steinberg, Epstein and Johnson 1997). In particular, young people receive very powerful messages that emphasise the compulsory nature of heterosexism, which in turn leads to circumstances where young people are pressured to demonstrate their heterosexual competencies. This is particularly pertinent for adolescent boys, where homophobia, characterised by homophobic name-calling and other bullying, becomes a significant feature of day-to-day peer group interaction (Durham 1999; Nayak and Kehily 1997). The consequences of being left to cope with these messages, as a predominant – and often the only – source of sexual information, is that children and young people become significantly prey to oppressive images and stereotypes of 'acceptable' sexual behaviour. These create anxieties and self-doubt, and oppressively internalised misunderstandings about personal attributes and sexual and social competencies (Bremner and Hillin 1993; Jubber 1991). This leads to circumstances where many young people overestimate the sexual knowledge, understanding and competencies of their peers (Moore and Rosenthal 1994). For some this leads to personal anxieties, retreat and sometimes solitude and depression; adolescence becomes a period of uncertainty and high anxiety. For others, these beliefs can significantly influence decisions to engage in abusive sexual behaviours.

In working with children and young people, social work and other professions are charged with the responsibility of: challenging these myths and stereotypes, countering them with more thoughtful and appropriate information and providing opportunities for the development of greater insight into how misunderstandings are generated. Working in this way allows children and young people to understand how myths and stereotypes enslave them in self-doubt, create personal anxieties that prevent them from reaching their potential and, for some, contribute to individual decisions to sexually abuse others.

A framework for therapeutic practice

In approaching therapeutic interventions with young people who have sexual behaviour difficulties, it is important to have a practice framework that centralises many of these social factors, as a context in which to understand how individual behaviours have been shaped and, sometimes, justified. The practice framework used by SIBS was developed through my doctoral research into the impact of sexual abuse on the lives of young men (Durham 1999). This research study was essentially post-structural in its method and analysis, having an emphasis on language and discourse. Jackson (1992) identifies three main themes of post-structuralism. First, language is seen as constructing, rather than transmitting, meaning and subjectivity is constituted through language. Second, there is a denial of the existence of an essential self outside culture and language. Third, there is no possibility of an objective scientific truth, and knowledges are seen as 'discursive constructs' (*ibid.*, p.26) produced from particular positions. From the outset, my research placed an emphasis on diversity and the uniqueness of individual experiences. In particular, the research established that gender, power and sexuality were significant issues in sexual abuse and that it was important to understand how these factors play out in their social context. However, as the research unfolded, young men were found to have had experiences, beliefs and feelings that they held in common. Uncovering such facets did not deny or compromise the uniqueness of each young man's experience, but rather served to highlight common struggles, concerns and fears.

In developing the framework, I was aware that whilst post-structuralism presents a challenge to the essentialist nature of structural theory, arguing that it homogenises groups of people and launders out diversity, it also has the danger of unseating some of the classic analytical concepts, for example, woman, class, 'race'. In this respect it has been criticised for breaking down and fragmenting the solidarity of oppressed groups, allowing space for traditional or classic oppressive relationships to establish increased potency, through being hidden within the tapestry of difference (Barrett and Phillips 1992). Furthermore, the statements from the young men who took part in my research presented a challenge to the post-structural notion of reality being mediated by language. The extent to which this occurs is related to the social context in which the language is used. In an oppressive social context of patriarchal relations, the use of particular types of language can invoke and carry forward social oppression and thereby significantly influence interpersonal power relationships. Individual words and phrases have the potential to invoke wider social understandings. In this sense, language potentially becomes a tool of oppression. Simple statements or even words could embody significant meanings, which directly relate to widespread and socially embedded oppression. It was shown for example, that the use of the word 'queer' in the context of adolescent peer group relations has a particularly powerful impact. It can make some people significantly more powerful and others significantly less powerful. The use of this word was shown to be capable of invoking multiple oppressive discourses about personal identity, and social misconceptions about the nature and impact of child sexual abuse. Equally, carefully chosen language can invoke positive discourses, such as citizenship, children's rights or positive personal identities.

In seeking a *rapprochement* that allows us in some way to reconcile these theoretical inconsistencies (essentially the contradiction between post-structural and structural approaches), and hold on to both common and unique experiences at the same time, a new approach for therapeutic practice and research is required. This approach seeks to allow diverse interpersonal language and individual experiences to be considered in a context of social oppression. This approach utilises Cooper's (1995) concept of 'organising principles', to allow for multiple dimensions of inequality and social oppression: 'Rather than basing analysis on axes of oppression, gender, class and race can be conceived as "organizing frameworks" or less systematically "principles" that over-determine each other in their operation and effects' (Cooper 1995, p.11). Racism, for example, is considered as it interacts with other structures of social oppression, such as age, gender or sexuality. No single aspect of social oppression is seen as an absolute determinant of social power. It therefore becomes easier to account for the complexities of interpersonal relationships, for example, between a white woman and a Black man, or between a white child and a Black woman. The white woman may have less power by virtue of being a woman, but may have more power through being white. Similarly, a white child may have more social power than a Black adult or, in certain circumstances, than a gay man. The location and social context of these power relationships can also be highly significant in determining their outcome.

I have drawn some of these theoretical considerations together to form the analytical framework, represented in Figure 5.1.

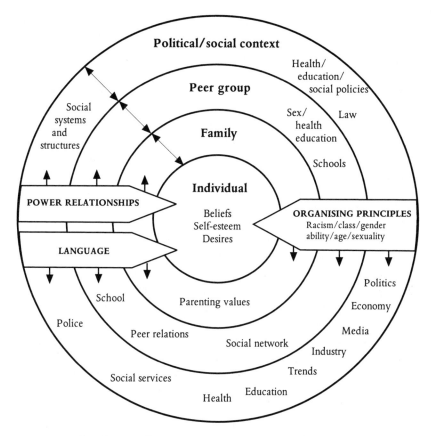

Figure 5.1 Analytical practice framework

The framework allows a study of power relationships at different but inter-related levels of social interaction, in the context of widespread oppressive social and political influences. At the centre of the framework, the individual is an agent of choice and action, with wishes, desires and beliefs. Individual experience, however, is subject to and created by interactions with others. Each level of interaction constitutes a site of learning and influence. Each individual is a member of each level and so not only receives its influence, but also contributes to its influence on others. This may, for example, be at a peer group level or at the level of the wider political and social context, where processes of hegemony and consensus involve each individual in receiving beliefs, carrying them forward within themselves, passing them on to others and so forth. The extent of the influence will vary according to many factors, some of which may relate to class, 'race', gender, sexuality, age or ability. The influence of each level is interdependent, and will vary according to the individual's circumstances, age and development.

The most immediate level of interaction is family and kinship. In most circumstances, for a young child this is the site of initial interactions, relationships and learning, and continues to have a varying influence over time. The next level of interaction is the social network of extra-familial relationships and interactions. Within this network is located the peer group and access to other close and intimate relationships, experienced through schools and possibly pre-school networks, social and leisure contacts and work or college. The three levels – individual, family and peer group – are located in the wider social and political context, which again influences and interacts with each level, and also contributes to the determination of interactions between the different levels. The framework explicates the apparatus of oppression and social disadvantage, as a context in which to understand diverse individual experiences. It allows an analysis of interpersonal power relationships and highlights the significance of language in mediating and carrying forward oppression, alongside recognition of the importance of power and sexuality. The framework has usefulness for a wide range of therapeutic practice, and in particular the arena of sexual abuse where issues of power, gender and sexuality are pertinent.

In working with young people with sexual behaviour difficulties, the framework allows us to examine the wider social and cultural influences on their decisions to behave in a particular way. By looking at the wider social messages a young person receives about how he or she should feel and behave, we can find clues about how a wide range of factors may have intersected and accumulated to precipitate the circumstances, thoughts, feelings and beliefs behind an abusive or inappropriate act. The framework also allows us to explore the power relationship between a person initiating inappropriate or sexually abusive behaviour and the victim. As over 90% of child sexual abuse is committed by males (Home Office 1997; Morrison, Erooga and Beckett 1994), the 'organising principle' of gender is a particularly significant aspect of the framework. It is therefore important to explore the concept of 'masculinity'.[1]

Masculinities

The concept of 'hegemony' has been used to describe dominant forms of masculinity (Carrigan, Connell and Lee 1987; Connell 1987). Hegemony was a term used by Gramsci in his development of work by Lenin (Joll 1977). In literal terms it means ascendancy, domination or leadership. Gramsci (1971) extended the concept to use it as an explanation of how one group in society dominates and subordinates another group. This is not dependent on economic and physical power alone, but has ideological dimensions, whereby large numbers of a subordinate group are led into accepting the values of the dominant group. Hegemonic masculinities are characterised by an essential control of the self, the environment and others, namely women, children and other men. Connell theorises a hierarchy of masculinities amongst men, 'hegemonic, conservative and subordinated' (1987, p.110), located within structures of power. He emphasises the importance of examining power relationships between men in order to understand men's relationships with women and children and, in particular, men's violence. Taking such a perspective forward, it is possible to conceptualise a more dynamic multiplicity of contested masculinites, interacting with other social oppressions. Masculinities are varied, shifting and changing across different historical, situational, cultural, temporal and spatial contexts (Cornwall and Lindisfarne 1994). Individual men or boys will present differing masculinities at different times and in different places and circumstances (Hearn 1996; Pringle 1995). Hearn suggests that the term 'men's practices' (1996, p.214) more accurately represents an understanding of the diversity of what men do, where, when, how and why.

There are tensions here. On the one hand there is an attempt to conceptualise a multiplicity of masculinities, which moves towards questioning the term 'masculinity' itself. On the other hand, it is recognised that there are dominant forms of masculinity that render other forms subordinate; dominant and subordinated discourses are produced mutually. (In addition, where there is subordination, there will be resistance.) However, there is no simple question of choice about which 'masculinity' to present where. There are particular forms of masculinity that are dominant in most circumstances and become the socially accepted norm. The negotiation of individual masculinities takes place in an oppressive social context in which heterosexism and homophobia are the norm (Nayak and Kehily 1997; Sedgwick 1990; Wolfe, Wekerle and Scott 1997).

Warner (1993) argues that most social theory takes a heterosexist perspective, in which heterosexuality is normalised and seen as functional to the social order, never requiring explanation, and that themes of homophobia and heterosexism pervade almost every document in our culture. As a consequence, other sexualities are marginalised, problematised and excluded. He further argues that a non-oppressive gender order can only come about through a radical change in the theorising and conceptualising of sexuality, with shifting styles of identity politics and the generation and valuing of new cultures. In following through some of the arguments put forward by Warner, it could be argued that in many ways the debate is predominantly about heterosexism. Particularly in adolescent peer cultures, notions of acceptable masculinities would appear to be at least a significant vehicle for, if not a fundamental constituent of homophobia. In this context, heterosexuality would appear to be a defining line in power relationships. In most circumstances, heterosexual forms of masculinity are more powerful than others.

Masculinities and sexual abuse

Within patriarchal relations, dominant or hegemonic masculinities are oppressively defined in terms of a restrictive range of acceptable behaviours (Durham
1999). The intertwining or conflation of biological sex and gender potentially
creates confusion and doubts for the individual. For the male, masculinities,
defined in terms of strength and power and natural domination, are not biological realities, and require constant nurturing, affirmation, and repression of
unacceptable 'feminine' behaviours (Connell 1989; Frosh 1993; Kaufman
1987a). In patriarchal relations, power bestows benefits, one way (the pre-
scribed way) to exercise power is to subordinate someone else. The greater the
need to emphasise or affirm masculinities, the greater the need to subordinate
someone else. Furthermore, the greater the extent to which it is done, the
greater the power, and hence the benefits, but also the greater the deception,
and ultimately, the greater the harm done to all. Sex, violence, power and
gender are combined to construct dominant forms of masculinities that are
invested in and expressed through the body, and are central to self-esteem and
identity.

For many men, the everyday experience of patriarchal relations is sufficient
to provide the necessary benefits and nurture for being male, although this is
not to deny the need for constant masculinising affirmations and access to 'legitimate and acceptable' closeness to other males. For other men, these benefits
are not felt. Other circumstances and negative experiences accentuate
self-doubts and repressed emotions and call into play the need for affirmation
through the use of a more overt force. Sometimes physical violence may suffice,
but for some the doubt is so great that affirmation has to be experienced
through the body, as physical and/or sexual violence and domination. There is
an illusion of, and subsequent disappointment with, power in these circumstances, which after a short passage of time thwarts the affirmation. This goes
some way to explain the repetition and escalation of men's sexual violence
(Kelly 1988). It has been argued that masculinities are particularly fragile
during adolescence. In adolescence the pain and fear involved in repressing
'femininity' and passivity start to become evident. For most of us, the response
to this inner pain is to reinforce the bulwarks of masculinity. The emotional
pain created by obsessive masculinity is stifled by reinforcing masculinity itself
(Kaufman 1987a, p.12).

These factors help us understand why the majority of sexual abuse is committed by males and why over 90% of referrals to SIBS of young people with
inappropriate or aggressive sexual behaviours are boys. The scale and prevalence of child sexual abuse cuts across all boundaries: class, gender, age, 'race',
disability (Herman 1990; Kelly 1988; MacLeod and Saraga 1991). The use of
the framework (see Figure 5.1) allows us to explore with a boy his received
beliefs about his 'masculinity', how this has influenced his thoughts and

feelings about being a boy or a man, and how this has been translated into action. It also allows us to consider closely the meanings, textures and dynamics of his interpersonal power relationships.

At this stage it is important to note again that whilst most young people who sexually abuse are men or boys, there are women and girls who also sexually abuse, or who have inappropriate sexual behaviours. Indeed, Appendix Two shows that just under 10% of referrals concerning sexual behaviour difficulties to SIBS were girls and young women. The practice framework has an equally important application to therapeutic work with girls. In a similar way to that in which boys receive oppressive messages and beliefs about their 'masculinity', girls receive oppressive messages and beliefs about their 'femininity'. The patriarchal construction of 'masculinity' is mirrored by an oppressive construction of 'femininity' that emphasises weakness, passivity and subordination to masculinity. Girls receive mixed and confusing messages about their identities and their sexual behaviours, and are often pressured into subordination (Carrigan *et al.* 1987; Kaufman 1987b; Steinberg *et al.* 1997). Again, as with boys, the framework allows us to understand and explore with a girl her received beliefs about her 'femininity', the influences on her thoughts and beliefs and how they are translated into day-to-day interactions. The approach described in the next section applies equally, therefore, to girls and boys.

Therapeutic intervention

This section presents a brief outline of the holistic therapeutic intervention schedule used by SIBS for children and young people with sexual behaviour difficulties. In discussing applications of the framework, two aspects of the schedule are considered in detail: first, engagement and setting ground rules and, second, sex and sexuality education.

Many writers have noted that children and young people who display sexual behaviour difficulties are themselves vulnerable, many having experienced a multiple range of family problems and various forms of abuse, but not necessarily (and not isolated) sexual abuse (Araji 1997; Cunningham and MacFarlane 1996; Morrison and Print 1995; Morrison *et al.* 1994; Ryan and Lane 1991). If this is the case, the appropriate intervention is one that challenges the inappropriate sexualised behaviours, but also provides a high level of support and guidance. This enables young people to begin to address the many problems in their lives and to develop a positive lifestyle, moving away from inappropriate sexualised behaviours.

Initially, the specific circumstances of the abusing behaviour need to be addressed and arrangements made for adequate supervision and the protection of others. During this assessment phase, a child or young person is taken through a process of being engaged in an agreement to undertake therapeutic work, which explores explicitly his inappropriate sexual behaviours. At this stage, the work moves on to explore the circumstances of the abusing, comparing the young person's description of his behaviour to the descriptions and statements which may have been made by the victim(s). It may be possible to map out a behavioural cycle or pattern that can be used to help the young person understand and interrupt their immediate abusive behaviour. This stage also involves an exploration of the young person's sexual history. At a later stage, this work is extended into a full exploration of the young person's predisposing thoughts, thinking errors and abuse-related sexual fantasies. Once an understanding of these circumstances has been established, it is important to take the young person through a detailed consideration of the impact of his behaviour on the victim (sometimes known as victim empathy or perspective-taking work). In addition, it is important to address any deficits in the child or young person's age-appropriate understanding of sexual behaviour and sexuality and related issues, such as sexual oppression, sexism, homophobia, etc. It is likely that an intervention will need to address the young person's own victim experiences, whatever they are, and to address the wider issues in the young person's life, which are likely to have contributed to the decision to sexually abuse. These may involve permutations of personal, peer and family-related issues. The work concludes with a comprehensive relapse-prevention plan.

Full theoretical considerations and details of interventions with young people with sexual behaviour difficulties, incorporating many aspects of this schedule, have been documented elsewhere (Araji 1997; Calder 1999, 2002; Kahn 1990; Morrison and Print 1995; Ryan and Lane 1991; Salter 1988). Araji (1997) has reviewed much of the relevant literature and has described a range of intervention programmes. Many of these programmes have a strong emphasis on the cognitive behavioural element, but often fail to take a sufficiently critical approach to gender and sexuality in a manner that adequately addresses a wider conceptualisation of the causes of sexual abuse (Durham 1999; Postlethwaite 1998).

It is important to note that an assessment of the child or young person needs to be accompanied by a comprehensive assessment of the family. The practice framework highlights that the family is an important mediator of wider social influences, as does the *Framework for the Assessment of Children in Need and their Families*, with its emphasis on a dynamic interaction between the child's developmental needs, parenting capacity and family and environmental factors (Department of Health, Department for Education and Employment and Home Office 2000; see Chapter Five). In particular the family assessment has to establish the extent of the parent's or carer's knowledge and acceptance of the reported inappropriate sexual behaviours and the extent of their motivation and cooperation with the planned assessment and intervention. It also has to assess the family's ability and willingness to supervise the child or young person adequately and to set appropriate boundaries for the safety and protection of all.

Engagement and setting ground rules

It is important to remember that even though a child or young person may have committed an extremely harmful act towards another child, he is still a child or young person himself. The framework allows us to understand aspects of the adult–child or adult–young person power relationship and translate it into meaningful action that will reassure him. It is also important to remember that the child or young person is likely to have suffered some form of abuse, loss or disruption in his own life, which may include sexual abuse. It is therefore imperative to adhere to the principles of anti-oppressive child- or young person-centred practice from the outset. Approaches to practice need to incorporate a critique of dominant social constructions of childhood that emphasise innocence and powerlessness and move towards alternative discourses of empowerment, based on children and young people's competencies (Butler and Shaw 1996; Butler and Williamson 1994).

In attending a therapeutic session about having committed a sexually abusive act, or behaving in a sexually inappropriate manner, a child or young person may be anxious, embarrassed or possibly afraid of the process. The practitioner's awareness of this is best stated and addressed as soon as possible. Equally, a child or young person may deny all knowledge of his alleged behaviours, or may be attending under duress, perhaps as part of a legal disposal or criminal conviction, or at the insistence of his parents. In gaining a child or young person's trust, a transparent approach is essential. The young person needs to know quite quickly how the practitioner is going to approach working with him, and what the ground rules are. He needs to be told that the intervention is about him and that an attempt will be made to explore fully the circumstances that have led to his reported difficulties and behaviours. The young person also needs to know that he will be supported through the difficult stages of the work and that the approach is not about punishment, but is about empowering the young person in a manner which allows him to consider his mistakes and make important steps towards an improved way of managing his life, without hurting others.

It is helpful at this stage to have a written agreement outlining the nature and purpose of the work to be undertaken. This agreement should inform the young person that he will be undertaking a programme of work in relation to specified behaviours and that he will be asked to talk in detail about his sexual knowledge, thoughts and fantasies. The agreement should also address the rules of confidentiality, stating that where possible, an appropriate level of confidentiality will be maintained. However, information relating to the actual or potential harm of the young person or another person may have to be shared with others in sufficient detail to ensure safety and protection. The agreement should also clarify the legal age of sexual consent.

The practice framework discussed earlier reminds us that careful and thoughtful use of language is important. Carefully chosen language can be empowering and pave the way for a young person to begin to think in a more positive manner. Careless use of language can be oppressive and move the young person in the opposite direction of negative thinking and resistance to change. For example, it is unhelpful to use the phrase 'young abuser'. I often wonder about the damaging impact on the young person of walking into the premises of services that adopt this phrase or use 'adolescent sex offender' in their project title and on their paper work. I recently read a report about a young person that had 'Adolescent Sex Offender Worker' under the practitioner's signature. We need to move forward on this and be more thoughtful and less oppressive in the way in which services are described. The framework allows us to see how language can invoke powerful discourses; these can be positive or negative. The phrase 'sex offender' or 'paedophile' carries considerable currency and for a child or young person, such phrases can potentially drain their confidence and belief in their own competence to move forward into an offence- or abuse-free lifestyle. The phrase 'young person who has sexually abused' is more helpful and less deterministic, as it immediately conveys a message of hope by separating the young person and the behaviour, whilst, importantly, not denying that the behaviour has been carried out by the young person.

There are many tensions at the early stages of this type of work. On the one hand, the practitioner will be attempting to remain child- or young person-centred, addressing the adult–child power dimension. On the other hand the child or young person may be resisting engagement and denying difficult and abusive behaviours that the practitioner knows have taken place. The practitioner has simultaneously to engage the young person and assert an authority that states, in no uncertain terms, that his inappropriate or abusive actions have to be addressed. It is not really possible to confront a young person about his behaviours, in a meaningful sense, until some form of therapeutic relationship has been established. The young person has to be supported in being able to withstand the confrontation, otherwise he is likely to close down and only engage at a shallow level, if at all. The practitioner needs to convey a respect towards the young person, alongside a belief that he can move forward from his behaviours and be different. The rationale behind the practitioner's actions and statements needs to be fully explained at each stage. There may well be resistance, disagreements or blatant denial. The principles of motivational interviewing (Miller and Rollnick 1991) are very helpful in managing this.

The goal of motivational interviewing is for the young person, and not the practitioner, to be facilitated to express concerns about the problem behaviour and to express arguments for change. The young person is encouraged to express both sides of his ambivalence and the arguments for change. The basic principles of this approach are that denial is a functional behaviour, and not a personality trait, and that motivation occurs in an interpersonal context between the practitioner and the young person. Accurate empathy on behalf of the practitioner is important; the style of the practitioner is a significant determinant of the outcome. Labelling and direct confrontation is considered to be unhelpful. The type of confrontation is more about confronting the client with himself; arguments are avoided, and resistance is diffused. In achieving this, it is helpful to express empathic concern about some of the immediate discomfort the young person may be experiencing, either about himself, what he has done or about other aspects of his life, for example, the impact of being moved away from home, or perhaps about family loss, or being bullied at school. The young person can then begin to understand and feel that the work to be undertaken is not about hurting or punishing him, but about helping him to make improvements in his life. The engagement process is the foundation of all work to follow.

Sex and sexuality education

It is important to establish an age-appropriate level of understanding of sexual knowledge for the child or young person and to encourage his ability to discuss his own sexuality. In helping young people understand issues about sexuality and sexual behaviour, it is important to have clearly stated values that take a holistic view of sexuality. (The book *Growing Up* [Meredith 1997] is an excellent source of sex education information for young people.) Children and young people should be encouraged to understand that sexual behaviour is not just about physical or genital contact, but includes physical, mental, emotional, individual, social, cultural, religious and political components, and that it is not necessary to have sex in order to express sexuality. They should be helped to understand that all forms of sexuality are equally valid: heterosexuality, lesbian and gay sexuality, celibacy. In discussing these issues, it is important to challenge oppression, misinformation and stereotyping. In undertaking this work, the framework can both provide theoretical underpinnings for the practitioner and be used as a direct work tool with the young person.

If the young person has been sexually abused, it will be necessary to address the impact of this as part of the work. At an early stage, a decision will have to be made about when this should be done. If a young person is highly traumatised by his abuse, then this may have to be addressed almost straight away. Whichever aspect of the work is being addressed, the other aspect will have to be kept in sight. It is helpful and important to inform the young person that most people who have been sexually abused do not go on to sexually abuse others and that it is necessary to explore how the young person's experiences may have influenced his subsequent behaviours and beliefs. It is important to understand that a prior experience of sexual abuse is neither necessary nor sufficient, in explaining the cause of sexually abusive behaviours (Durham 2003; Grubin 1998).

Using the framework, the practitioner can draw out a specific configuration of the young person's own beliefs and feelings about his gender and sexuality, possibly accompanied by looking through and discussing images in newspapers and magazines. In doing this, the young person can be helped to develop a more critical approach to gender and sexuality. Specifically, and importantly, the framework can be used to help young men explore their beliefs and understandings about their masculinity, how this relates to their sexual behaviour and how it may shape their understanding of femininity. As we have already discussed above, this is closely related to the social generation of homophobia and compulsory heterosexuality, particularly in male adolescent peer relations. An anti-homophobic approach, which acknowledges all aspects of sexuality and sexual feelings, will assist the young person in feeling able to challenge some of these images and received beliefs. It is important to acknowledge that young people are often oppressed into being afraid to admit that they have not had many sexual experiences and may therefore overstate their knowledge and competence, believing that having the right image is more important than being truthful about what they need to learn.

Similarly, the framework could be used to explore the influences on peer relations, exploring the origins and perpetuation of social oppression and power differentials in interpersonal relationships, taking in issues of oppression and pressure, based on age, class, gender, sexuality, racism and disability. In looking at issues of power, the young person needs to understand the concept of 'informed consent'. To give informed consent to a sexual act, a young person: has to be old enough to understand what they are consenting to; have enough knowledge and information; be in a situation where it is just as easy to say 'no' as it is to say 'yes'; not feel under any pressure. The issue of pressure will need to be fully explored, in the context of the young person's peer experiences, where image and identity is particularly significant and can therefore potentially lead a young person into making mistakes (Moore and Rosenthal 1994).

The framework allows us to examine how young people may have internalised oppressive stereotypes, beliefs and misunderstandings, through which, in some ways, they may have become able to justify their actions to themselves, or may have generated powerful motivations for committing the abuse. For example a boy living, for whatever reason, in fear of his self-perceived heterosexual 'inadequacies' may engage in behaviours geared towards heterosexual affirmation. He may have beliefs about his own inadequacies or incompetence through being oppressed as a 'child' (Archard 1993) within a chaotic family, or a family characterised by sexual aggression and domestic violence. He may have felt more powerful, or more like a 'real man' or 'one of the boys' through committing sexual acts with a weaker, younger or less powerful person. The framework can be used to explore the dynamic power differential between the young person and the person he abused. This may lead to greater insight, with the young person being helped to see where he is located within the multiple influences and discourses which may have shaped his thinking, leading him into a situation where he made the decision to sexually abuse or behave in a sexually inappropriate way. The framework effectively gives the young person a map through which to interpret and negotiate the past, present and future landscape of his sexuality. It can assist him in negotiating positively about the future influences on his behaviour. These applications of the framework are drawn together in Figure 5.2.

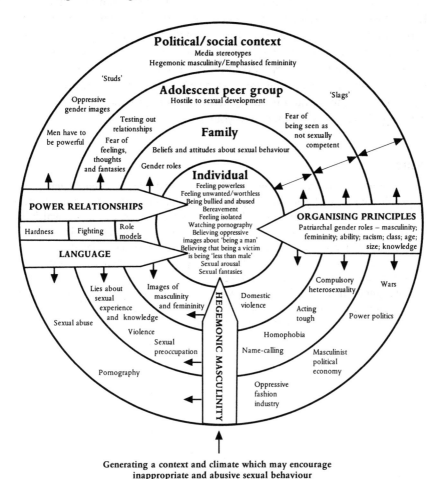

Figure 5.2 The Social context of young people's inappropriate and abusive sexual behaviour

Conclusion

This chapter has discussed an analytical practice framework for a holistic approach to therapeutic work with children and young people who have sexual behaviour difficulties. In particular, the chapter has explored an application of the framework to the process of engaging a young person in that work and to the provision of sex and sexuality education. The framework allows the practitioner to address his or her power relationship with the child or young person and emphasises the importance of a transparent approach to the work, which explains the process from the outset and maintains a high level of respect, whilst acknowledging that some behaviours are problematic. In working through issues directly related to the young person's sexual behaviours, the framework conceptualises the social context of sexual behaviour. Its anti-oppressive approach allows a full exploration of abusive power relationships and circumstances of compulsory heterosexuality, homophobia and peer pressure and how they may have influenced a young person's decision to behave in a sexually inappropriate or abusive manner. The framework provides a theoretical underpinning for the practitioner, and provides helpful ideas for working directly with children and young people.

Note

1   It is important to acknowledge that there are incidences of children and young people being sexually abused by girls and women. It has been argued that there is widespread social and professional denial of female child sexual abuse, which has contributed to its under-reporting (Elliot 1993; Saradjian 1998), denial of the act of abuse taking place or denial of the responsibility of the woman committing such an act. Sexual abuse committed by males or females is likely to entail an abuse of power and responsibility and leave a child feeling hurt and guilty for what has happened. Throughout the rest of the chapter, when referring to children and young people, masculine terminology will be used. This should not be taken as a denial of the existence of abuse committed by girls and women.

Chapter Six

Working in a Multi-agency Context
Children's Services Development Groups

Robin Hill

Introduction

This chapter outlines the birth of multi-agency children's services development groups in a local area in Warwickshire during the second half of the 1990s, placing this in the context of the re-emergence of community development in a new guise during this time. The chapter considers how new initiatives in this field can be linked to this resurgent movement and how this model of service development may be developed to assist social services departments and their partner agencies in their future work together.

Background

In 1994, Warwickshire County Council Joint Care Planning Team, which was designed as a mechanism for bringing together the work of health, social services and other agencies, recommended the establishment of multi-agency configurations within the county's five districts. These would focus on the provision of services to specific user groups, especially after identifying where gaps in services existed, and would make suggestions as to how these gaps might be filled. In the area in which I work, we established a range of such groups and I took responsibility for convening those responsible for coordinating children's services. I had already worked in a front-line children's team as a social work supervisor for three years within the district, but my only contact with other agencies had been on a case-by-case basis until then, so the time seemed right to try an approach which at that time was not familiar to what is a large rural district, forming half of the geographical area of Warwickshire. Such an approach had historical antecedents.

Working backwards

Working collaboratively with other agencies, and acknowledging the community dimension of social work is neither new nor radical. The Seebohm Report (1968), for instance, strongly encouraged the newly born social services departments in the early 1970s to establish mechanisms for working with voluntary organisations and other statutory authorities. There was then much activity for more than a decade in establishing posts and projects both at a neighbourhood and authority-wide level in which social workers and other staff within departments often played a key role. These initiatives ran alongside other government-driven projects, including the dozen or so community development projects in a number of areas of disadvantage and deprivation. Inaugurated in 1969, they targeted those communities which were regarded 'through ill-fortune or personal inadequacy [as] suffer[ing] from a multitude of inter-related problems and deprivations which cannot be resolved by uncoordinated support from a series of separately organised services' (Loney 1980).

The publication of the Barclay Report (Barclay 1982) attempted to provide further impetus to such an approach, yet it was published at a time when the Thatcher government was shifting the emphasis from collective responsibility towards individualism. By this time the aspirations of the community development projects were widely considered to have failed and the main impetus within the Barclay Report was contained in the debate between the academics whose minority reports in appendices took polarised approaches to the concept of community social work. Brown, Hadley and McGrath argued in favour of social workers being based in small patches within the communities which they served, whereas Pinker resisted the notion of social workers participating in neighbourhood work. 'Although the Barclay conclusions were seen by some as an unsatisfactory compromise, the advocacy of community social work represented a real attempt to return to some of the earlier Seebohm ideals, and update and rescue them' (Webb and Wistow 1987, p.225). However these writers go on to suggest that the term 'community social work' may have been misleading; they query whether the Barclay approach of a bottom-up needs-based approach to planning and an individualised service-packaging approach to social care can be carried out by a single worker or profession.

A number of other factors mitigated against the advance of Barclay's vision of community social work in the mid-1980s. First, it became clear that patch teams were too small to be able to operate as effective units for the delivery of children's services within localities; managers needed more flexibility in deploying workers with different skills across a larger geographical area. Second, where social workers had sought to use their statutory powers, for example by applying to the court for the removal of children belonging to a specific family within a community, they would no doubt be greeted subsequently with fear and suspicion if they sought to undertake preventive work within that same community. Third, community work itself was becoming discredited and politically unpopular within the ruling Conservative Party, as the need for greater accountability and clarity about outcomes took precedence. All of this was coupled with widespread misinterpretation of what community social work sought to achieve, and scepticism about whether social workers possessed the necessary skills to undertake the tasks required:

> [Community social work] was different to community development in its emphasis on individualising its clients. Instead community social work sought to mobilise the collective resources of the community as part of a social care strategy… However there was little in social work training, based largely on individualised service delivery, to prepare practitioners for this task. The language of management rather than community informs the practice of community social work, for example, social care planning. This is at odds with the humanist principles of social work. (Powell 2001, p.66)

At the same time, unsurprisingly, the children's agenda in social work narrowed to a focus on child protection, in response to the crisis in public confidence occasioned by high-profile public enquiries following the deaths of children who were well known to social services departments, and recognition of the widespread scale of sexual abuse of young people, which had lain undisclosed over many years: 'As Social Services budgets shrank, more emphasis was placed on [these] statutory duties than on the human relations task of helping clients and their families to live in the community' (Jones 2000, p.184). A retreat into casework followed and dominated the next decade, during which the Children Act (1989) was implemented, and most social services departments divided their functions between children's and adult services. From the mid-1980s until the mid-1990s most departments interpreted multi-agency work as being relevant only within the context of casework with individual children and their families. Warwickshire, for instance, had redeployed its handful of community work posts within fieldwork teams and most preventive work was done on a single agency basis. The ideas contained in Twelvetrees' textbook on community work, which was first published in 1982, seemed very out of fashion when a second edition appeared in 1991:

> However, a community social work approach has to be department-wide. It is virtually impossible to sustain it on any other basis…[it] is a value system concerned with enabling, empowering and involving the community, facilitating the growth of mutual aid, modifying or changing the system, team work, cooperation between different departments and the breakdown of unnecessary professional distance. (Twelvetrees 1991, p.75)

Harris charts how the philosophy of the Seebohm Report, which was to 'enable the greatest possible numbers of individuals to act reciprocally, giving and receiving service for the well-being of the community' (Seebohm 1968, cited in Harris 2002, p.268), had been replaced by New Right philosophies which emphasised the need for freedom and choice for citizens, leading to the breaking of the monopoly of public services and the targeting of services for those unable to provide for themselves: 'Notions of community and collectivism were replaced by an emphasis on enterprise and individualism' (Harris 2002, p. 270).

The re-discovery of multi-agency work

By 1994, the 'cult of the individual', with its concentration on privatisation, profit and market forces, was no longer in the ascendancy in British society. Harris provides an account of how active citizenship, a more compassionate variant of Thatcherism, began to be endorsed as a key theme in Conservative policies in the early 1990s (Harris 2002, p.270). Against this backdrop, in December 1994 four practitioners and managers from social services and health and two from education held a speculative and tentative first meeting, seated around a large blank map of our local district, on which we plotted the comparatively sparse provision of services which was at that time available; mainly our own offices, interspersed with some playgroups, a few summer activities schemes and one after-school club which had recently been started by a new primary school head teacher. Although most of us had already worked in the district for some time, we had never met before to pool knowledge and discuss common issues in this way and it seemed somewhat self-indulgent to draw up a wish list of provision that we would like to see in our district, ranging from parenting and self-help groups and playschemes, in areas where none existed, to transport schemes and toy libraries. There was one thing of which we were all certain: none of our agencies had the spare capacity to undertake much developmental work on our own.

There was, however, one emergent opportunity; a few months earlier, I had instigated a successful application that had been worked up and submitted by social services managers for joint social services and health funding for a children's services development officer, who was due to commence her duties, on a part-time basis, in January 1995. We therefore decided to meet again after she had joined us and in the meantime we agreed to collect statistical data relating to our respective areas of work. We also offered to find out information about sources of funding to develop new services and to invite representatives from the local Council for Voluntary Service, the police and the Pre-school Playgroups Association (now the Learning Alliance.) It was decided to convene a separate meeting to discuss gaps in provision for young people aged 16 and over, as their requirements were identified as being distinct from those of younger children. It was certainly unusual for the Social Services Department to have any contact at all with the Youth/Community Education Service, or the sports and amenities officers in the District Council, yet we quickly discovered that they were running leisure activities from which young people referred to social services could benefit. For instance the District Council was subsidising transport from remote villages to attend swimming sessions at leisure centres in the major centres of population during school holidays. We were able to sponsor children to join this scheme at minimal cost, where previously we had provided one-to-one sessional workers to take children to the same activity!

The next meeting was attended by fourteen representatives from seven different agencies. There was sufficient enthusiasm for the re-discovery of multi-agency work to enable several different sub-groups to be established in order to develop specific areas of interest. These included the coordination and development of new play schemes, parenting groups and some provision for young people in a couple of specific geographical areas. It felt as though community work had been re-born!

In April 1995, we held the inaugural meeting of the group which would look at gaps in provision for 16–18-year-olds (later extended to 16–21-year-olds). Agencies in attendance included the Community Education youth work team, the Housing Department, the Young Homeless Project from an adjacent district, the Youth Justice manager, the Drugs Advisory Service and the Centrepoint (national housing campaigning charity) regional development worker, who was particularly supportive of the new forum. She commissioned an immediate task for the group, namely a survey of homeless young people to be conducted amongst all agencies and we rapidly agreed to establish a multi-agency sub-group to discuss the housing needs of this age group.

At the second meeting of this group, we received a presentation from a project officer who had researched the health, recreational and sexual advice needs of young people in the district. It became clear during the ensuing discussion that there was plenty of enthusiasm and support both for the development of an advice and information service for young people and also for a mobile youth club facility to reach those living in remote villages scattered across the district. Both issues had been identified by agencies separately for some time, but there had seemed little prospect of success until it became clear that a number of agencies working together might be able to achieve what none had been able to do on their own, either because they did not recognise the needs identified as their 'core business', or because they did not feel that they should be the lead agency in taking the initiative to address those needs.

The Centrepoint worker encouraged one of the Community Education workers to submit some proposals to a subsequent group meeting, as this appeared to be the best mechanism for harnessing and demonstrating multi-agency support. A sub-group was readily established and a substantial bid was submitted to health and social services joint finance to employ a project worker to develop an information service. The strength of support for the bid from so many quarters meant that the funding panel agreed to sponsor the proposals at the expense of a number of smaller bids for single-agency projects.

The project evolved over the next couple of years into an independent voluntary organisation known as 'The Depot', which not only attracted funding from charities and local businesses, but also became charged with the responsibility for delivering the county's 'Signposting for Choice' strategy within the district. This was a considerable challenge in the light of the geography of the area and was achieved through the acquisition of a second-hand double-decker bus, which was converted, painted and fitted with computers and a private counselling area. The bus proved extremely popular, especially in villages that had no facilities of any kind for young people. Whilst it is now sadly off the road, due to mechanical failure, 'The Depot' still maintains an advice and drop-in centre in a barge moored on the River Avon for young people, whilst the new manager is currently looking at other ways of reaching isolated young people, including the provision of a smaller mobile centre and the development of a website.

Whilst the group for services for younger people, now called the Children's Services Development Group (0–16), continued to identify gaps in existing provision, a third group came into existence, focusing specifically on the needs of children with disabilities. Whilst this group lasted for only a couple of years it made one very important contribution to services for this user group. For several years social services had run a play scheme for disabled children each summer, with negligible support from parents or any other agency, including the school where the scheme operated, which charged the full market rate for the use of its premises. As many of the young people attended this school anyway, the location was far from ideal and some resentment had grown up around the scheme. The local SCOPE representative drew our attention to the lack of opportunities for integration into mainstream activities for disabled young people within the district; the school holidays should have provided a golden opportunity for such young people to take part in some activities of their choice, rather than being offered no alternative other than attending a segregated play scheme at their own school. In summer 1996, we decided not to run the scheme again, but to employ a coordinator to recruit individual workers who would accompany disabled young people to facilitate their participation in mainstream leisure opportunities. We funded this through money that had been earmarked for providing new day care services for disabled children, but which had never been used. Within three years the scheme had developed into a stand-alone voluntary organisation named ILEAP (Integrated Leisure Education Activities Project) and is now able to attract considerably more funding than statutory sources can provide. Regrettably the disability group did not continue beyond 1998. It was hoped that the mainstream groups would be able to stimulate projects for this user group, but they have largely failed to do so and it is hoped that the group might be revived in the future.

Two other highly successful multi-agency initiatives generated by the children's services development groups have been the 'Taking Care Project' (which is featured in Chapter Seven) and the 'Confidentiality Initiative', which was suggested by the head teacher of a secondary school. She was concerned about what information it was appropriate for school staff to pass on to other professionals when approached by young people in confidence. The discussion on this topic spawned another sub-group, which, in turn, led to two multi-agency conferences and a series of focus groups involving young people themselves. At the end of this process guidelines were prepared, launched and distributed to many organisations working with young people across the district. The process was facilitated by a social work lecturer, who subsequently published several articles in the house journals of the agencies involved. The leaflets remain in use in schools, youth clubs, at 'The Depot' and in social work teams.

The children's services development groups (0–16) and (16–21) have each continued to meet on a quarterly basis since their inception in 1994/5. (Their aims and objectives are included in Appendix Three.) There are eight meetings evenly spaced throughout the year. Some of the initiatives generated are relatively small, but still commendable, for example, the distribution of credit card-sized leaflets on contraception to young people. Others are still at the planning stage, for example, providing an appropriate multi-agency response to young people who feel suicidal.

The social policy context of the development groups

Looking back on the successful development of these groups, we seem to have been fortunate in riding the tide of the re-emergence of seeking collective solutions to individual problems. By March 1996 there was already a renewed enthusiasm for collaborative working, as evidenced by the Department of Health that local authorities would be expected to provide Children's Services Plans in order to promote 'the kind of holistic, multi-agency strategies that are increasingly recognized as necessary to enhance the well-being of children' (Utting 1998, p.32). This announcement was accompanied by guidance, which explained that the plans would attempt to broaden the concern of social services planners beyond the population of 'children in need', as described in the Children Act (1989), to a wider concern with all potentially vulnerable children in localities. Strategic planning would henceforth need to be based on a reliable and updated knowledge base, an analysis of need and the supply of services, the views of users and the local community, consultation with other agencies, monitoring and feedback. During the previous year the Department of Health had published a collection of research findings, which recommended that when families had been the subject of a child protection investigation, they should also be assessed as to whether the children were 'in need' (Department of Health 1995).

New Labour

In May 1997 the Labour Party was returned to power, whereupon the context for joint agency work acquired a new impetus, framework and language. Guidance issued in 1998 underlined the importance of joint planning, in order to cultivate shared values, to make a commitment to long-term goals, and to develop joint assessment procedures, protocols between agencies and pooled budgets (Department of Health 1998c). The White Paper on 'Modernising Social Services' (Department of Health 1998b) was followed by the Quality Protects initiative (Department of Health 1998a), with its emphasis on tackling child poverty and social exclusion. Sure Start, which targeted large amounts of money on specific geographical areas in order to provide services predominantly for pre-school children, was announced in 1999, as part of the National Childcare Strategy and Early Years Development and Childcare Partnerships. In 2000 Connexions was launched, to replace the Careers Service and to coordinate advice and support services for teenagers approaching school-leaving age and beyond. In February 2001, the Children's National Service Framework, intended to draw together health and social services, was also announced. Meanwhile multi-agency Youth Offending Teams had been created and their remit has been broadened to include preventive work with those young people who are identified as being at risk of committing offences. The Children's Fund, which is intended to provide funding opportunities for new initiatives to serve young people aged between 5 and 13, has also been introduced, on a phased basis, in all local authority areas. Single regeneration bids have made substantial new resources available for the redevelopment of communities.

Development group meetings have provided opportunities for existing agencies to learn about these changes and fresh initiatives, and also for those who are representing the new services to meet with existing agencies to discuss what is already in place locally and to plan how gaps might be filled. Although there are more opportunities for funding, greater sophistication and professionalism is now needed to obtain this money. Group meetings have thus become opportunities for sharing information about what is available and pooling expertise about how to present information (for example, through the production of business plans) in such a way that funds can be successfully obtained. Simultaneously the groups have become the local manifestation of a number of corporate initiatives within Warwickshire. A Policy for Young People was launched in 1996 and the 16–21 development group became the district's Local Action for Youth Group, in line with this policy. Subsequently the Crime and Disorder Strategy was launched, and the development groups agreed to report to the strategy's steering group and to allow their objectives to be included within the strategy's annual report. In the late 1990s central government encouraged local authorities to set up Local Partnership Teams;

when such an arrangement came into existence the development groups were joined to it. This team has now been superseded by the new statutory Local Strategic Partnership, which is an alliance of representatives of all public services, voluntary sector and business interests within each area. As part of the preparation for this metamorphosis, the local partnership officer undertook a survey of what constituent members felt about the development groups (see Appendix Four). It was clear from these responses that the groups remain valued; there is a consistent attendance of 15–20 people at each meeting.

New approaches to community development

Although we did not realise this at the time the groups were being developed, they have in fact come into existence at a time when community development was coming back into fashion:

> although the term is disdainfully absent from most policy guidelines, we appear to be witnessing a renaissance for community development in Britain. There is money for community projects and community sector activities generally, new compacts are appearing in relations between the statutory and voluntary sectors, and there seems to be a genuine commitment to involving communities in both the planning and delivery of public services. (Gilchrist 2003, pp.16–17)

Sharper definitions of community development, too, have appeared in recent years:

> Community Development is seen as a set of techniques (such as outreach and 'planning for real' exercises) rather than a body of expertise which incorporates a specific value system relating to social justice... (Gilchrist 2003, p.21)

> [It is defined as] building active and sustainable communities based on social justice and mutual respect. It is about changing power structures to remove the barriers that prevent people from participating in the issues that affect their lives. (Standing Conference for Community Work 2001, quoted in Gilchrist 2003, p.22)

One of the key objectives within these new definitions is 'capacity building', in which the community is facilitated and enabled to take responsibility for dealing with its own issues. This approach has driven a number of the initiatives that have arisen from the children's services development groups, including the parenting projects and the Taking Care Project. Barter has developed a paradigm that applies the concept of community building to child protection work:

> Hence the focus of attention includes an emphasis on ensuring that children's protection services and programmes support a process of community

building. It is recognised that for far too long community has remained as an afterthought, not necessarily integrated into services, programmes or public child-serving organisations. (Barter 2001, p.267)

Children's services development officer

Posts which provide a link between social services and the voluntary sector have been in existence at least since they were recommended by the Seebohm Report (1968). When the opportunity arose to establish such a role in Warwickshire, through joint finance with health in 1994, there was both enthusiasm for the new initiative and speculation about what the new person might achieve. In other parts of the county mainstream funding was not made available when the joint finance grant expired. However in the district that is the location for the account in this chapter, it was decided to make the half-time post permanent, in view of the particular success of the post-holders in developing new projects, linked to the children's services development groups.

The first occupant of the post worked with the chief officer of the Council for Voluntary Service to obtain funding for 'The Depot', as well as developing a number of specific parenting and other projects, and still works on a consultancy basis to advise on future provision and to make further applications for funding. The second occupant continued the work and also developed and obtained funding for ILEAP from BBC Children in Need. The current post-holder has established substantial child care facilities in a large isolated village, where there is much child protection work, and has also bid successfully for resources for a district-wide project to develop parenting work. (The district twice missed out on funding from the Sure Start government initiative, which targets significant resources in concentrated areas with the aim of alleviating deprivation amongst families who have pre-school children. However these disappointments did not deter the local community and other agencies from making bids to other sources, and the development officer was able to undertake many of the practical tasks involved in following this through.)

In common with the rest of the country social work posts have been difficult to fill recently and it would be hard to argue that the children's services development officer post does not represent 'best value', not only because of the substantial resources which the incumbents have attracted, but also because of the substantial amount of goodwill generated towards social services, both amongst other professionals and in the community. It is significant, however, that none of these post-holders has been a qualified social worker. Our previous experience has shown that it is very difficult to combine the roles of community builder and front-line children's social worker and indeed the children's services development officers have sometimes needed to emphasise that they are not social workers in order to gain the trust of the communities with whom they are working. This experience suggests that social services departments need to invest, even at a comparatively modest level, in staff who have the skills, time and motivation to employ techniques associated with community development, in order to assist communities to protect and make provision for the children within them.

Some principles of multi-agency work

During the past eight years we have learned much about running this type of multi-agency group. First, one important feature of the early meetings was that they were structured in such a way that creative ideas could be released. Although we later introduced more formal agendas, at the early stages we tried to make sure that no-one would be inhibited about putting forward new ideas, however unrealistic they might have seemed, and that everyone's contribution was acknowledged. It is important to allow the members of such groups to decide upon how often the meetings will be held and what the terms of reference are. However, it is equally important to dispel negativity, especially amongst those who use such phrases as 'That will never work' or 'We tried it once, but it never got off the ground.' Sometimes one agency will mistakenly assume that it has a monopoly in developmental work in one particular area. For instance the identification and establishment of new play schemes lends itself to a multi-agency approach, but we found initially that one agency felt rather sceptical about the value of the multi-agency sub-group which was set up. However its staff agreed to join and soon became valued members.

Second, the chair of the development group needs to be skilful in gauging whether it is the right time to suggest that a sub-group be formed to take an idea forward and also to know when to put something 'on the back burner'. For a couple of years we knew that our district would benefit from a young carers' project; this had been well researched, but no-one was coming forward to develop these proposals. We therefore quietly dropped the topic from our agenda, so that we did not focus on failure. Then, suddenly, a newer member heard about a highly successful young carers' project in an adjacent county; we placed the item back on the agenda, ensuring that representatives from those agencies likely to be involved were in attendance at our next meeting. A sub-group was quickly formed. This became the steering group that was able to bid for some money which social services had already put aside but which would not be released until it could be responsibly utilised. The group found a suitable local voluntary agency to sponsor the project, a worker was recruited and another new service was launched in the district.

Third, the chair should ensure that a warm welcome is extended to all new participants, some of whom will be new to the area, and will have been encouraged to attend on the recommendation of other agencies. The new members should be given the opportunity, if they wish, to speak briefly about their work, even if this is not on the agenda. Their names should then be added to the minutes circulation list, unless they expressly ask not to be included (which rarely happens). Some new attendees may not join the group regularly, but a liberal distribution of minutes will ensure that information about agencies, projects or people who are new to working in children's services in the area gains a wide readership, and this will help in networking amongst professionals and agencies.

Fourth, meetings should aim to attract a range of staff at different levels within organisations working in the area. They should not be set up as a lateral grouping of, for instance, solely practitioners, first-line managers or middle managers within the agencies represented. The head teacher who started the confidentiality initiative reminded us that, in order to be successful, the policy would need to have the approval of policy makers within agencies, as well as contributions from those who worked face-to-face with young people on a daily basis.

Fifth, success breeds success, so there should be ample opportunities at meetings for those whose projects have made significant progress, and who have set up a new service successfully, to be able to share what they have done with their colleagues in other agencies. Nevertheless, it is equally important for individuals whose projects are struggling to feel free to discuss their difficulties and to receive some encouragement and practical suggestions from other participants. Needless to say, no-one should be made to feel that they have let people down if their project is not an unqualified success.

Sixth, if social services is to be the lead agency in coordinating the group it is vital that chairing, attending and minuting is prioritised by the staff involved. Our district has found it useful to have two managers working in unison to share the chair's role, which makes allowances for emergencies or caters for the possibility of one person moving on.

Finally, it is important to prevent the group being taken over or subsumed by a particular topic or initiative whose aims may, in part, coincide with what the group aims to do, but which, in reality, has a much narrower focus. Multi-agency fora that concentrate specifically on, for instance, youth offending, drug misuse or work with under-8s are valuable configurations in their own right. A development group will want to establish close reporting links with such initiatives, without being wholly absorbed by one particular topic.

Looking forward

So where are we now? We have re-discovered community development as a method of enabling citizens to work in a collaborative way. The old techniques of empowering people to identify needs in their neighbourhood or communities of interest and then working towards meeting them have been harnessed to more sophisticated modern frameworks of accountability, planning and reviewing. This is all implemented within the context of a multi-agency framework in which the whole is greater than the sum of its parts. The groups are still evolving; we have changed the age bandings to 0–13 and 14–21, and we are looking towards involving young people themselves, in the light of the advent of the national Youth Parliament and a set of local youth fora that have been established by the Community Education service working with voluntary organisations in the area. We aspire towards direct representation on the Local Strategic Partnership by young people themselves, who will also have the opportunity to decide how grants may be spent on new services that will also be developed by young people.

Individual casework or groupwork with families in areas of poverty can cause unintentional division, for instance where a social services department funds a service for one family in a street where neighbours may be living in similar deprivation, but are not known to the agency, or where it runs a group for some young people or their parents, but not others. Re-introducing the community dimension to social work seeks to redress this balance by stimulating the development of new services that will be available to all families within the neighbourhood. Meeting with other agencies on a regular basis in the way described in this chapter ensures that strong foundations are laid for this approach, and it is hoped that this time it may be sustainable in the future, regardless of political and ideological changes within society.

Chapter Seven

Taking Care
Helping Children Learn to Keep Themselves Safer

Ann Seal

Introduction

It could be argued that the issue of children's safety should be at the centre of any community's priorities. Although this is an admirable aspiration, its implications in terms of prevention strategies are not always identifiable in concrete policy and practice. In the UK, for example, the main emphasis has been on providing services for children who have suffered harm[1] or who are seen to be at risk of suffering significant harm. Harm includes abuse but also refers to other experiences that may be detrimental to children's development and well-being (Children Act 1989). In many instances, this could be characterised as a shutting-the-stable-door-after-the-horse-has-bolted approach, with social services departments as the main agencies carrying the responsibility for implementing it. It has become increasingly clear, however, that we cannot protect children from harm by surveillance and protection alone. The UK has much to learn in terms of being more creative and proactive in relation to the prevention of abuse, from other countries, such as the United States, Canada, Australia and New Zealand. Experiences of preventive education in these countries will be discussed later in the chapter.

Keeping children safe from physical dangers (preventing accidents) and from harmful diseases has attracted media interest and investment from government and voluntary organisations for many years, with high-profile national campaigns being commonplace. Health visitors, among other professionals, are actively involved on a day-to-day basis with these aspects of preventive work. Saving children from physical injury or death in this way is given high status and priority, and no doubt saves many lives a year. Prevention of harm, while unanimously agreed to be of utmost importance by agencies involved in caring for children, does not attract the same commitment in terms of funding, policy or practice. Without a more nationally coordinated effort in prevention, the outlook for the UK's children in this regard might be quite bleak. Part of the difficulty in seeking to accord greater emphasis to harm prevention is the lack of research into effective ways of preventing harm to children and the difficulty of establishing how the outcomes of intervention in the longterm can be assessed (Finkelhor and Strapko 1992; Krivacska 1990).

Given the multitude of risks and hazards faced by children, and that many of the experiences they have impact negatively on their overall development and well-being (NCH Action for Children 2002), prevention has to have a greater prominence in policy and practice. Responsibility for keeping children safe lies with adults who care for them until they are competent to make decisions for themselves about safety, or until they reach a position of equal power with an individual who might abuse them. One criticism of prevention education is that it fails to recognise this adult responsibility and, instead, puts the responsibility for keeping safe from abuse on the shoulders of the child (Bagley and Thurston 1996; Kitzinger 1990; Melton 1992). The counter-argument is that providing information to children may help to protect them and that they have a right to developmentally appropriate information and knowledge (Haydon 2002). Although the responsibility for abuse to children lies with the perpetrators of abuse, there is a 'community' dimension to responsibility, a more general responsibility for the welfare of children: 'for children to be safe, the community must be safe. All community organisations should be encouraged to accept a role in providing a safe environment' (Bagley and Thurston 1996, p.312). Meeting children's needs should be seen as an expression of their entitlements or rights and the wider community has a role in seeking to meet them (Hill and Tisdall 1997).

The remainder of the chapter will look at children's rights, as set out in the United Nations Convention on the Rights of the Child, and their applicability to preventive education in the UK. This consideration of children's rights will be placed in the context of what we know about children's experiences from the available evidence. Evidence from other parts of the world, where preventive education is more widely used and tested, will be reviewed and the key messages from research in this area will be distilled. A history of one example of preventive education – the 'Taking Care Project' – will follow, together with an account of the processes of change and development it has undergone.

Abuse of children in the United Kingdom

Large numbers of children in the UK suffer from harmful experiences each year. This evidence puts into context the need for a prevention strategy. In the report *Childhood Matters* (1996), the National Commission of Inquiry into the Prevention of Child Abuse (NCIPCA) found that children are harmed by a variety of different incidents and experiences, ranging from isolated occurrences to long-term maltreatment. In addition, the numbers of children affected are likely to be far greater than the evidence in this report suggests, as many children do not tell anyone about what has happened to them; surveys among adult survivors of abuse regularly show that less than half told anyone at the time.

The Commission adopted a broad definition of abuse (derived from Gil 1970): 'Child abuse consists of anything which individuals, institutions, or processes do or fail to do which directly or indirectly harms children or damages their prospects of safe and healthy development into adulthood' (NCIPCA 1996, p.2). Using this definition as the baseline, at least 1 million children and young people are harmed each year:

- at least 150,000 children annually suffer severe physical punishment

- up to 100,000 children each year have a potentially harmful sexual experience

- 350,000–400,000 children live in an environment which is consistently low in warmth and high in criticism

- 450,000 children are bullied at school at least once a week

- in 1992 there were 4.4 million children living in poverty, one in three of all children in the UK

- many of the effects of child abuse are long-lasting and persist into adulthood.

(NCIPCA 1996, p.9)

Children's rights

The United Nations Convention on the Rights of the Child, ratified by the UK government in 1991, contains several articles that are pertinent to protecting children from harm and outline children's rights in this regard. For example, Article 17 states that children 'should have access to information and material …especially those aimed at their social, spiritual and moral well-being and physical and mental health…' and Article 19 states that 'State Parties shall take all appropriate legislative, administrative, social and educational measures to protect the child from all forms of physical or mental violence, injury or abuse…' (United Nations 1989)

The idea that children have human rights, and equal human rights to adults has not been embraced fully in the UK thus far. The UK lags behind some other European countries when it comes to observing the rights of children in schools, for example, in respect of having their voices heard and playing a role in decision-making (Lansdown 1996).

Prevention education: an international view

Prevention education programmes about child sexual abuse are widespread in the United States, having originated there in the late 1970s. The rationale for such work is that large numbers of victims exist, most of them unidentified. The assumptions underpinning programmes are that many children could avoid victimisation if they had appropriate information, and that prevention programmes can be inexpensive and highly cost-effective (Finkelhor 1986). The notion that children can avoid victimisation needs to be handled sensitively in prevention programmes because children who have not avoided victimisation must be clear that the responsibility for what has happened to them lies with the perpetrator of the harm. In the context of unequal power relationships, many children are not going to be able to keep themselves safe from harm, but the hope would be that, through what they learn in preventive education, they may be able to talk to trusted adults about their experiences and seek help.

In the mid-1980s both Australia and New Zealand were looking to implement preventive education programmes in their schools (Briggs and Hawkins 1994). The Australian police and education departments most commonly adopted the 'Protective Behaviours Programme' from the United States. The New Zealand authorities opted to invest heavily in developing their own new materials, which they felt would be more culturally appropriate, and these were introduced with parent involvement, teacher training and teacher support. The majority of primary schools in the Republic of Ireland have implemented the locally developed 'Stay Safe' programme since 1991. This is a culturally sensitive, developmentally staged curriculum for abuse prevention that includes bullying and abuse as linked forms of victimisation and incorporates assertiveness training and enhancement of self-esteem. In Canada preventive work in schools has been widespread in relation to violence awareness since the mid-1990s. Teachers there have found that 'general anti-violence work has opened the door to disclosures of direct and indirect abuse' (Hague, Kelly and Mullender 2001).

Prevention education: key messages from research

Bagley and Thurston (1996) reviewed approximately 3000 articles, book chapters, monographs and reports concerned with the prevention of child sexual abuse. Some key messages from this research are outlined below, with some additional comments as to the relevance of some of the points:

- It is important to get the message over that it is morally wrong for sexual encounters between a child and an adult to occur.
- Teacher training is important.

- Parents need to be involved. Parents can provide constant reinforcement and clarification of learnt themes. They can also provide support for the very small number of children who may be distressed following implementation of a programme. Children will get the feeling that their parents are on their side and subsequent communication may be improved.

- Sex education is important. If children do not have knowledge about sex-related matters they may not understand the significance of what has happened to them and may not have the necessary language to tell someone about it. If adults persist in feeling awkward about raising issues about sex, children learn that it is something not to be discussed with adults.

- Self-esteem may be a prerequisite to assimilation of information. In some studies, children with higher self-esteem showed more improvement after the intervention. This raises a challenge for preventive education as research has shown that children with low self-esteem are more likely to be victims of abuse.

- It is important to teach children problem-solving strategies. Younger children in particular are more unrealistic and compliant in the solutions they offer to sensitive problems presented to them. Girls' solutions are more likely to be less confrontational and more planned than those of boys. Teaching problem-solving strategies, and practice, should aid consistency in choosing effective strategies when required.

- Some of the concepts are difficult for young children to grasp. Studies have shown consistently that older children make more gains in knowledge than younger children.

- There may be difficulties for children in discriminating against 'bad' sexual touches if other 'bad' touches are allowed e.g. physical punishment.

- Preventive education changes what a large number of children say they will do, but may not actually change their behaviour in an abusive/dangerous scenario.

- Themes and concepts need to be revisited regularly.

- Role play is a particularly effective method for reinforcement and learning, especially with younger children.

In addition to the research findings drawn together by Bagley and Thurston (1996), Finkelhor and Strapko (1992) found that prevention programmes facilitate children talking more openly about their experiences, including their experience of abuse. MacIntyre *et al.* (2000) reported that programmes considered most successful/progressive are: well integrated within the school curriculum; adopt a range of methods and are not just didactic; deal with cultural and ethnic diversity; are well resourced; have the support of teachers, students and parents; include tackling racism and bullying.

Bearing in mind the history of lack of prevention work in the UK, but placed in the context of the evidence as stated above, the steering committee of the Taking Care Project took a bold and innovative step when it put its plans into action.

The background to the Taking Care Project

In the late 1990s, staff in Warwickshire Social Services Department had concerns about the safety of children in a village when they were made aware that a registered sex offender was being released from prison to accommodation overlooking a primary school playground. Social workers worked with the children in the school, alongside teachers, using *'Taking Care' with Toby and the Puppet Gang* (Adams and Gifford 1991). This is a package of materials that can be used in either a treatment or preventive way with children aged 3 to 8 years. It consists of several stories on a video of a puppet show, colouring sheets and role-play activities.

The intervention was well received by children, parents and teachers and a multi-agency steering group was set up (see Chapter Six), chaired by a children's team manager from social services, to look at how the programme could be extended to children across the area. Other members of the steering group included the senior nurse for child protection, the principal education social worker for the county, the manager of the Sexualised Inappropriate Behaviour Service (see Chapter Five) and a family centre senior social worker. Additional advice came from a consultant psychologist (who was a co-author of the *Toby and the Puppet Gang* package) and a university lecturer in social work. A successful funding application was made to a health source and two part-time coordinators were appointed to commence work in September 1999. The posts were for three days per week, term-time only. The two coordinators were both from health visiting backgrounds, although the posts were open to professionals from any of the following backgrounds: primary teaching, social work, school health, psychology and health visiting.

The first year of the Taking Care Project

Eleven schools were selected to take part in the project. They were chosen for a variety of reasons, including the following: social services staff had concerns about referral rates for children in the area; geographical spread; different sized schools were included in the sample and also one special school. Head teachers were contacted and visited by the coordinators. All schools approached agreed to take part, although one school limited the amount of work carried out and would only allow the coordinators to work with children in year 1, and limited work with them to road safety and stranger awareness.

In five of the schools all children aged 4 to 7 took part in the project; in four schools only children in year 1; in one school only years 1 and 2; and in the special school all children in Key Stage 1. Reasons for this were usually due to numbers of classes per year group in the school. The coordinators based themselves in a school for a whole day or half a day and worked with one class after another. Four sessions were offered to each class of 45 minutes each, for four weeks. Teachers were asked to be present in the sessions and to join in the discussions. Topics covered included road safety, stranger awareness, good and bad touching, good and bad secrets and telling adults (see Table 7.1).

Table 7.1 Taking Care Project programme of work (4–8-year-olds only in 1999/2000; 4–11-year-olds from 2000/01)	
4–8-year-olds	**8–11-year-olds**
Toby and the Puppet Gang	*Protective Behaviours*
4 x 45 minutes	4 x 45 minutes
Topics covered include: • road safety • stranger awareness • good/bad secrets • good/bad touching • telling adults.	Topics covered include: • rights and responsibilities • feelings and emotions • feeling safe • early warning signs • fun to feel scared • networks and persistence • strategies for safe action/choices • using the network and review.

Parents' meetings were held before every programme commenced. Parents were given the opportunity to see video clips that might concern them. The times of these meetings were chosen by the school. Some took place after parents dropped children off in the morning, some before children were collected in the afternoon and some took place in the evening. Attendance by parents was generally poor, regardless of the timing of the meetings. Where the head teacher and/or a class teacher was present the coordinators felt the meeting was more successful in engaging parents in discussions and in giving them the message that this was something the school felt strongly about and to which it was actively committed.

A research project was carried out by a university to evaluate the effectiveness of the intervention and to assess the reactions of parents, teachers and head teachers. Interviews were conducted with a sample of children (79 in total) from nine participating schools, before and after the coordinators worked in the classroom. Head teachers (10), teachers (19) and parents (63) were surveyed by questionnaire. Positive results were identified by the research.

The main areas of change for the children were increases in their knowledge about crossing the road safely, personal safety, touching and bodily integrity. Before the intervention, 47% of children did not know where a safe place to cross a road would be, with an additional 7.3% vague. Only 22% specified that lollipop person/zebra crossing/pelican crossing/traffic lights were safe places to cross before intervention and this had risen to 53% after intervention. Not only were there more correct answers post-intervention, but at this time 72% were able to give their answer without difficulty compared with 40% beforehand.

When asked 'What is a stranger?', 44% of children before intervention said it was someone you don't know and this rose to 74.7% afterwards; 30% thought it was a man before intervention (11% after); 10.5% thought it was a monster before intervention (4% after). Whilst most children before and after input would not take sweets from a stranger, a small proportion before would take sweets (13.4%) or go in a car with a stranger who offered them sweets (3.7%). After the intervention no child said they would accept sweets or go in a car with a stranger.

In relation to questions about good and bad touching, children prior to intervention were largely unaware of these concepts with 75.6% responding 'don't know' to the question 'What is a good touch?' This reduced to 20.3% afterwards. When asked 'What is a bad touch?' approximately 85% of children before intervention described smacking and examples of bad behaviour, with only 2% mentioning touching the private parts of their body. Afterwards, 31% said touching the private parts, with a much smaller number mentioning examples of bad behaviour, and 47% said smacking.

Encouragingly, teachers, head teachers and parents overwhelmingly agreed that the programme of work was beneficial to the children: 90% of head teachers said the programme was beneficial to the children, with the remaining 10% stating that 'some aspects' were beneficial; 84% of teachers felt it was beneficial with 16% saying 'some aspects'. When parents were asked if they believed the programme had been beneficial to their children, nobody said 'no'; 76% said 'yes'; 21% said 'some aspects' and 3% said that they could not comment. Fifty-seven per cent of parents commented that their children had been positively affected by the work, with only 10.5% of parents describing some form of negative feedback, although in no instance did this amount to any form of emotional distress. Approximately one-third of parents and teachers felt that the programme had increased the self-esteem or confidence in the children. Seventy-four per cent of teachers indicated that they would be happy to continue with the work after the coordinators left, with only 5% saying that they would not be happy to do so, but this has happened in very few cases.

The *Toby and the Puppet Gang* package that was used was designed for 4–8-year-olds so it was necessary for other materials to be sought for the older primary children. The coordinators were asked to source something suitable and their inquiries led them to the *Protective Behaviours* programme, for which they undertook basic training.

Protective Behaviours

The Protective Behaviours programme originated in the USA in the early 1980s and spread from there to Australia, Canada and the UK. It has two main themes:

- We all have the right to feel safe all the time.

- There is nothing so awful that we can't talk about it with someone.

The process used by the programme enables individuals to recognise what feeling safe means to them and then to identify their own signs of feeling unsafe. It highlights the link between rights and responsibilities and the need to take responsibility for our own feelings and behaviour. The process encourages individuals to have fun and adventures (if desired), whilst observing others' rights at the same time. Strategies for safe action and choices are explored along with identification of a network of adults who can help. Using the network and checking that it works are also covered, as is the importance of persistence. *Protective Behaviours* is used in a wide variety of settings in the UK: by professionals working in the fields of child protection, youth justice, crime prevention, domestic abuse, substance abuse and counselling.

The second year of the Taking Care Project

In the second year, the coordinators were funded to work two days per week during term-time following grants from the Social Services Department and the County Council. A further five schools became involved with the project and work was extended to children aged 8–11 years in three of the original schools. An adapted Protective Behaviours curriculum for Key Stage 2 was used with the older children (see Table 7.1). Parents' meetings were not always held prior to commencement of *Protective Behaviours* work, a decision taken by the

head teacher, as none of the written materials make direct reference to inappropriate sexual contact. Teachers are encouraged to give specific examples of
physical and emotional abuse and inappropriate sexual behaviours to the
children during discussions about appropriate and inappropriate behaviour.
This important message was discussed in class however, as were issues around
inappropriate physical punishments. That said, it is worthwhile to open
dialogue with parents about why the school is involved with the project and the
importance of the messages contained within it and the coordinator always
offered to run a meeting for parents if the school wanted one.

Many interesting and valuable discussions ensued in classrooms as a result
of using the new Protective Behaviours materials. The programme provided
flexibility in being able to move in directions led by the children. As a result,
different points were raised by each class, but all of the children still heard the
key messages in each lesson. A willingness to follow the children's agendas is
very important and requires confidence in the subject matter. Bullying was a
commonly occurring theme that children wanted to talk about. Where teachers
became actively involved in discussions the coordinators felt the sessions were
more effective and this doubtless gave the children the message that their
teacher had an understanding of the issues and empathised with them.

Although teachers had said during the first year that they would be happy
to continue with the work without the project workers present, it became
apparent that few were doing so. One of the key problems was lack of 'ownership'. In response to this problem, the coordinators completed a *Protective
Behaviours* extended training course during the second year and made plans to
be mentored to become trainers in the use of the programme themselves. The
aim of this was to be able to run multi-agency basic training courses in *Protective
Behaviours* and to run in-service training for teachers so that they felt confident
to carry out the curriculum work with the children and to continue the themes
in class themselves. This was consistent with an integrated whole curriculum
approach to safety which research has shown to be valuable (MacIntyre *et al.*
2000).

No formal evaluation of the programme was carried out during the second
year, but teachers were encouraged by children's responses to the work and the
coordinators felt that children were benefiting from the intervention. This
assumption was made because children engaged in very open discussions, were
able to put their own views and opinions forward in front of their peer groups
and said they enjoyed the sessions.

The third year of the Taking Care Project

Funding continued to be a problem, with grants being made again by the Social
Services Department and the County Council. During the first term of the
academic year the programme continued in schools as before, with two new

schools joining the project. The coordinators carried out some multi-agency Protective Behaviours training under supervision. Reviewing the practice of working directly with children, it became apparent that few schools could benefit unless an army of staff was recruited and trained. A new way of working, that empowered teachers to do this work themselves in personal, social and health education time, was required, together with constant reinforcement of the themes and messages. It was decided that new curriculum materials needed to be written for schools so that every year group had different work to complete based on the themes of Protective Behaviours. The topics could then be revisited annually for maximum reinforcement and retention by pupils. One of the coordinators moved out of the area at the end of the first term and the steering group decided that the project should continue with the remaining coordinator working alone for the time being.

A presentation was made to the Area Child Protection Committee (ACPC) and a one-off award was made to the project to enable it to continue into its fourth year on the understanding that the project sought alternative sources of funding for the future. A decision was made to seek charitable status for the project as a stand-alone organisation.

The fourth year of the Taking Care Project

Multi-agency Protective Behaviours training continued and, by the end of the second term of the fourth academic year, 183 professionals had received basic training and ongoing networking/support from the coordinator. This was seen as a valuable 'add-on' to the work in schools and benefited children in need who came into contact with professionals outside school, for example, with social workers, staff working for the 'Young Carers' charitable organisation, domestic abuse staff, school health staff and health visitors. The training has been evaluated very highly by staff attending and follow-up groups have indicated that the Protective Behaviours process is being widely used.

Much time was spent developing new curriculum materials for schools based on the Protective Behaviours approach, but with some additional elements. Schools that committed themselves to the project were expected to implement a specific curriculum following free training for all teachers and support staff. The coordinator supported the use of the materials by the teachers themselves. All children began to be taught the key messages in each year they were at school, thereby building and consolidating their knowledge and confidence year after year. It was anticipated that staff would find some additional strategies for managing children's behaviour throughout the year based on the principles of Protective Behaviours.

Early on in the first term of the fourth year, potential trustees met with the steering committee to discuss setting the project up as a charity. Potential sources of funding were identified and bids were drawn up. In-service training for schools commenced with six schools planned to join the project and receive training and support over the academic year. The coordinator attended school staff meetings regularly to provide further information/clarification about matters arising from the original training or to assess progress in delivery of the programme in school. Support can be given in the classroom setting, for example to a teacher who is newly qualified or who has a specific concern about the delivery of a particular session. Final drafts of the new materials were made so that schools could begin to use them following training. An evaluation of these materials will follow before getting them professionally published. Plans will also be made for a research project to be carried out to assess the new materials.

Discussion

There have been some problems and pitfalls. Funding has been the most significant concern to the steering committee. After the first year, funding has never been secure for more than a few months at a time. This not only led to feelings of insecurity about the future of the project, but also led to difficulties in making any long-term plans or commitments. It has been difficult to access and pay for fund-raising expertise. It has been frustrating to hear from all the key agencies involved how worthwhile the project is, but that none of them can fund it as part of their 'core business'. It is hoped that turning the project into a charity will mean that funding can be secured for periods of a few years at a time.

Getting schools to commit fully to the project has also been difficult, hence the change in strategy. Schools were glad to have the project workers come in and do the work with the children, but were not continuing with the work after the project staff left, despite expressing a willingness to do so. The issue was largely one of ownership and should improve with the changed way of working. A problem noted earlier was that in one school the head teacher wanted to 'cherry pick' which parts of the work to accept. Having had that experience, the coordinators decided that they would not work with a school again which was not able to give an undertaking that it would receive the whole package. They would, however, work with the head teacher to try to move forward to a position of acceptance.

Training teachers is difficult to do unless access is given to an in-service training day. Primary schools in the area only have five of these training days each year and some of them are taken up with compulsory training. Schools usually take them at the same times, at the start or end of term or joined on to half-terms. This makes it difficult to give training to all of the schools wanting it during the year, unless they are prepared to be flexible about when they take a training day.

Whilst there have been pitfalls and problems, the project has also moved forward by changing and developing from the time it started. This has been due to an ongoing process of formal and informal evaluation through action and practitioner research. The nature of the work has lent itself to an organic process of change, owing to its largely untried status in the UK. One of the major challenges for the coordinator has been endeavouring to translate research findings and evaluation into effective interventions and the outcome of these interventions will take some time to become apparent. As with all prevention work, long-term assessment will provide some of the answers. A need to remain responsive and creative is important so that the project continues to change and develop in the future.

Working with parents whose children are involved in the project would be an interesting new venture, and it is hoped that this will take place in the near future. It is also hoped that other means of evaluating children's learning will be developed, rather than restricting research methods to interviews.

Attention needs to be paid to meeting the needs of children with disabilities and to those from different cultural backgrounds. This has not been addressed formally or evaluated yet, emphasis having been placed on school teachers and special needs assistants to reinforce messages learnt in class and to ascertain levels of knowledge and further input required.

One of the major benefits for the coordinator has been the opportunity provided to work effectively in a cooperative multi-disciplinary team. The steering committee has voiced this sentiment on many occasions too. Networking opportunities provided by running multi-agency training sessions benefited not only the coordinator but also the training course participants and resulted in increased learning and liaison. This is something that is frequently commented upon in course evaluations.

Conclusion

This chapter has provided an overview of the extent of harm that children suffer in the UK and put into context the rationale for the development of a preventive approach to child safety. It has outlined how such an approach was implemented in part of Warwickshire, providing an account of the progression of the project from its infancy through to its fourth year. It has also commented on the more widespread use of such programmes in some other parts of the world and how prevention programmes can assist in acknowledging children's basic human rights. Lessons have been learnt from research into prevention of abuse and the main findings have been discussed.

The difficulties faced have been described, along with an explanation of how the project has grown in response to research, evaluation and experience. One of the main lessons for the coordinator has been that the length of time to implement a new project should never be underestimated. At the outset four years would have sounded like an excessive amount of time to have reached the current position, but with hindsight it has been a period of continuing change and development, offering exciting opportunities for all those who have been involved. The steering committee feels that the project has come a long way.

It could be argued that the best way to prevent children from coming to harm would be to stop the perpetrators of harm in the first instance. Unfortunately, this is an idealistic dream and we have a duty to put in place measures that will help children to understand which behaviours are unacceptable and to give them strategies for getting help sooner rather than later so that any damage done to them is limited. By emphasising to children that they have a role to play in prevention, it could be said that we are placing the responsibility for their safety on their shoulders; it is the obligation of those involved in prevention education to ensure that children understand that they are never responsible for the actions of others.

Note

1 The word 'harm' refers to the impact on the child of a particular behaviour, not the 'act' itself (as in the use of the word 'abuse'). 'Harm' is the term that is used within legislation and is a broad concept that includes abuse but also includes other behaviours that affect individuals.

Chapter Eight

Recognising and Celebrating Children's Cultural Heritage

Mandy de Waal and Satwant Shergill

Introduction

REACCH is an acronym for a project that produced a protocol for ensuring that children from minority ethnic backgrounds have their cultural needs assessed, met and monitored by social services. REACCH represents: *R*ecognizing (making a good assessment) and *C*elebrating (highlighting its place, importance and relevance) *C*hildren's *C*ultural *H*eritage (including language, diet, religion, ritual, community inclusion). At the heart of REACCH are several aspirations: to make a difference to the lives of children from minority ethnic backgrounds; to improve their life chances; to help them combat racism; to help them make and maintain links with their communities; to help them to enjoy and be proud of their heritage; and to give them the skills, the information and the confidence to celebrate their difference. REACCH owes its existence and success to the acknowledgement that, in a county with small minority ethnic populations, services to minority ethnic children were unlikely to match their needs fully. Special processes were regarded as essential in order to ensure that the best quality services possible were delivered.

Origins of REACCH

The starting point for the social services department was to examine what it was currently doing. This information, however, was not readily available or at least not in a format that could be used to identify potentially problematic aspects of practice. There was a good deal of anecdotal evidence of the problems the department was experiencing in this area of work, but nothing tangible. The department was still getting to grips with ERKM (Ethnic Record Keeping and Monitoring) systems and, whilst the quality of data was improving, it was not wholly reliable. At best, it told us nothing more than the number of Black and minority ethnic children in the system and even this basic level of information, as we identified later, was not entirely accurate. The department needed to examine how assessments on Black and minority ethnic children were being conducted and how cultural needs were being determined and met. Following that, a process would have to be developed that achieved the desired standard – a holistic assessment where 'race', culture and identity was fully integrated into care planning – and, finally, ongoing monitoring systems would have to be in place to ensure that this standard was maintained.

In early 1999, Warwickshire Social Services Department commissioned an audit of all cases involving children from minority ethnic heritages (de Waal 1999). The audit concentrated on a particular district within the authority and the purpose of the audit was to identify more detailed information. The objectives of the audit were to look at the quality and accuracy of assessments in relation to 'race' and cultural needs, and the extent to which specific needs were identified and met. Apart from some small pockets of good practice, the audit showed that social workers generally lacked confidence and expertise in handling cases involving minority ethnic children. One aspect of this was poor and inaccurate recording of ethnicity, parentage, cultural needs and socialisation. The audit made recommendations for improving services for these children and young people: the establishment of a protocol for the use of consultants; the use of an assessment and monitoring form for racial and cultural needs; support for social workers; training and support for foster carers; and improved links and working in partnership with Black communities and the Black voluntary sector. In February 2000, the Social Services Department commissioned the author of the audit to look at a process to meet its recommendations, a process which would seek to ensure that a quality service to minority ethnic children depended less upon which social worker worked with them. The acronym REACCH was adopted, for the reasons explained in the introduction to the chapter.

The issues

It was obvious from the outset that in order to improve services to minority ethnic children, assessments had to improve. In particular: recording of ethnicity had to be more accurate (no more use of 'mixed race', 'black' or 'white' which gives no useable information); understanding of 'cultural needs' had to be built upon; social workers had to comprehend and acknowledge racism and its impact on children and families; there needed to be some appreciation of the value of the extended family and the wider minority ethnic communities in building resilience and confidence in Black children; and there had to be a way of getting social workers to pick up on cues that might indicate those children who had identity issues that might need to be addressed. For example, one file reported that a child had low self-esteem, seemed isolated and was in danger of being excluded from school. This mixed parentage child, in an otherwise all 'white' family, might have been demonstrating identity confusion or experiencing rejection, but the social worker was unable to translate these behaviours into a possible need for some direct work on identity. Thus, 'REACCH' had to deliver accurate, precise, detailed ethnicity recording of the wider family and full, informed and holistic assessments. Those assessments then had to translate into action, into care planning which integrated cultural needs into overall service objectives.

The difficulties were obvious. With small minority ethnic populations in Warwickshire, most practitioners lacked the range of experience that might have made them confident and knowledgeable in working with minority ethnic children. The audit had highlighted some areas of poor practice that were being masked by this lack of knowledge and experience, an issue that would become more apparent and controversial as the project progressed. Initially, training seemed the obvious solution to such problems. However, the small number of cases raised the question of how effective any training could be, if it could not be translated into direct practice experience. After training, practitioners might wait months or even years before they had the opportunity to work with minority ethnic children. In addition, a rolling programme of training would be needed to take into account staff turnover and the funding for this was likely to be problematic.

In this situation, whilst training was recognised as an important learning tool, there was a clear need for a reference manual that would go beyond the impact of a two-day training course. The manual would be aimed at social workers and would preferably be written by a social worker, who could understand what information was required and how it should be presented. Social work already involves detailed form-filling and recording, and social workers would not have time to sift through pages and pages of additional information. In dealing with complex and sensitive issues, the need for clear, concise, jargon-free language was paramount. The manual was not envisaged as having responses to all of the specific issues that might arise; each case would have to be considered and responded to on an individual basis. Instead, the manual would guide social workers to where responses could be found and enable them to respond, based on their own informed judgement and expertise. It would not, for instance, get into specifics arising from age or culture; the information needed to be presented in such a manner that it would be applicable across all age ranges, ethnicities, cultures and religions. In addition, given the rapid pace of change in social work, the manual would have to be in a form that would not be easily outdated by new research, government policy or departmental practice. Finally, whatever shape or form this manual was to take, it would need to be accessible to all social workers within the social services department.

Aims of REACCH

What REACCH wanted to achieve was the provision of opportunities for each minority ethnic or mixed parentage child or young person:

- to interact with a culturally and age-appropriate peer group in a suitably positive and encouraging environment and to experience regular structured and unstructured socialising and/or play within the group setting

- to receive appropriate supervision and input from suitably qualified staff confident and able to offer support and/or counselling as necessary

- to be offered positive reinforcement of Black culture, history, art and achievement, appropriate to age, understanding and ability

- to be integrated in and have communication with the wider Black communities (preferably locally, depending on what was available), through attendance at religious or cultural events and festivals as appropriate to that child's cultural, religious and ethnic heritage

- to link, when appropriate, with a mentor, independent person or older friend of similar ethnic origin

- to have access to suitably qualified direct identity workers who can help in dealing with any identity issues, confusion or rejection

- to have access to a wide variety of resources, appropriate to age and understanding, which positively reinforce and provide information about minority ethnic heritage.

Where were the experts and the resources to achieve these aims? Unless REACCH made access to direct work, resources and services easier, better assessments were unlikely to lead to better services.

Finding solutions

Working with a small steering group, the consultant recommended a three-pronged solution. First, a 'Race' and Cultural Needs Assessment Form: this is a tool for use primarily by social workers and is designed to help them identify the issues that may impact on cultural needs, such as language, diet, health, racism and religion. It is completed for every minority ethnic child looked after by or known to the department, and appears in every file as part of the care plan. This complemented the new Assessment Framework (see Chapter Four), which was about to be launched, and was described by the Assessment Framework Project Manager at the time as a 'how to' guide; a tool which would show social workers how to take ethnicity and culture into account when completing the Assessment Framework.

Second, a training manual, *Children First*, was produced (de Waal and Foster 2001). A social worker who felt apprehensive or unsure about the issues faced by a minority ethnic child could use this book as a refresher guide in identifying possible areas of concern. The information then acquired could in turn inform the use of the 'Race' and Culture Assessment Form. *Children First* gives social workers basic information and guidance in making assessments of minority ethnic children and has chapters entitled 'Why bother with "race", culture and identity?', 'What is identity and what is identity work?', 'Answers, where to find them and what to do with them'. This training manual has now been given to every social worker in children's teams in Warwickshire.

Third, *specialists and resources*: in spite of training manuals and assessment forms, there would remain a paucity of confidence and up-to-date expertise in determining cultural needs. What many social workers required was access to a consultant who could talk over children's needs with them and help them develop an understanding of what the issues were for the child and how they might best be met. A REACCH consultant was available who would meet and discuss children's needs and provide each social worker with a written report on their discussions. In addition, a list of direct workers who could be called upon was drawn up and a large resource library was funded by the department, containing books, games, puzzles, masks, paint and CD-roms in order to assist a practitioner working with a child or young person identified as having cultural needs. Warwickshire Social Services Department was positive about the use of consultants in relation to 'race'. The use of Black consultants was not new to the department. Previously, they had been used extensively for training within the department at all levels, leading to the development of the department's Race Equality Policy and Procedures (held on the intranet at Warwickshire Social Services). Although the department already employed three Race Equality Development Officers, it was acknowledged that this area of work was quite specialised and required the input of someone with detailed knowledge and experience of working with both social workers and children. However, social workers would remain as case managers for minority ethnic children. They would consult with children and young people to decide what information went on the assessment form and work plan and would coordinate services and resources.

Putting the REACCH project into practice

Having had the project approved and adopted, a number of workshops were held to brief social workers on REACCH and to invite them to contact the consultant. Simultaneously, a list of all cases relating to children of minority ethnic heritage was compiled and the consultant began meeting with social workers. The process that was instigated was as follows:

- Social worker assigned case relating to child of minority ethnic heritage who had either been identified as a child in need or who had recently been placed in foster care.

- Consultant advised of allocation and contacts social worker.

- Social worker and consultant discuss the case, identify issues relating to the child and any issues specifically highlighted by the family and other significant people, and agree on the content of the 'Race' and Culture Assessment Form. Where older children or young people were involved, it was vital that their views were sought directly.

- Consultant writes REACCH report and sends it to social worker.

- Social worker completes the 'Race' and Culture Assessment Form together with the child and family (if appropriate) and work plan and sends it to consultant.

- Work plan implemented as part of normal case management.

- Consultant monitors case by contact after three months.

At the beginning of the project, social workers required a fair amount of support. The consultant's meeting with the social worker sought both to gauge the social worker's grasp of the issues and to inform her or him of the process. Although the consultant wrote the REACCH report, it reflected joint decisions with the social worker for moving this part of the work forward. Had the consultant not written the report, on occasion, vital information or issues would have been omitted. It became clear that, in some instances, the 'Race' and Culture Assessment Forms were not being completed or they were completed but not implemented. Two large cabinets of books, videos, toys and games remained untouched. Most importantly, there were 'looked after' children who had not had a proper assessment of their cultural needs. In general, social workers appeared not to have embraced the REACCH project. Some had little knowledge of the process, of who had commissioned it, of why it was important to act in accordance with its aspirations, and to whom they were accountable should they not do so. What was needed at this juncture was more and better publicity about REACCH, better implementation and more robust monitoring.

Pushing on

Until this stage of the process, the REACCH consultant had been an external, independent specialist. This had its drawbacks. Who was this consultant and how did she fit into the department? What status did she have? Why was she asking about social workers' practice? There appeared to have been insufficient publicity within the department and, although the consultant explained her brief, some social workers were reluctant to engage with the task. If REACCH was to become embedded as part of Children's Services, a full-time REACCH coordinator had to be appointed, who would be a permanent member of staff, available at the end of a phone and known throughout the department – a resource for social workers. The coordinator needed to be given the status of a senior social worker and the title 'project manager' in order to attract the right calibre of applicant and to give credibility to the work. The creation of the project manager's post was to become the key that would unlock wider departmental ownership of REACCH. The project manager would not only provide written REACCH reports but also check regularly with social workers that work plans were being executed and changes were under way that would have a positive impact on children's lives. The project manager also needed to be part of a wider monitoring process, undertaken by a REACCH panel.

Interviews were held and a REACCH project manager was appointed at senior social worker level. As soon as she was in post, written information was sent to every social worker in all of the children's teams informing them of the appointment, and arrangements were made for the REACCH project manager to visit teams and brief them about the post. Arrangements were also made for the REACCH project manager to meet with every social worker who had a case relating to a child of minority ethnic heritage. There was an added incentive for social workers to meet with the project manager; the progress of every case relating to a child of minority ethnic heritage would be monitored by the REACCH panel. This panel was established as a multi-agency monitoring and advice forum that meets monthly with social workers to discuss any issues, create action plans and monitor progress. The REACCH project manager advises social workers when a child will be considered by the panel and helps them prepare. The panel consists of:

- Children's Services manager (Chair)
- REACCH project manager
- Senior social worker (Fostering Team)
- Senior social worker (Long-term Team)
- Senior social worker (Leaving Care)
- Representative from Education Department
- Representative from Child Psychology
- Independent member.

The REACCH panel does not simply monitor the progress of children. Rather, it has become an advisory panel for social workers. They can bring their cases to the panel for discussion about issues facing a child, aspects of case management and draw on panel members' combined expertise to consider how best to meet a child's needs. Although the panel makes recommendations, overall case management rests with the social worker.

The best measure of success is whether or not the REACCH process has made a difference to children's lives. Improving the quality of assessments of the needs of minority ethnic children, enhancing the skills of social workers, disseminating expertise, better case monitoring, a growth in confidence for social workers – these are all worthwhile and valuable by-products. However, first and foremost, the needs of these children must be properly assessed and fully met. The evidence to date suggests that REACCH works. All of the REACCH reports have picked up the needs of minority ethnic children, most of whom are of mixed parentage, with many living away from home.

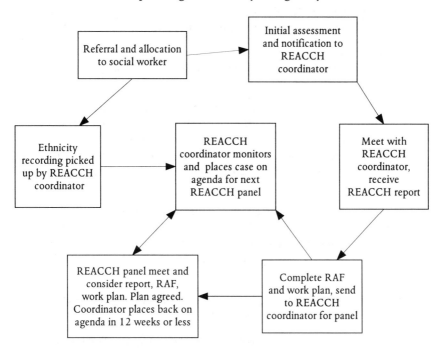

Figure 8.1 From referral to monitoring by the REACCH panel

REACCH was a bottom-up initiative and it has worked well. For local authorities with small minority ethnic populations the issues raised in meeting the needs of minority ethnic and mixed parentage children are potentially complex and far-REACCHing. Children need to be given opportunities early on in their lives to explore and celebrate their cultural heritage and have their cultural needs incorporated into overall case planning, not added on as an afterthought or not addressed at all. It is equally vital to have a skilled and committed workforce. Although a process like REACCH cannot solve all of the problems, it does point in key directions. By focusing on the outcomes (the well-being of children) and bringing committed and creative individuals together, as happened in Warwickshire, the life chances of these children can be maximised. The remainder of the chapter provides an example of the process.

REACCH report for social worker 'X'

1. Introduction

1.1 This report is in respect of YY, a 9-year-old girl of mixed parentage (birth father Indian Hindu, birth mother white English).

1.2 She is currently on an interim care order, having been removed from both parents who are living apart due to, *inter alia*, neglect, failure to protect and more recently rejection by her birth father.

1.3 She is in a stable foster placement with experienced, mature (59 and 67) white carers in 'X' city. She attends a mainly white school and her best friend is also white.

1.4 YY has a close attachment to her mother with whom she has not had contact since September of this year. It was YY's wish to return to live with her mother but a residential assessment completed in August of this year suggested she would be incapable of caring adequately for her daughter and the option of rehabilitation is no longer viable or being pursued.

1.5 YY has recently been forcefully and openly rejected by her birth father with whom she lived for 10 months. She has five half siblings, all of whom are Indian Hindu and has an extended Indian family. Her birth father is reluctant to have any further contact with the social services department.

1.6 YY is a bright and intelligent child, aware of her mixed parentage, aware of her identity, father's religion and heritage.

1.7 YY has had the benefit of some identity work which was successful in introducing YY to Indian dress, culture and language.

1.8 The long-term plan is for YY to be moved to a permanent placement.

2. 'Race' and Culture Assessment Form (RAF I and II)

YY needs to have a 'Race' and Culture Assessment Form completed as soon as possible. In view of her recent life events and the significant changes which have recently occurred, any interventions to address 'race' and culture must be sensitive to her current situation. The RAF should include the following:

2.1 YY to have access to her own resources which show positive images of children from minority ethnic groups, particularly mixed parentage children. These can be games, toys, books, computer CDs, maps, face paints, masks, dressing-up clothes, dolls or puppets.

2.2 YY needs to have further identity work, preferably from the same worker who can help YY express her feelings about her 'race', culture and skin colour. She has not participated in any identity work since March of this year. It is essential that YY does not perceive her Indian heritage as an added on part of her otherwise 'white' life. This can only be achieved by her regular, meaningful, enjoyable and rewarding interaction with the Indian/Hindu community.

2.3 Although the identity worker may be unable to involve birth parents in any identity work, efforts should be made to approach the extended family, both paternal and maternal, and seek their cooperation.

2.4 Any identity work, especially that which includes investigation of the extended family, must be tied in closely with ongoing life story work for YY. Photographs, memorabilia, religious objects and clothes might be obtained which can facilitate both life story and direct identity work.

2.5 As part of her identity work, use could be made of the local Hindu community where there is a regular women's group. Further advice on this can be sought from the local community coordinator.

2.6 YY's carers should be encouraged to facilitate play and use of the above resources and to promote a positive home environment which values YY's heritage. It is understood that the current carers have been supportive and cooperative so far in promoting mixed culture and have regular contact with an Asian family.

2.7 In view of her birth family's inability and unwillingness to care for her, family-finding for YY should already be under way. YY has expressed a wish to remain at her current placement where she is settled and feels part of the family. The placement is not ideal. YY would benefit from living in a culturally mixed area where she could attend school and interact with children from a similar background, and who resembled her. More importantly, YY needs to be part of a younger, mixed 'race' family preferably Indian Hindu/White. There are well known difficulties in finding families that meet these criteria but all efforts should be made.

2.8   YY is now of an age where her participation in, cooperation with and enthusiasm for any plan will be crucial to its success. She needs to be able to express her hopes and concerns about her culture, identity and future, have those feelings acknowledged and acted upon where possible. She is also, at this time, fairly positive about her culture, religion and identity. While she remains in this frame of mind, the above recommendations must be actioned.

2.9   A copy of the completed RAF needs to be sent to the REACCH coordinator.

2.10 Please ensure that the foster carers' key workers are informed of the work you are planning to do. The foster carers will need to be supported throughout this process.

3. Additional resources

To supplement your existing skills and expertise you will also need:

3.1 A copy of *Children First* by Mandy de Waal and Shirley Foster (2001), which forms part of the REACCH project and to which you will need to refer to complete the RAF.

3.2 Resources as mentioned in 2(a). *It is very important that these resources are for YY's own use and belong to her. She should be encouraged to write her name on them and take them with her should she move placement.*

3.3 If her foster carers require resources to inform them about issues affecting mixed parentage children or information about the culture of her birth father, they too should be provided with suitable resources for their own use. The same stipulation regarding ownership applies.

3.4 As soon as the RAF is received, arrangements will be made to contact the former identity worker to continue her work with YY.

4. Monitoring and revision

4.1 Copies of the completed RAF will be sent to the REACCH coordinator. Another copy should be placed on YY's file and should be the subject of review during supervision.

4.2 It may be that some of the plans you have for YY do not bring the desired results or the RAF may in some other way need revision. Please read carefully the chapter 'Success?' and 'What if Everything Fails?' in *Children First* before you revise the RAF.

4.3 Should you need to revise the RAF, please send a revised copy to the REACCH coordinator.

4.4 You will be advised as soon as this case is on the agenda for the REACCH Panel. You may contact the REACCH coordinator at any time about this report and its contents.

The social worker in this case completed a RAF and a work plan that needed the input of a direct worker. A direct worker was identified who was an Indian woman with many years experience. An extract from her report says:

> I met with YY and her carers on three separate occasions and with YY's birth mother. During my work with YY I have addressed the following:
>
> religious festivals
>
> Asian dress
>
> Asian music and dance
>
> dietary needs
>
> Asian language.
>
> I began my work by introducing YY and her carers to a variety of books containing information on different religious festivals and positive black role models. YY expressed a particular interest in Asian dress. I therefore felt it would be beneficial for YY to visit 'X' city, which is the heart of the Gujerati community. During this visit, YY had the opportunity to visit several shops and we purchased an Asian outfit and accessories. She really enjoyed this visit and commented how lucky she was to be of Asian heritage because she loved Asian clothes, food and jewellery. I also gave her some Asian dressing-up clothes. To promote her interest in music and dance, I bought YY two Asian films, which also gave positive images of Asian life and culture to YY and her foster family.
>
> YY also told me that she missed eating Asian food so I took YY to an Indian restaurant during our visit to 'X' city. I purchased a variety of ingredients and utensils and taught the carers and YY how to cook her favourite dishes. This session also enabled the other foster children to get involved and have a

positive experience about cooking Asian food. This was particularly useful to YY (who was initially very negative about Asian food).

I believe that YY has thrived on the input she has received to meet her cultural needs. I strongly feel that YY has developed an appetite to learn more about Asian culture.

It would be beneficial to YY and her carers to have a point of contact to get assistance and advice in continuing to meet YY's cultural needs. This would also enable the carers to have up-dated information on events and cultural festivals that YY can attend.

Shortly after this report was written by the direct worker, YY moved to another long-term placement. Her case was considered by the REACCH panel and the following recommendations were made:

- that YY's carers continue to take YY to festivals and events in the area which are compatible with YY's 'race', religion and culture

- that YY's carers be given factual information on India, the Hindu religion, culture, language and diet

- that YY continues to access direct work as necessary

- that YY is encouraged to access Asian clothing, magazines, music, videos, etc.

YY continues to express an interest in her Indian heritage. She is positive about her mixed parentage and as long as she is provided with access to the things which interest her and she has some contact with the Asian community this positive attitude may well remain.

Chapter Nine

Family Placements
Matching Needs and Services

Rebecca Johnson and Phil Sawbridge

Introduction

Services for 'looked after' children are crucially important for all local authorities. First, for these children the local authority assumes the responsibility of parenthood and the quality of services provided will be a crucial factor in their future life chances. Second, the largest area of expenditure in Children's Social Services in Warwickshire is within the Family Placement Service. Finally, the consequences of failures within the system and the high level of public interest make providing family placements for children extremely hazardous for local authorities. This chapter describes how management information was used to develop a commissioning strategy to meet the needs of this group of children.

Management information

There has been an increasing emphasis in the delivery of social services on being able to provide convincing evidence about what works best in improving outcomes for services users (Office of Public Management and Department of Health 2003). As a consequence, management information systems are becoming increasingly important. When used appropriately, such systems provide the tools for extracting and manipulating data, and rendering information that is meaningful and valuable to a range of audiences, leading to the claim that 'improved availability and quality of information can improve an organisation's competences' (Johnson and Scholes 1999, p.475). Within Warwickshire Social Services Department, for example, the client records management system, 'Care First', holds a wealth of information about service users and service provision (see Chapter Two). Using 'Business Objects', a query/reporting/data analysis tool, information held on 'Care First' can be interrogated in order to obtain aggregate and detailed management information. This enhances the capacity to monitor and support performance across children's services, to undertake audits to ensure that procedural requirements are being followed and to plan, develop and evaluate services. In addition, providing such information demonstrates the Social Services Department's accountability to external stakeholders, in particular, the community it serves and also to an increasingly information-hungry central government.

Despite the advantages gained by using management information to inform practice, there are limitations to what quantitative analysis can achieve; it has been viewed more as a method for investigating problems than for solving them (Quade 1989, p.175). Management information has the capacity, then, to open issues for further scrutiny: 'thorough exploratory study may suggest questions, or act as a starting point for unforeseen lines of enquiry' (Robson 1993, p.283). The minimal amount of qualitative data held on management information systems means they can only be 'a starting point for understanding the complex and dynamic needs and experiences of the children and families who typically come to the attention of child welfare agencies' (Melamid 2002, p.20). Mindful of these limitations, the starting point for the 'Matching Needs and Services' project, centred on Warwickshire's Family Placement Service, was that the information available raised questions about the service's future direction, which called for further investigation. The project was designed to enable us to 'get beneath' this information so that more informed recommendations could be made for the planning, commissioning and delivery of services for children and their families.

Background to the project

Services for 'looked after' children are crucially important for all local authorities. At the time of writing, there are 408 children 'looked after' by Warwickshire County Council of whom approximately 88% are living in family placements: in foster care, placed for adoption or the subject of a care order and placed with a parent or a person with parental responsibility. This area of work accounts for 58% of all expenditure in children's social services.

Against this general background, the immediate context for the 'Matching Needs and Services' project was the 'Best Value' initiative (Department of the Environment, Transport and the Regions 1998), introduced after the 1997 general election as one of the main mechanisms through which central government drives its objective of achieving better performance from public sector organisations. Under this initiative, local authorities are required to review key services on a cyclical basis to ensure that they are needed, that they are delivered efficiently and benchmarked with the best comparable services, that stakeholders' views are sought and considered and that services could not be provided more effectively by others. From a planning perspective, there have been concerns that family placements, as a key area of strategy, might be being developed on the basis of the practice wisdom of managers within the service, rather than the principles of Best Value. These were key factors in the development of the 'Matching Needs and Services' project.

The primary objective of undertaking a matching needs and services exercise within Warwickshire's Family Placement Service was to promote improvements in the matching of foster carers with children 'looked after' by the local authority, and to develop the service in accordance with 'Best Value' principles. As the project progressed. it became much broader as it became clear that the development of services for 'looked after' children could not be separated from development of services for all children. To promote the interests of 'looked after' children there needs to be an effective continuum of services that includes services designed to prevent the need for them becoming 'looked after' in the first place and to support them when they move on. However, at the outset the aims of the project were as follows:

- To investigate the nature and extent of the demand for the services provided by Warwickshire's Family Placement Service.

- To examine the nature and extent of the supply of available carers.

- To consider ways of creating a more effective balance between what is required and what is provided.

- To draw conclusions from the research and recommend a strategy for the future commissioning of services.

Methodology

The project's methodology was adapted from two source materials: the *Matching Needs and Services* practice tool developed by the Dartington Social Research Unit (1999), which is being utilised widely in social services, and *Planning and Providing Good Quality Placements for Children in Care*, developed by the Department of Health (2001c). Following the principles of the *Matching Needs and Services* methodology, a longitudinal sample was selected, case-level research was undertaken and a multi-disciplinary working group defined common need groups. The publication *Planning and Providing Good Quality Placements for Children in Care* was used as the basis for designing the research questions. In contrast to the *Matching Needs and Services* methodology, a great deal of information was collected about all aspects of the experiences of the children in the sample in order to assess needs, circumstances and trends more effectively. This aspect of the project was prompted by wanting to ensure that the findings from the research were translated into actions and strategies that could be evaluated and that would lead to better outcomes for children. Little *et al.* (2002) point out that the *Matching Needs and Services* approach falls short of 'orthodox taxonomical formulations', but that it should be viewed as a tool to support the initial stage of the planning process. We believe that our approach has taken us beyond the Dartington model and that we are well placed as a result to progress to the development of a sound and effective commissioning strategy for children in need. This aspect of the project is explored later on in the chapter.

The project began by mapping the current demand for service. This was achieved using two methods. In the first phase, in-depth research was undertaken into the circumstances of 100 consecutive children who started to be 'looked after' following 1 September 1998. By selecting a consecutive group, the spectrum of need was more representative; taking a cross-section of 100 currently 'looked after' children would have resulted in over-representation of children who had been in the system for a long time. By selecting a retrospective sample, it was possible to assess the consequences of interventions offered by various agencies. The key dimensions examined were: the children's needs, their circumstances on referral, services offered or used by the children and their families, placement details/issues and the outcomes of placement activity. The second phase of mapping demand incorporated statistical analyses of Warwickshire's 'looked after' population and a general analysis of the needs of children and families in Warwickshire. We then scanned the contemporary environment to enable us to develop a view about emerging legislative requirements and professional ideologies, which may impact on service requirements in the future.

The overall purpose of mapping demand was to:

- establish a clearer picture of the groups of children who require placement and what type of placement they require

- determine what support packages/services are most appropriate for addressing the needs of these groups and exploring options for the delivery, or change, of these services

- clarify the policy objectives and thresholds, adopted by agencies to moderate demand, that provide the context for service provision.

The second stage of the project was mapping the supply of services. This involved:

- looking at the budget available for meeting the needs of young people in Warwickshire

- analysing our existing foster carers

- examining various elements of other placement options available, e.g. residential care

- exploring service availability from other agencies to establish whether their services are appropriate and accessible

- evaluating the impact of services by looking at the outcomes for children in care

- exploring service quality for 'looked after' children, including the results of any consultation carried out with them, their families or carers

- finding successful ways to increase the supply of foster carers, to recruit and retain effectively and to ensure sufficient support services are in place.

Key findings and recommendations

The project produced key findings that led to recommendations, based upon the research evidence, for improving and developing services to meet the needs of children in Warwickshire.

Over 90% of children who had a 'looked after' episode in Warwickshire were known to social services beforehand. This is slightly more than Packman, Randall and Jacques (1986) found in their seminal study of 361 children admitted to care over a 12-month period, in which 80% of children were known to social services before they were accommodated.

Approximately half of the children who required a placement in Warwickshire did so on an emergency basis. A great number of these were short-term, one-off incidents. Packman *et al.* (1986) found in their study that three out of five children returned from care within a short time, some of them within a matter of days or weeks. Taking this information into account, it can be suggested that children are more likely to become 'looked after' if they have a social worker, and that, on occasion, the 'looked after' process is being used as a form of family support. To address this, where a child becomes 'looked after' in an unplanned way, the episode is now treated as a respite placement and recorded as such on the client records management system. The placement is then seen as a family support service and the risks of it drifting into becoming a long-term arrangement are diminished.

Warwickshire's care population has increased by 25% since 2001, with a current rate of 37 children 'looked after' per 10,000 of the under-18 population. While Warwickshire still looks after considerably fewer children than the national average of 54 children per 10,000 at 31 March 2002 (Department of Health 2003c), this increase has brought the authority more in line with activity across a 'family' of comparable local authorities.[1] Key factors in explaining Warwickshire's rising 'looked after' population are the substantial increase in starting rates, from 16 per 10,000 in 2001 to 22.5 in 2002, a decrease in ceasing rates, from 18 to 17 per 10,000 over the same time period, coupled with the fact that young people are being 'looked after' for longer periods of time. This rising demand threatens the long-term stability of the service and makes it almost impossible to meet our own standards of service provision for children once they become 'looked after'. With these factors in mind it is crucial that strategies are developed to contain and, if possible, reduce demand to restore equilibrium. In order to prevent young people becoming accommodated for indeterminate periods, all episodes involving a young person being assessed as requiring a substantive placement, including all permanent placement moves, are now authorised locally by the most senior manager. This encourages careful and reflective case planning that is designed to meet the best interests of the child.

In making efforts to reduce the 'looked after' population corresponding efforts need to be made to ensure that the needs of the child and her or his family are not ignored. As Packman *et al.* warn:

> Too sharp a focus on the gateway to care can narrow and distort notions of 'prevention'. Rather than seeking to prevent disruptions, stress and harm to children and their families – to which admission to care *may*, in some cases, be a positive and appropriate response – the term becomes equated simply with prevention of *admissions*. (Packman *et al.* 1986, p.194, original emphasis)

It was evident that young people aged 10–17 are more likely to require accommodation. At 31 March 2002, this group represented 56% of Warwickshire's 'looked after' population, but only constituted 45% of the general child population within the county.

The research highlighted the extent to which teenage boys are a particularly vulnerable group. At 31 March 2002, young males aged between 13 and 17 constituted 23% of Warwickshire's 'looked after' population. They also accounted for 24% of all placements the Family Placement Service were involved in making during 2001/2002. In addition, young males between 13 and 16 years made up 20% of our sample of 100 placement episodes. Ward and Skuse (2002), in their study of children 'looked after' for 12 months or more, found that teenagers were one of the groups particularly vulnerable to having a high number of placements in the first year of being 'looked after'. From our study it was apparent that teenage boys, in particular, are more likely to suffer disrupted placements: 25% of the young people in our sample who experienced a placement move were of this age and gender. In response, we proposed the design of a menu of placement services which social workers will be able to access specifically to address the needs of this particular group.

Another group at risk are children of single carers: 'In Britain today one family in four is a lone parent family and one child in three will spend part of their childhood in a lone parent family' (Rowlingson and McKay 2002, p.1). Many of the young people in our research sample had come into care from a home situation where there was only one parent (39%). In the study by Packman *et al.* (1986) the proportion was similar (40%). Bebbington and Miles (1989) also found this trend in their study. They looked at the background of

2165 children entering care and found that only one-quarter of children had been living with both parents. On the basis of their investigation, they stated that 'living with one adult only is the single greatest risk factor' (Bebbington and Miles 1989, p.354). Wigan Social Services Department (2002), in conjunction with Dartington Social Research Unit, also found when researching the cases of 100 newly 'looked after' children that family breakdown was a major factor in the lives of these young people, with only 27% of their sample living with two parents prior to placement. One of the recommendations made to prevent some of the children in Warwickshire requiring accommodation was that a menu of family support packages, including regular respite provision where appropriate, should be developed to ensure that support is delivered before situations reach crisis point.

Citing the work of Sinclair and Little (2001), Little *et al.* state that in children's services 'there is not only no acknowledged taxonomy of children in need but also a dearth of information about the characteristics of the children, their life trajectories and the outcomes of interventions with which to develop one' (Little *et al.* 2002, p.28). The taxonomy of children in need developed by Sinclair and Carr-Hill started with identification of the antecedents of need, for example, deprivation, abuse or (wilful) neglect and then correlated this with other factors such as the causes of need, for example, family circumstances, the place of residence and pattern of services received (Sinclair and Carr-Hill 1996). Following this work and the introduction of the Children in Need (CIN) Census, the Department of Health CIN categories were introduced which classify children in relation to causation of need, for example, abuse or neglect, parental illness. In order to gain better insight into the circumstances of young people coming into local authority care in Warwickshire, five categories were developed, which describe the purposes that placements are intended to meet for young people: 'their needs'. Further work is needed to develop these categories so that detailed guidance can be produced to assist social workers when planning a child's placement and support. Any such developments would need to take account of progress made nationally in developing an established or recommended taxonomy of children in need. In the future, the recruitment of foster carers could be informed by these categories. Table 9.1 provides some brief details of the need categories and provides a proportional breakdown of the needs of young people in our sample.

The value of categorising children in this way is that the categories are based upon the assessed needs of the child rather than the issue that they initially present to the Social Services Department. If a young person's needs were defined as 'sanctuary', for example, the placement would need to be designed to meet that need and the focus of the care plan would be fixed on securing their immediate physical safety. If a young person's category were defined as 'abuse', the purpose of the placement might be any of the four categories highlighted in Table 9.1 and the focus of the care plan would not be apparent without further inquiry being undertaken.

Table 9.1 Categories of need

Need	Purpose of accommodation	Placement provided	Nature	Percentage of sample with this need
Sanctuary	To protect the child from harm	Foster care	Short term	26
Maintenance	To preserve the continuity of permanent arrangements	Respite care	Long-term arrangement	17
Immediate physical and emotional care	To respond to a disruption in normal care arrangements	Foster care	Short term	52
Long-term health need	To provide specialist care for a child with life-threatening/ limiting, or other complex health needs	Respite care or residential provision	Long term	2
Unmet psychological need	To provide specialist care for a child with emotional or psychological difficulties, or whose carer has these	Residential provision, respite or foster care	Dependent upon individual progress	3

The research highlighted that a child's mental health needs are often not considered when planning a placement, unless the needs are profoundly obvious. Mental health was only taken into account in a quarter of placements made in our sample. Ward and Skuse, in their study of children 'looked after' for 12 months or more, found evidence to suggest that mental health issues, specifically behavioural disorders, were not always recognized appropriately by social workers (Ward and Skuse 2002). Given the levels of trauma experienced by many 'looked after' children, this suggests that mental health awareness training is required for staff to enable them to assess young people appropriately and to plan the most effective care package.

The research also highlighted that on many occasions children did not receive any information about their forthcoming placement. In the sample only one in five young people received information about where they were going before the placement was made. An opportunity to increase the chances of the placement being a success is missed if young people do not feel part of the planning and decision-making. To rectify this, a general information sheet will be given to all children who are accommodated on an emergency basis. When a child is placed on a planned basis, arrangements are in place to ensure that she or he receives written information about her or his prospective carer prior to placement, in the form of the carer's profile, and that a pre-placement visit takes place. Performance against this requirement is monitored and reported.

Within Warwickshire, a large majority of children are placed with foster carers or for adoption (77% at 31 March 2002). However, there are significant differences across the county in the proportion of various placement types used. Although some local variation may be appropriate, the local authority is under increasing pressure from central government to deliver a consistent service, with local variety being pejoratively described as a 'postcode lottery'. County-wide and local targets are, therefore, being established in order to promote consistency of placement use across the county. For example, targets will be developed around kinship placements (placements with family or friends), children placed out of the county boundaries or in agency placements. Linked to this, is the need to explore the possibility of commissioning a block contract with a voluntary sector placement provider within Warwickshire. This would serve two main purposes: to promote local connections for children placed outside their community and to minimise the numbers in costly and hard-to-control out-of-county placements.

Using our client records management system we routinely gather information on the numbers of placements experienced by 'looked after' children and the number of these that break down. A total of 336 foster placements ended between 1 April 2001 and 31 March 2002. Of these it was reported that 55 ended as a result of placement breakdown (16%). Problems with this information include the fact that there is no clarification in Warwickshire on what constitutes a placement breakdown and it cannot be easily determined what actions, if any, are needed when a placement comes to an end. Ward and Skuse found considerable variation in their study when looking at placement disruptions in six local authorities, and stated that differential use of terminology was a key factor (Ward and Skuse 2002). To remedy this, a definition of what constitutes a placement breakdown will be developed so that consistent and accurate information can be gathered on the reasons why placements break down, in ways that will assist planning and service development.

Family support services should be considered as support to any member of a family. Services should be designed and directed appropriately in order to make the most positive impact upon the capacity of a family to sustain itself. This research found that a great number of support services provided to children in need were provided solely by social services: 81% of services provided prior to placement were from social services, 80% during placement and 82% post-placement. These figures were derived from categorising all of the services that a young person or their family were receiving. They suggest that strategic managers, teams and units must work towards engaging partner agencies, in particular health and education services, in the commissioning, planning and provision of support services on an individual case basis.

Since the implementation of the Children Act (1989), there has been greater recognition that short-term fostering can help in preventing the break-down of family relations (Aldgate and Bradley 1999). The use of short-term placement agreements, designed to support families by providing planned periods of short-term respite, has been consistent over the last few years at approximately 7 children per 10,000, notably lower than the national average. This suggests that Warwickshire does not maximise the benefits of this service for children in need. Many of the children who receive short-term placements in Warwickshire are disabled children. Aldgate and Bradley (1999) highlight in their study that while respite care has traditionally been a service for disabled children, other children in need could benefit from receiving planned short-term fostering. Aldgate stresses that the use of respite care has unique advantages: 'used properly, it could become a sophisticated service which is delivered…to promote the welfare of children in touch with social services' (Aldgate 1993, p.105). A particular strength of short-term fostering is that it promotes working together with parents, often a successful way to improve children's welfare and to accomplish positive outcomes for families (Aldgate and Bradley 1999). In Warwickshire, part of the overall preventive strategy is to increase the number of non-disabled children who receive short-term place-ments as a family support service. As mentioned earlier, lone-parent families in need could be one group to benefit from this service.

Of the children in our research sample, 42% were accommodated as a result of their parents' behaviour, with a further 9% being accommodated as a result of their parents' health. It appears that this trend is not uncommon. In a study undertaken by the East Coast Area Health Board and Dartington Social Research Unit (Dartington Social Research Unit 2003), on social services waiting list cases, it was found that the greatest need of the 90 young people in the sample (29%) was for their parents to be provided with services that would support them in providing better care for their children. In a study in Gloucestershire, it was found that 62% of children:

...had needs around the quality of parenting they were receiving... Many parents have major physical and psychological needs which were not addressed and had a profound impact on their well being and capacity to parent. To address these needs adequately demands, firstly, that they be recognised and acknowledged... Addressing parents' own needs requires a close relationship with adult services in both the planning and provision of services. In developing adult services' thresholds an explicit strategy will be needed to take account of parenting responsibilities and the impact of unmet adult needs on children and child care services. (Boushel *et al.* 2002, pp.17 and 41)

Wigan Social Services Department also concluded from a *Matching Needs and Services* project that improved emphasis was needed on certain elements of preventive work, in particular, that work needed to be better focused on adults (Wigan Social Services 2002). Tailoring services to meet the needs of parents, in some instances, can reduce the need for a child to become accommodated, making the overall impact of services more effective. Within Warwickshire, adult and children's services will work together to agree a common vision for how parents can be supported in their role. This may result in revisions to Warwickshire's current thresholds for adult and children's services.

This research highlighted numerous variations in practice across Warwickshire. For example, differences were found in the rate at which children move through the assessment process. In one district, close to 100% of referrals result in an initial assessment, whilst in another the figure was only 39.3%. However, only 5.5% of initial assessments resulted in a core assessment in the first district, whilst the figure in the second was 24.4%. While recording practice does make a considerable impact on perceived performance in this area, it cannot fully explain such differences. It was also evident that there was a lack of consistency in the proportion of children who move from assessment through to service provision, or in the proportion of children who start to be 'looked after' as a result. In a third district, for example, it was estimated that 21% of core assessments undertaken in 2001/2 resulted in a child becoming accommodated, while in a fourth the figure was much higher at 73%. There is a need for a constant stream of initiatives designed to promote consistency, thereby ensuring that services are provided equitably and to a high standard.

Foster carer recruitment activity decreased significantly during 2001/2, while the numbers of children 'looked after' increased. At 31 March 2002, only 293 foster care households were approved to provide placements for 405 children 'looked after'. The recruitment of foster carers differs greatly across the county, as does the numbers of children 'looked after'. We have proposed the development of local targets for the number of carers that a district should have at any given time. These targets will take into account differences in socio-economic circumstances and the nature and size of districts' 'looked after' populations. Providing a target figure is designed to stimulate the development of a range of initiatives to attract new carers to meeting local needs.

The research has identified that while almost 7% of Warwickshire's 'looked after' population is Black or of minority ethnic origin, only 2% of foster carers are. Ensuring that we have the right foster carers, including the right ethnic mix, is key to the matching needs process. Targets might be set for the ethnic composition of foster carers in each locality. The ethnic mix of the local population in each area would influence targets. The value of setting a target is that desirable outcomes can be clearly signposted and success criteria are identified which are consistent with service objectives.

Carers aged 50 or over were identified as major providers of placements for young people aged 10 or over. Of carers aged between 50 and 59, 33% of the young people they cared for were aged under 9 and 67% aged 10–17. As a result of this, foster care recruitment is likely to be specifically targeted at carers of this age group and inquiries and applications from this group are being fast-tracked.

In order to fulfil plans to offer increased respite, including providing respite to children 'looked after' in an unplanned way, efforts need to be concentrated on recruiting specialised carers to provide these placements. Until the supply of these carers meets demand, applications for prospective respite carers need to be prioritised.

Word of mouth is reported as the most successful method for recruiting foster carers. Research indicates that 'word-of-mouth' contact (through existing foster carers) remains a well-regarded source of new recruits (Shaw and Hipgrave 1989). One study found that 46% of carers heard of fostering through friends, relatives or work. It concluded that 'the experience of past and current carers is crucial in shaping a public image of fostering' (Triseliotis, Borland and Hill 2000, p.55). The Social Services Inspectorate's inspection of foster care services reinforced the importance of word-of-mouth as a powerful means of attracting new foster carers (Maddocks 2002). In response to these findings, Warwickshire has encouraged carers to introduce friends and relatives and when they do so, they receive a one-off reward payment.

This research has highlighted that a great number of carers who leave fostering did not provide placements during the year prior to departure. Of the mainstream foster carers who retired or resigned between April and September 2001, over 50% had provided no accommodation for 'looked after' young people during the year ending September 2001. In future the use of foster carers will be tracked to make sure that resources are maximised. An occupancy target will be set to ensure that all carers are utilised effectively and take advantage of the benefits of a new fee-paid scheme.

The research reinforced the recommendation made in Warwickshire's Best Value review of the Family Placement Service that improvements need to be made in the quality and reporting of management information in the Fostering

Service. This will be achieved through the development of a minimum dataset, which will ensure that key information impacting on the service is routinely monitored to assist service development and planning.

What next?

Warwickshire's matching needs and services project report has been publicised to policy makers within children's services and the document is available as source material that is of interest to key stakeholders. The research evidence also has wider significance for service planners within the County Council. The work will be useful to other departments undertaking 'Best Value' assessments, as source material for the Social Service Inspectorate and the Audit Commission and as a model of service planning that is of interest to the wider social work profession. The model itself has the potential to be applied widely within the social services sector.

As mentioned earlier, the key to this project was ensuring that the research findings were used as an aid to developing strategies, services and initiatives that will have a positive impact on the lives of children in need in Warwickshire. To this end, a stakeholder event, involving professionals from the County Council, social services, education, health, the police and the voluntary sector was held. The aim of the event was to bring professionals together to explore the needs of children in Warwickshire, to agree a vision for children in need and to develop shared aims and objectives for achieving this vision. The Matching Needs and Services project report was used as the starting point to prompt discussion and to provide professionals with evidence about what is happening currently to children in need. The knowledge provided by the report was used as the basis for identifying key areas for service development and developing responses geared to promoting improvements. This forum was used to share ideas, set priorities and foster commitment to improving services for children. Following this event, a similar event was held with young people who have been engaged with social services at some point in their lives. This event paralleled the professionals' event and was used to test young people's opinions on what the professionals thought were the key needs. A commissioning strategy for children in need will be produced, based upon the material produced during these events.

Conclusion

Despite the initial focus on Warwickshire's Family Placement Service, this research revealed the need for a broader approach to planning, commissioning and delivering services that will prove beneficial for all children in need, not just those 'looked after'. During the course of the research, it became clear that efforts cannot be limited to improving services for 'looked after' children. To have the greatest impact upon their lives, a range of services is required to support children in need before they enter public care (see Chapter Four). For 'looked after' children, services need to be designed to deliver the best possible outcomes. Resources need to be deployed to maximum effect and that necessitates moving away from the current position of directing resources at the highest level of need, without paying attention to the potential benefits of early intervention. By adopting this approach, the numbers of children who become 'looked after' can be minimised, the harm suffered by those who are 'looked after' can be reduced and 'Best Value' can be demonstrated to stakeholders.

Note

1 Our comparative family of authorities consists of Bedfordshire, Cambridgeshire, Cheshire, Derbyshire, Gloucestershire, Hampshire, Leicestershire, Northamptonshire, Nottinghamshire, Oxfordshire, Somerset, Staffordshire, Suffolk, Wiltshire and Worcestershire.

Chapter Ten

Developing an NVQ Assessment Centre for Foster Care

Sylvia Vickers

Introduction

Competent and confident foster carers improve the quality of care for vulnerable children and young people. As a key contribution to developing the competence and confidence of its foster carers, Warwickshire Social Services Department introduced National Vocational Qualifications following a comprehensive review of the Fostering Service in 1998. The NVQ scheme was set up both to 'professionalise' the Foster Care Service and as part of the department's 'retention of carers' strategy.

This chapter will review some of the research and literature on the NVQ in Social Care and the development of NVQs for foster carers. It will consider the main policy documents that have brought NVQ and professionalisation of foster care into prominence. It will also explore the development of the Warwickshire (Foster Care) NVQ Assessment Centre and its overall NVQ strategy for foster carers, and discuss a number of themes that have emerged from moving in this direction. User feedback is provided, some of the barriers to the use of NVQ in local authorities are set out, issues associated with becoming an approved 'stand-alone' assessment centre and taking on partners are opened up, and, finally, outcomes are highlighted and analysed.

Review of key policy developments

In the early 1980s, central government considered that the UK was falling behind the rest of the world in terms of vocational qualifications. It commissioned a Review of Vocational Qualifications in England and Wales and a Working Group Report (1986) recommended the introduction of National Vocational Qualifications (NVQs) to address what were seen as weaknesses in the, then, current systems of vocational qualifications (see Qualifications and Curriculum Authority [QCA] web document *The Story of National Vocational Qualifications*: www.qca.org.uk/nq/framework/story_nvqs.asp). From that point onwards NVQs became qualifications that reflect the skills, knowledge and understanding an individual possesses in relation to a specific area of work. Amongst other things, the Working Group's report concluded that there was no understandable overall pattern of vocational qualifications and there were considerable overlaps, duplication and gaps in provision. The report highlighted barriers to accessing vocational qualifications and stressed that existing assessment methods leaned towards testing knowledge rather than skill and competence. One of the key weaknesses identified was that there was insufficient recognition of learning gained outside formal education and training. To address these issues the Working Group proposed that a clear, coherent and comprehensive system of vocational qualifications should be developed that represented a statement of competence and were relevant to the work and needs of the individual.

Following the publication of the White Paper *Working Together: Education and Training* (HMSO 1986), the National Council for Vocational Qualifications (NCVQ) was set up. The council developed NVQs that consisted of five levels in eleven occupational areas and it was expected that the majority of employers would accept NVQs as evidence of learning. There was a concern with ensuring that these qualifications observed strict standards and this concern led to a review, which was undertaken by Gordon Beaumont in April 1996. The review found widespread support for the concept of NVQs amongst employers, with over 80% considering that competency-based standards were suited to vocational qualifications. However, the review report identified room for further development and, in particular, found that the language and structure used in the standards, against which competence was judged, was difficult and complicated.

A number of changes since 1996 have impacted on the development of NVQ. The NCVQ produced a revised version of the *NVQ Awarding Bodies' Common Accord* (NCVQ 1997) (now *The NVQ Code of Practice* 2002), which includes customer service standards. Standards-setting bodies[1] were encouraged to write standards in plain English and were given freedom in terms of format and presentation of the material. They were also encouraged to adopt a more flexible structure of an NVQ by having mandatory and core units thereby giving candidates greater unit choice. These bodies were also required to define which national occupational standards must be assessed in the workplace. However, there was still a lack of a coherent system of vocational qualifications which needed a framework of competence-based qualifications. This was developed by the Qualifications and Curriculum Authority (QCA: www.qca. org.uk/nq/framework/story_nvqs.asp) so that NVQs are now firmly established as competence-based qualifications that reflect the skills, knowledge and understanding an individual possesses in their specific area of work, with the NVQ framework providing a structure for them.

The general developments in vocational qualifications over a number of years have had a marked impact on social services staff but this was given added impetus with the publication of the government's White Paper *Modernising Social Services* (Department of Health 1998b). The White Paper stated that social care had been one of the fastest growing employment sectors in recent years with a workforce at that point numbering around 1 million. Although they worked with very vulnerable people, 80% of the members of this large workforce had no recognised qualification or formal training. One of the key themes in the White Paper was 'Improving Standards in the Workforce'. In this regard, it signalled a new statutory body called the General Social Care Council, which would develop occupational standards, and the development of a national training strategy by the new Training Organisation for the Personal Social Services (TOPSS).

The General Social Care Council began its work on 1 October 2001 and has developed codes of practice, one for social care workers and one for employers of social care workers, both of which are intended as contributions to raising the standards in social care services. TOPSS works with a range of partners, including awarding bodies for NVQs in Care. Awarding bodies are jointly responsible to the QCA for the assessment methods of NVQs, for their implementation and for the approval of centres who wish to offer assessments for NVQs. The QCA published *the NVQ Code of Practice* (NCVQ 2002), which replaced the *NVQ awarding bodies' Common Accord*. The code is designed to promote quality, consistency, accuracy and fairness in the assessment and the award of all NVQs. It is meant to ensure that standards are maintained in each occupational area and across awarding bodies from year to year.

Within this framework, the 'Caring for Children and Young People' award is a Level 3 award.[2] Further new 'modernising' objectives were identified for children's social services as part the government's plans for radical improvement. These led to the first national training strategy for England. The aim of *Modernising the Social Care Workforce* (TOPSS 2000b) was to create a child care workforce which was available in the required numbers and skill mix and competent to meet the needs of service users. There would be a framework of qualifications linked to occupational standards together with a commitment to lifelong learning and continuing professional development.

Included in the recommendations and targets for action, by 2003, was the goal of 50% of the child care workforce achieving NVQ Level 3. Foster carer training was required to target these key areas:

- induction/pre-approval training

- looking after children – adopting a child development approach

- attaining NVQ Level 3 'Caring for Children and Young People'.

It was also made clear that progress on the training provided to foster carers would be closely monitored (www.topss.org.uk/summaries/childpq2.htm)

Occupational competence and service standards

Occupational standards for foster carers were introduced as an attempt to ensure that the needs and rights of children and young people are met and respected; that foster carers provide effective and appropriate care; and that organisational structures and policies underpin good practice (Fostering Network 1999). The Care Standards Commission introduced National Minimum Required Standards and these aim to: detail minimum standards below which no provider should operate; ensure protection of service users; safeguard the health, well-being and quality of life for service users; provide standards that are robust, measurable and enforceable (Care Standards Commission 2002). These service standards provide a guide against which practice can be measured because: they describe best practice in particular areas of work; they are statements of competence; they provide managers with tools for workforce management and service quality control. Two sets of national standards exist which overlap: service standards and occupational standards; these are the basis for training and qualifications.

TOPSS has produced a guide to the links between national occupational standards (in NVQ) and service standards. This means that when a foster carer achieves an NVQ award, she or he demonstrates that she or he meets the UK National Standards (service standards), which focus on the quality of her or his foster care. Competency-based assessment of foster carers also provides a standard for assessing a foster carer's skills and abilities and identifying their learning needs. The areas covered during the assessment overlap service standards and NVQ. The comparison of the National Service Standards and the National Occupational Standards shows that they match closely with each other.

An NVQ for foster carers fits well with the government's *Quality Protects* initiative (Department of Health 1998a). The initiative's intention of transforming the management and raising the standards of children's services meshes with the enhancement of foster care practice through the implementation of an NVQ for foster carers. The NVQ's emphasis on observed, competent practice is integral to developing the Foster Care Service. Furthermore, it provides an opportunity for foster carers to gain a national qualification that recognises their knowledge, skills and competence against national standards. The changing nature of the foster care role requires such a competent workforce: 'People who work in social care are called on to respond to some of the most demanding, often distressing and intractable human problems' (Department of Health 1998b, p.84).

Developing an NVQ assessment centre

As we have already seen, one of the key reasons for introducing the NVQ award for foster carers in Warwickshire was to professionalise the Foster Care Service and produce a competent workforce which would 'improve the experiences and outcomes for children and young people looked after away from their own families' (TOPSS 2001, p.1). As part of a major review of fostering services in Warwickshire in 1998, an NVQ pilot scheme for foster carers was established and funded from the children's services' budget. A group of seven placement support carers and three social workers were trained to assess a candidate group of 15 senior carers. Placement support carers and senior carers are salaried foster carers employed by the Social Services Department for 30 hours a week and have full conditions of service. They were appointed at the same time as the NVQ scheme was launched and the role and requirements attached to being an NVQ candidate or assessor were written into their job descriptions. Ideally, foster carers should have achieved the award themselves before becoming assessors, but special circumstances applied at the beginning. In the future, foster care assessors will be NVQ-qualified before becoming assessors. It was agreed that the placement support carers would work towards their own award as soon as they had successfully completed the assessments with two candidates each.

'Caring for Children and Young People' was a new award provided by the awarding body, City and Guilds. It is a Level 3 award, which is the equivalent of two 'A' levels or an access course. Candidates must complete 12 units of competence to gain the award. This is the first professional qualification available to foster carers.

Taking soundings

Before launching an NVQ scheme in Warwickshire, a variety of agencies across the country, where NVQ had been introduced for foster carers, were consulted. Some schemes were still in place but many had been discontinued. A number of problems were identified:

- The foster care award was considered more difficult to assess than other NVQs. For example, direct observations by the assessor could be intrusive, given the location of assessment in the foster care home. Observation visits could be carefully planned, but placement difficulties could sometimes prevent the visit from going ahead.

- There were also myths surrounding the NVQ. Some foster carers thought it was just another college training course; others wanted to do it but thought they might fail. (NVQ candidates do not 'fail' – they are either competent or 'not yet competent'.)

- Some candidates in other agencies said they felt isolated and unsupported. It was a new learning experience for them as adults and they 'didn't want to show themselves up'. Their accounts indicated that candidate support is a key component to the success of an NVQ scheme and should be an integral aspect.

- In some parts of the country schemes lacked senior management support, were severely under-funded and failed due to a lack of resources or the inability to employ qualified assessors with job knowledge. Other schemes lacked 'champions' to push NVQ forward in their agencies.

- Some schemes lacked structure and had not developed a candidate tracking system, so they were unable to monitor the progression of some of their candidates.

- Many of the schemes visited did not introduce timescales for completion of the award, which are absolutely essential to maintaining momentum and making the best use of assessor time. If candidates are allowed to put their award 'on hold' for a month or so, they can lose motivation, enthusiasm wanes and it is much more difficult for them to get back into it again.

Developing an NVQ strategy for foster carers

A three-year strategy was written that included the need for a selection process, induction of new candidates, timescales for completion and proposed intake targets. It also identified the need to provide support and mentoring, good communication processes, underpinning knowledge workshops and a robust candidate achievement tracking system. The pilot group in Warwickshire was set up in June 1998 and became a satellite centre, linked to the main Warwickshire NVQ Assessment Centre that provides the Care Level 2 awards for adult services.

Several of the agencies visited expected their candidates to complete their award within 12 months. However, feedback from these candidates was that this was insufficient time, given the nature of the foster care task and the difficulties of 'direct observation' by an assessor, which is one of the main methods of gathering evidence of competence. As a result of this candidate feedback, and given that this was a new and untried award, the pilot group was given 18 months to complete the award. This timescale meant that each unit had to be completed within six weeks and it took into account placement difficulties. The other issue for the pilot group was that their assessors were being assessed concurrently themselves. It was recognised that the process would be much slower for the first three months, until the assessors had achieved their own award.

NVQ assessors must hold the Training and Development Learning Board (TDLB) qualification D32/D33 which demonstrates that the person is competent to assess NVQs and they also need to have occupational competence.

The strategy identified two candidate intakes a year, in spring and autumn, providing 20 places for foster carers each year. Clearly, one of the main difficulties was having sufficient assessors. The NVQ for foster carers is still relatively new and to begin with there were very few qualified assessors with occupational competence available in the Midlands. It was clear that we needed to 'grow our own' assessors, as soon as the first group completed their awards, which would not be for 18 months.

An NVQ newsletter was launched, to precede the first two intake groups. It was circulated to all foster carers and invited them to apply for a candidate place. Group Two, which was the first opportunity for mainstream carers to undertake NVQ, was planned for spring 1999, but the level of interest was unknown. Selection criteria were established and were clearly identified in the newsletter. Information was given in the newsletter that work on the award would take up to four hours a week and 18 months to complete. It was clear from the outset that carers have conflicting priorities, which may mean they have to take shorts breaks away from working on the award, but it is still achievable within the time allowed. It is costly, in terms of the foster carer's time and the department's resources, for a candidate to achieve the award and so it is important to ensure that prospective candidates are committed to completing the award within the agreed timescales, unless there are extenuating circumstances.

Prospective candidates are required to foster for Warwickshire for one year before undertaking the award and to give a commitment to attending the award's underpinning knowledge training and its support meetings. They have to complete an application form and say, in about 250 words, why they want to pursue an NVQ award, outlining how they will make time to do it and what support they will get from their families. They are also informed that their application needs to be supported by their supervising social worker who needs to confirm that, in terms of any placement issues, it is an appropriate time for them to start work on the award.

At this early stage it was not known whether foster carers would want to be assessed by one of their peers or whether they would prefer a social worker as their assessor. A mixed model was adopted, with peers, social workers and external foster care assessors being recruited. Candidates in this group could identify which 'assessor group' they preferred but not the actual assessor. Social workers were given opportunities to become assessors as part of their own professional development. However, major difficulties arose when other work priorities impinged on the work with the candidates. Subsequently, it was decided that NVQ assessment could not be 'bolted on' to a heavy workload and that only part-time social workers would be recruited to undertake assessments.

Furthermore, the lack of qualified assessors with occupational competence in the locality meant that it was necessary to 'buy in' external foster carer assessors from a college over 30 miles away. Communication with and assessment visits by these external assessors presented some difficulties, partly because of the distance involved and partly because the paperwork used by the college was different to that required by the centre. Nevertheless, the external assessors made substantial efforts to meet the centre's requirements and have made significant contributions to the development of its work.

Candidate induction

An induction process is essential to candidates feeling that they have made a positive start on their NVQ. However, the induction meeting can be quite daunting. There is a plethora of information and unfamiliar jargon that can sometimes leave candidates feeling overawed. Moving beyond this into a sound induction into NVQ helps the candidates to feel confident about taking responsibility for their learning and assessment, and it enables them to recognise their skills and knowledge. Candidates are now linked with a mentor from the induction onwards, to support them through the award.

Candidates are registered with the awarding body, City and Guilds, when they submit their first unit and there are monthly 'verification dates' for the submission of units to the assessment centre internal verifier. The role of the internal verifier is to conduct internal quality assurance of the assessment process. It is important that all units are individually verified when they are completed because it enables the internal verifier to check that the assessment process has taken place properly and she or he can give clear feedback on the assessors' performance as their candidates progress through the award.

Support and mentoring

Some carers have not undertaken much written work since leaving school and can become anxious. Consultation with carers from other agencies identified that one of their main concerns was about feeling NVQ would expose their academic weaknesses, or that they might become isolated. Therefore, when the scheme was set up in Warwickshire a comprehensive support programme was put in place. This comprises: local support groups which meet in each district every six weeks to look at ways of gathering evidence for a particular unit and to discuss any other issues; county-wide portfolio-building days, a requirement of the awarding body, which are held four times a year to update candidates and give advice about completing their portfolios; and mentoring.

It is important that candidates feel as comfortable as possible in the learning process, which was why a mentoring scheme was put in place. Mentors guide and support candidates with visits and/or telephone calls for as long as they need them. The introduction of the scheme has been especially important for candidates with particular needs. For example, this type of support has enabled candidates with dyslexia to complete their award. The mentors are foster carers who have already completed their own award. The role of a mentor is to help the candidate look at ways of gathering evidence for their portfolio. Most units require 'direct observation' by the assessor as the main assessment method. However, there are one or two units where this is not possible, such as the child protection unit and the emergency aid (life-saving) unit. For these units, other ways of providing evidence of competence are required. Clearly assessors and mentors have different roles but before the mentoring scheme was introduced assessors would often need to undertake the mentoring role as well as the assessment. As well as having the potential for role confusion, this became very time-consuming. The introduction of mentors has enabled the roles to be clarified. There is a written job description and training is provided. The possibility of a recognised qualification for mentors is being investigated.

Underpinning knowledge training

As part of the consultation process it became clear that most agencies were linked with local colleges for assessments, as well as for underpinning knowledge training. Historically, expertise in NVQs has been located in colleges; however, there were some difficulties with this approach. College assessors may have occupational competence in work-based settings that enables them to deliver NVQs but it is unlikely that they will have 'job knowledge' in fostering, unless foster carers are recruited by colleges as assessors or workers with an up-to-date knowledge of the fostering task. In Warwickshire there is a comprehensive Foster Care Training Programme in place. All carers are required to complete four core training courses: Making Placements Work, Child Protection, Caring for Other People's Children and Promoting Equalities. These courses were revised to ensure that they met underpinning knowledge requirements for the NVQ award. The county-wide training programme also provides other relevant training courses as part of the Underpinning Knowledge Programme, which are all delivered in-house.

Doing an NVQ is not training. Some foster carers may be capable of being assessed as competent without having any further training, but, in practice, there may be some skills that need more development or some subjects where greater knowledge is needed and training can help (National Foster Care Association 1997, p.8). Therefore, it is important that underpinning knowledge is available to support whichever units are selected by the candidate. The award consists of more than 26 units, some of which are more relevant for residential workers than foster carers. Therefore, candidates were given a choice of 19 appropriate units. The Foster Care Training Programme was reviewed and additional courses provided to ensure that in-house training covered all the underpinning knowledge requirements for the selected units. If specialist carers such as Emergency Duty or Family Link carers need to complete a different unit, additional underpinning knowledge workshops are provided.

The underpinning knowledge programme is supported by distance learning material if carers are unable to attend courses. Opportunity to access underpinning knowledge 'on-line' will be available to foster carers within the next two years. The development of an interactive website for NVQ foster care candidates is planned, which will enhance support and mentoring. It will also provide opportunities for candidates to discuss issues on-line, including ways of gathering evidence for particular units, and this should reduce isolation. E-learning is emerging as a new model and can be developed effectively to deliver underpinning knowledge on-line.

Candidate tracking system

It was essential from the beginning to have a robust candidate tracking strategy in place. The Candidate Achievement Tracking System (CATS) used by the centre monitors equal opportunities, maintains candidate records, tracks the progress of candidates and their achievements. It also records assessor visits and produces a wide range of reports on all aspects of the verification process. City and Guilds (the Awarding Body) requires NVQ Assessment Centres to have effective tracking systems in place.

User feedback

Over 100 candidates, almost one-third of the foster carers in Warwickshire, are now registered with the scheme. Thirty-three candidates have achieved the award, at the time of writing. Many of them have said how much they have enjoyed working with the centre, want to continue to be involved with NVQs and have gone on to train as assessors or mentors. There is a great deal of enthusiasm for the scheme from foster carers, which is very encouraging, and they are excellent advocates for NVQ with their peers. Foster Home Annual Performance Reviews take place on a formal basis, once a year, to review and appraise the foster home activity during the last year. These reviews are presented at the Fostering Panel and in them many have outlined how NVQ has had an impact on fostering practice. It has helped carers to recognise the skills they already have and also enabled them to examine their practice.

NVQ newsletters, which are distributed by the assessment centre twice a year to all foster carers, have carried the following quotations from foster carers

- 'I thought it would be really hard work, but thoroughly enjoyed it and found everyone really kind and helpful.'

- 'NVQ is really worthwhile. It makes you think about your practice, which benefits those you care for. There was a real sense of achievement to receive this award. The support I had was excellent.'

- 'I found NVQ to be a really rewarding and reflective experience. It war only when I was gathering evidence that I realised what a valuable job we do as carers.'

- 'NVQ helps me to recognise the skills I have as a foster carer and learn about other areas. I found the First Aid course really useful.'

- 'If I can do it you can.'

Feedback from foster carers is that the NVQ scheme has also provided them with an on-going support network that has enabled them to share experience and good practice. Many carers consider that having the NVQ qualification has enhanced their status and that when they attend case conferences and meetings they feel much more like professional partners with their social work colleagues.

The Director of Social Services holds an awards ceremony for staff and their guests twice a year. This is a very important event for foster carers who have gained their award, as it denotes public recognition for their achievement. The centre's twice-yearly NVQ newsletter publishes photographs of carers receiving their certificates from the Director.

Approval as a stand-alone centre

The NVQ scheme originally operated as a satellite centre to the main Warwickshire NVQ Assessment Centre and on two consecutive visits by the City and Guilds external verifier was awarded an 'A' grade status. On the second of these visits, the centre was deemed a 'Centre of Excellence' and City and Guilds recommended that application should be made for the assessment centre to become an NVQ centre in its own right. This was a significant development, as it was one of the first dedicated NVQ assessment centres for foster carers in the country.

Approval was a lengthy process, requiring the production of 72 pages of evidence for the centre's portfolio. Approval was granted in April 2002, which enabled the centre to operate independently and offer the NVQ Level 3 award 'Caring for Children and Young People'. Scheme approval was granted to offer the Assessor Award, D32/D33 (now revised and called A1), which means that we can train our own assessors in-house to City and Guilds standards. We will also be able to offer other awards, if required, which will be particularly important as we begin to take on new partners from other agencies.

Partners

Since the Warwickshire (Foster Care) NVQ Assessment Centre became a stand-alone 'Centre of Excellence', other agencies have registered with us for the full package of assessment, underpinning knowledge training and support. Partners include independent agencies, the Health Authority, Barnardos and family support worker candidates. There are robust systems in place that enable the centre to provide a full candidate package for partners. A complete underpinning knowledge programme for partners is provided at their own locations, using distance learning material delivered as an underpinning knowledge workshop to candidates by a centre trainer. The 'on-line' learning material, mentioned earlier, will also be available to partners in due course, as will the interactive website for NVQ candidates. Regular support meetings and mentor support is also provided as part of the package.

Budget costs

The NVQ programme for foster carers in Warwickshire is well resourced and has the commitment and support of senior managers in children's services. This support has been absolutely essential in establishing a robust structure for delivering NVQ. The Social Services Training Support Programme (Department of Health 1998d) has provided grant allocations to local authorities to support the training of foster carers and NVQ programmes, which has helped with the costs of over £1000 for a foster carer to achieve the NVQ Level 3 award, including registration, assessment and verification, support, mentoring, full underpinning knowledge training, the portfolio and resource materials.

Future plans for the centre

The centre is exploring the use of 'paperless portfolios'. Whilst this approach may not suit all candidates and assessors, it will add another dimension of choice for some. This approach will link with the proposed computer-mediated communication and distance learning, mentioned earlier, which is being developed to provide underpinning knowledge.

Impact of NVQ

There is little written information available at this stage about the impact of NVQ on practice. However, some research has been undertaken by Manchester Metropolitan University into the link between NVQ activity and the quality of services (Sargeant 2000). It was a small-scale study that explored the relationship between social care workers' experiences of an NVQ qualification at Level 2 of the Care awards and their knowledge and practice: 'the findings suggest that, although it was possible to identify some associations between NVQ progression, knowledge of care practice and competence, these are not always clear' (Sargeant 2000, p.639).

One social services department undertook a major review of its domiciliary service. It was concerned about the impact of the growing private sector and whether it could compete in terms of quality and cost. They invested a substantial amount into NVQs and, although they had no 'hard evidence', it was considered that the quality and effectiveness of the service had been increased (Joint Initiative for Community Care 1998 p.12). However, as schemes develop, it will be important to measure the impact of NVQ on quality and effectiveness. It is envisaged that we will begin this in Warwickshire through the foster care supervision process.

Barriers to completing NVQ

The Joint Initiative for Community Care's *Caring with Competence* (1998) was a report about barriers to completing NVQs in social services departments in England and Wales, with suggestions for overcoming them. The findings identified in this report included the importance of high-quality assessors, of 'NVQ champions' and of NVQ assessment centres. The report noted a reluctance to set targets for completion and difficulties in obtaining sufficient work-based assessors. It identified inadequate financial resources and the marginalisation of NVQ activity, as well as the effect the culture of a department can have and the significance of the personal interest of directors of social services. One of the difficulties experienced by foster carers is that placement difficulties can mean putting their work for the award on hold for a short time. However, this rarely necessitates exceeding the candidate's expected completion date.

Conclusion

The establishment of an NVQ scheme for foster carers in Warwickshire is already achieving its stated aims: 'to professionalise the Foster Care Service' and to play a significant role in the 'retention of foster carers' strategy. Foster carers are demonstrating their occupational competence through NVQ. The quality of care provided to children 'looked after' by foster carers in Warwickshire is very high. This was identified in a Best Value review and an audit of the service against the UK National Standards and the National Care Standards. However, evaluating the impact of NVQ on practice is clearly an area for future development.

Achieving the NVQ qualification has enhanced the self-esteem of foster carers and enabled them to consider themselves as professional colleagues. It also appears to have had an impact on retention of carers – fewer than half the number of foster carers retired or resigned from the service during 2002/3 than in previous years. Clearly, the NVQ process cannot claim all the credit for this but, based on consultation with foster carers, it is certainly a contributing factor.

The NVQ, together with the introduction of the new fee-paid scheme (which pays carers for their skills), has enabled the department to offer 'career opportunities' for foster carers. There are three payment levels in the fee-paid scheme, which are all linked to competence and training. Level 3 is also linked to NVQ. It is a requirement that one partner in the household holds an NVQ qualification to enter the scheme at this level.

The introduction of NVQ qualifications for foster carers in Warwickshire is producing a competent and confident foster care workforce which will improve the outcomes and life chances for 'looked after' children.

Notes

1 Standards-setting bodies are required to develop national occupational and service standards that capture the wider aspects of competent performance.

2 'A level 3 award is for work that demands competence in a broad range of work activities, carried out in a wide variety of settings. Most of the work is complex and non-routine. The worker has considerable responsibility and autonomy, and is often required to guide or control other people' (National Foster Care Association 1997, p.4).

Chapter Eleven

Change... and More Change

Chris Hallett

Introduction

In the final chapter of a companion volume on developing good practice, I considered the prospects and possibilities in community care services for adults (Hallett 2001). I highlighted the changes that had occurred over a relatively short time-span and outlined many further changes that were on the horizon at that time. On reflection, my views on the impact of those changes on social work and social care in adult services share many similarities with the repercussions of changes that are taking shape in children's services:

> The amount of change initiated by legislation and central government policy built up to a furious pace across the closing years of the twentieth century, often leaving front-line managers and social workers reeling from the lack of time for consolidation or for taking stock. (Hallett 2001, p.175)

In the early years of the twenty-first century there has been a similar plethora of government activity in relation to children's services, again often leaving managers and social workers feeling desperate for a period of consolidation. This is unlikely to occur in the short to medium term, with many more government initiatives in the pipeline. As these initiatives take shape, there is likely to be more emphasis on partnership in the delivery of services and greater involvement in decision-making by young people and their parents.

A future vision for children and families

The needs that children present are likely to become more complex, even though the number of children in the population is likely to fall, certainly until 2011, when it is likely to plateau at around 11.3 million in the UK (Association of Directors of Social Services 2002, p.3). *Tomorrow's Children*, a discussion paper issued by the Association of Directors of Social Services (2002), highlights the factors that indicate the probability of children's needs increasing in complexity.

The health of children

- an increasing number of disabled children, as more children with low birth-weight survive
- the increasing incidence of childhood cancer
- the incidence of mental illness (10% of 5–15-year-olds are thought to have mental health problems)
- the incidence of drug abuse (12% of 11–15-year-olds are thought to have misused drugs in 1999).

Socio-economic factors

- the increase in the number of children living with one parent
- nearly 14% of households in England live in poor housing
- a significant number of children suffering from emotional or psychological maltreatment
- a high teenage pregnancy rate
- an increasing number of unaccompanied asylum-seeking children entering the country.

These factors begin to indicate the challenges that will be faced by social workers and social care staff. Whilst the number of children and families receiving services might decline, the complexity of their needs is likely to be greater and to require a higher level of input and resources.

In Chapter Two, Lord pointed to the importance of vision in strategic development. *Tomorrow's Children* outlines a vision for the future, in response to the factors outlined above.

Healthy children

- increased life expectancy
- reduction in the rate of children admitted to hospital
- better nutrition
- increased physical activity

- decreased morbidity
- better dental health.

Increased achievement

- increased personal achievement in school, leisure and community
- a wide contribution to society.

Identity

- children with a strong sense of personal identity and self-esteem.

Decrease in poverty

- a decrease in the number of children living in low-income households.

Greater protection

- decrease in the number of children suffering harm
- decrease in accidents
- decrease in the use of illegal drugs
- decrease in involvement in and fear of crime.

Inclusion

- a reduction in the number of children in public care
- increased access to mainstream education and training
- reduction in anti-social and criminal behaviour
- fewer exclusions from school.

Transitions

- a decrease in the number of young people aged 16–19 not in education, employment or training.

Greater involvement

- children should be seen as citizens and have a much bigger say on the key issues that impact on them.

Better environment

- enhanced places to play
- better places to live.

In its paper, the Association of Directors of Social Services outlines how that vision can be achieved through more integrated, holistic and seamless service delivery that is embedded in the development of community partnerships, with a focus on outcomes for young people. The government has also been formulating proposals in a consultation document, *Every Child Matters* (Chief Secretary to the Treasury 2003).

Every Child Matters

The Green Paper *Every Child Matters* (Chief Secretary to the Treasury 2003) is the government's response to the publication of Lord Laming's report on the inquiry into the death of Victoria Climbié (Department of Health 2003a). These publications mark significant events in the discussion of the direction that children's services will take in the next decade and beyond. In addition, in 2003 responsibility for children's social services moved from the Department of Health to the Department of Education and Skills. This shift by central government to align children's social services with education is reflected in *Every Child Matters*.

This document, with the government aiming to introduce legislation to effect change from 2004, sets out a framework for improving services for all children and their families: to protect them, to promote their well-being and to support them in developing their full potential. The key proposals are:

- To develop integrated teams with professionals from all agencies based in and around schools and children's centres.

- To remove legal, technical and cultural barriers to information-sharing and facilitate effective communication.

- To establish a clear framework of accountability at national and local level, in part through the appointment of a Children's Director in every local authority responsible for children's services. The delivery of children's services would then be integrated within Children's Trusts, by 2006 at the latest. These trusts would normally be part of the local authority and report to elected councillors.

- A lead elected councillor for children in each local authority.

- A new duty to promote educational achievement of young people in public care.

- The abolition of Area Child Protection Committees with new duties on police, health professionals and others to safeguard children and a requirement on them to come together in local Safeguarding Children Boards.

- Children's services to be judged through an integrated inspection framework, overseen by the Office for Standards in Education.

- A national campaign to recruit more foster carers.

- A workforce reform package, which would aim to make working with children an attractive career and to improve the skills and effectiveness of the children's workforce.

- The appointment of an independent Children's Commissioner to champion children's views.

These proposals set out a framework for change; they throw down a challenge to achieve change for children and young people. They focus on their well-being through their being healthier, safer, achieving more, enjoying life, being economically stable and making a positive contribution to society. However, there is also an analysis in the Green Paper of factors that militate against these aims, such as low income, parental unemployment, poor parenting, poor schools and protective mechanisms that have let children down. The Green Paper argues that there are strong foundations already in place and gives a range of examples as supporting evidence from the 'Sure Start' programme, the 'Early Years and Child Care' initiative, the raising of school standards and increasing participation in post-16 learning.

Next, *Every Child Matters* sets out its vision to improve parenting and family support through developing better, and universal, parenting services, accompanied by specific targeted support such as family mediation services and relationship stress counselling. If these supportive approaches, based on voluntary partnership arrangements between the state and parents, are unsuccessful, compulsory action through Parenting Orders would be a last resort, if parents were condoning their children's anti-social behaviour, such as truancy or offending. The Green Paper also sets out a clear intention to support better substitute parenting through fostering and adoption and addresses issues such as skills, support, recruitment and retention.

The government's specific responses to the Victoria Climbié Inquiry are set out in Chapter Four of *Every Child Matters*. The emphasis is on improving early intervention and providing effective protection for children. The need for better information sharing between agencies is set out, with each child having an identity number, enabling vulnerable children to be identified, referred to services and tracked. The intention of developing a common assessment framework for children across all agencies is signalled as one aspect of the bringing together of professionals through multi-disciplinary teams located in and around schools, children's centres and primary care centres. Such arrangements are seen as conducive to providing a rapid response to the concerns of teachers, child care workers and others. By seeking to ensure that child protection procedures are working effectively and facilitating earlier intervention, it is hoped that children will not fall through the net.

It is clear the government considers it necessary to bring about structural changes at national and local level to deliver the vision in the Green Paper. Legislation will be required, with the aim of having someone responsible for children at local and national level so that lines of accountability are clear. The government wants to see services for children integrated 'within a single organisational focus' (Chief Secretary to the Treasury 2003, p.67). This will involve integrating children's services in a Children's Trust under a Director of Children's Services. Key services that would fall within the remit of the Children's Trust would be education, social services and health but they could also include Connexions and Youth Offending Teams. At the national level there would be a Minister for Children, Young People and Families within the Department of Education and Skills, who would also have a coordinating role across government departments. A new Children's Commissioner would be seen as an independent champion for children.

The final chapter in the Green Paper acknowledges the challenges faced by people who work with children and the need to develop a higher status for careers within a skilled and flexible workforce. Two new bodies are to be introduced: a Children's Workforce Unit which will develop a pay and workforce strategy and help develop a Sector Skills Council to implement elements of the strategy.

The future vision for children and families set out by the Association of Directors of Social Services in *Tomorrow's Children* and that in the Green Paper *Every Child Matters* have a number of strikingly similar ideas: healthier children, greater social inclusion, integrated systems, better partnership, a safer environment and a focus on better outcomes for children and families. The government has set out radical proposals concerning how this might be achieved. In the remainder of the chapter, I shall focus on the changes that have taken place in social care delivery and social work practice, as discussed in earlier chapters, and reflect on the contribution made by these changes in preparing the services for the future change agenda. Finally, I will consider what services might be like for a young person and her or his family as they access them over the next decade.

Change...and more change

In facing further changes in children's social services, there is much to provide encouragement in terms of how change has been tackled thus far. For example, in Chapter Two, Lord outlines the important role of strategic planning and how this has changed over the years, moving from departmental strategic plans to a broader partnership agenda with planning across agencies. The latter approach recognises that no one agency can provide all that may be needed in complex situations involving children. Lord also argues that strategic planning should be underpinned by values and outlines how Warwickshire closed its children's homes because of a belief that family life is best. Lord goes on to state: 'Children are also thought to need to be part a wider local community.'

The importance of communities is elaborated by Hill in Chapter Six. Community development has come in and out of fashion in social work over many decades. Hill argues that social workers should persevere with the concept. At first glance this is surprising. As social work became squeezed by resource constraints and the narrowing of priorities, community development was seen as a luxury rather than essential use of social workers' time. However, Hill argues that the rewards can be great:

> We have re-discovered community development as a method of enabling citizens to work in a collaborative way. The old techniques of empowering people to identify needs in their neighbourhood or communities of interest and then working towards meeting them have been harnessed to more sophisticated modern frameworks of accountability, planning and reviewing... Re-introducing the community dimension to social work seeks to redress this balance by stimulating the development of new services that will be available to all families within the neighbourhood. (pp.108–9)

The Taking Care Project outlined in Chapter Seven by Seal is an example of a new service that emerged from the framework outlined by Hill. Seal sets out the difficulties and rewards involved in getting preventive work on to the agenda and introducing techniques like the Protective Behaviours programme, which originated in the USA.

The emergence of community development to a position of greater prominence in the future is not a foregone conclusion, even though *Every Child Matters* advocates this. Quiggin, in Chapter Four, captures the ambivalence about community strategies in her discussion of the use of the Assessment Framework:

> The Assessment Framework's emphasis on family and environmental factors, however, is a definite improvement in that it discourages social workers from adopting an individual pathology model and implies that the 'community' is a legitimate area of social work support. However, I feel this is unlikely to lead to a return to the community action model, given the current under-funding of social services departments, the national recruitment crisis and the renewed

focus on child protection following the report into the death of Victoria Climbié. (p.80)

Quiggin is right to highlight the resource issues, given her concern with the possibility of inadequate assessments resulting from resource deficiencies, linked to the potentially bureaucratic nature of some features of the assessment process. Clearly resources are important but so is a balance in approaches, recognising, as Quiggin does, that assessment is not the totality of service provision. The role of community development and community involvement can assist greatly, especially in preventive services, whilst leading to greater social inclusion.

Tuck's contribution (Chapter Three) emphasises the value of systematic initial and core assessments outlined in Quiggin's chapter. He draws out the importance of risk assessment associated with child protection and his risk assessment model extends the Assessment Framework. Whilst Tuck's model is still in the early stages of implementation, the importance of identifying risk and then managing it should not be underestimated as a significant aspect of the more widespread changes that need to be implemented.

Durham (Chapter Five) looks at the complex issues arising in work with young people displaying sexualised inappropriate behaviour. Again, assessment is the first important step in taking forward change, but Durham goes further in outlining the value of therapeutic counselling in managing risk more safely and achieving better outcomes for young people. Durham states:

> The young person also needs to know that he will be supported through the difficult stages of the work and that the approach is not about punishment, but is about empowering the young person in a manner which allows him to consider his mistakes and make important steps towards an improved way of managing his life, without hurting others. (p.91)

De Waal and Shergill also outline a change in service provision through the REACCH project, which led to better outcomes for children from minority ethnic backgrounds. They state:

> Children need to be given opportunities early on in their lives to explore and celebrate their cultural heritage and have their cultural needs incorporated into overall case planning, not added on as an afterthought or not addressed at all. It is equally vital to have a skilled and committed workforce. Although a process like REACCH cannot solve all of the problems, it does point in key directions. By focusing on the outcomes (the well-being of children) and bringing committed and creative individuals together, as happened in Warwickshire, the life chances of these children can be maximised. (pp.131–2)

Implicitly underpinning the contributions is the significance of a skilled workforce in delivering services. Lord (Chapter Two) goes back to 1978, when the Director of Social Services in Warwickshire, Bob Bessel, 'believed passionately that if excellence in social services provision was the goal, excellence in the workforce was a key means of achieving it. The workforce had to be valued and had to be seen as requiring investment' (p.29). In 1978 there were few qualified social workers. Now there are many and the workforce is generally more highly qualified and skilled. Vickers (Chapter Ten) extends the importance of workforce issues by outlining the significance for foster carers of the introduction of NVQs: 'Competent and confident foster carers improve the quality of care for vulnerable children and young people' (p.151). Vickers argues the case that the introduction of an NVQ for foster carers has 'professionalised the foster care service'. This is a significant change, as foster carers spend considerably more time with vulnerable young people in their care than social workers. If foster carers' expertise can be developed, the outcomes for young people should improve.

Another major change in social services is outlined by Johnson and Sawbridge (Chapter Nine): managing information. This area of growth in capturing, analysing, evaluating and using information has expanded the knowledge base used for planning. The government, through the introduction of performance indicators, has added to the plethora of data requirements in its efforts to control change in social care performance and outcomes. However, Johnson and Sawbridge add a cautionary note: 'Despite the advantages gained by using management information to inform practice, there are limitations to what quantitative analysis can achieve; it has been viewed more as a method for investigating problems than for solving them' (p.138). Management information has the capacity, then, to open issues for further scrutiny. The matching needs and services work, which they report, initially looked at the family placement service but broadened out as it became clear that the development of services for 'looked after' children could not be separated from development of services for all children. Thus, a continuum of services needs to be considered, from prevention to care through to leaving care. In considering the optimal use of services, Johnson and Sawbridge introduce categories of need and issues concerning how those categories can be matched to service delivery. The innovative nature of these categories offers scope for further consideration of relating needs to service provision. This illustrates the value of information, both quantitative and qualitative, in planning, commissioning and delivering services.

The future

So how might children's social services be provided in the next decade? As has already become clear, maintaining the status quo will not be an option and it is likely the Green Paper *Every Child Matters* will form the basis of legislation. I envisage much closer and more multi-disciplinary ways of working through Children's Trusts, accountable to the local authority. The setting of national standards for expected outcomes for children and their families, as a result of intervention, would go some way to meet service users' higher expectations. The need for child protection, public care and meeting children's needs will not disappear and the need to safeguard children will be as prominent as ever, but the bringing together of the knowledge, skills and competence of various professionals in seamless service delivery will go some way to achieving better outcomes for children, manifested in a more enriched and fulfilling life.

As a first step in this direction, in 2002 the Department of Health set out the challenge of integrating children's systems and in Warwickshire work commenced on this goal in 2003. The proposals set out by the Department of Health for an integrated children's system envisage a seamless service across professions and agencies with effective management of information, with, for example, a single assessment process. Lyndon and Payne, in their work on introducing this approach in Warwickshire, describe the integrated children's system as a joined-up way of working, which is not an information technology project but needs information technology to make it work. It is not just a vision for social services but spreads across all agencies working with children. They outline their vision for the integrated children's system as:

- a system that is supportive, accessible, available, flexible, easy to use, and is in line with technologies that users are likely to be familiar with outside of the Social Services context.

- a system where users are better rewarded for the information they gather and in return are given further information as tools to enable better outcomes.

- a system where better information sharing across agencies and teams will reduce the need for repeated assessments but still increase the quality of work being done with children, young people and their families.

(Lyndon and Payne 2003)

In short, for staff it would be about working smarter not harder.

During the next decade Lyndon and Payne's vision will have been fully implemented within a Children's Trust that brings together education, child health, youth justice and Connexions as the key agencies providing services for children. What other developments will take place?

Local offices are likely to disappear, as the capital and revenue costs of running an office become so high as to be no longer economical. Many people might be working from home, with a communication network that is more efficient and rapid in response. Schools may be used as the main centres for contacts with children. Most first contacts for a service might come through the Internet and an interactive discussion between the social worker and referrer will no doubt be feasible. Information will only need to be given by service users on one occasion, as it will be feasible to share it with other professionals electronically. One multi-disciplinary assessment will be completed in a timely manner and the need for repeat assessments will be a thing of the past. The assessment will lead to a plan of intervention, shared electronically with the young person and their parents. Better sharing of information with young people and their parents will lead to their greater empowerment in the process. More empowerment will lead to better services and a higher level of satisfaction. This greater involvement of the young person and their parents in designing and contributing to service delivery will lead to greater ownership and motivation in achieving change in young people's lives. This fits neatly with anticipation of the expectations concerning the range and quality of services being higher in the future. It would be the type of service response that it is hoped will become the norm; a seamless, cohesive and multi-professional approach, with easy access to information held. If this service response can be achieved, children will be kept as safe as possible and become more included in society.

Conclusion

This chapter, and indeed the book as a whole, has been about developing good practice in the changing context of children's social services. The changes of the past, and likely developments in the future, have been considered. The one certainty is that change will continue as the Green Paper *Every Child Matters* is turned into legislation. In highlighting the potential for developing good practice, each chapter makes the case for seeing change as an opportunity rather than a threat: an opportunity to enhance quality and achieve better service outcomes for children and their families. This willingness to embrace change as an opportunity should stand social work in good stead, as it maintains the value base established through practice over many years and seeks to ensure that every child really does matter.

The European Foundation for Quality Management (EFQM) Excellence Model

Simon Lord

The EFQM (Business) Excellence Model, referred to in Chapter Two, is a framework that enables an organisation systematically to assess and improve the quality of its performance. The framework comprises nine criteria against which to assess performance. The first five criteria are referred to as 'enablers', the inputs that are needed for any organisation to conduct its business. The enablers are Leadership, People, Policy and Strategy, Partnerships and Resources, Processes. The remaining four criteria are referred to as 'results'; what is achieved by the activities of the organisation. The results are People Results, Customer Results, Society Results and Key Performance Results.

There is a sophisticated system of scoring how well the organisation performs in each of the criteria, and how well they interrelate with each other, particularly with regard to enablers and results criteria. The criteria have different weightings within the scoring system to reflect their differing importance.

The EFQM assessment process starts with the organisation itself producing a submission document. This is then assessed by a team of trained EFQM assessors who also visit the site. A final score is awarded for the organisation and feedback arrangements are made. From the assessment the organisation will be able to understand its strengths and the areas for improvement in its overall performance and thereafter can plan accordingly. Progress can be measured at further subsequent submission and assessment.

The EFQM model enjoys an impressive reputation, is extensively used in both the private and public sectors and is constantly being improved and developed.

Appendix Two

Analysis of a Sample of 248 Referrals to SIBS of Children and Young People Reported to Have Initiated Inappropriate Sexual Behaviours During the Five-year Period 1997 to 2001

Andrew Durham

Introduction

This appendix supplements Chapter Five, by providing an analysis of referrals to the Sexualised Inappropriate Behaviours Service (SIBS) over the five-year period 1997 to 2001. The analysis focuses on the referrals of children and young people reported to have initiated some form of inappropriate sexual behaviour, looking at the children's and young people's histories, and the nature and circumstances of the behaviours carried out. Four detailed composite case studies are also provided.

Definitions

It is difficult to reach final concluding definitions of inappropriate sexualised behaviours and child sexual abuse that are able to encompass and accurately reflect a vast range of unique individual experiences. Influenced by the work of Kelly, Regan and Burton (1991), Finkelhor *et al.* (1986) and Morrison and Print (1995), broad and lengthy definitions of inappropriate sexualised behaviours and child sexual abuse, presenting a range of options and defined behaviours, were used in this study of referrals:

Inappropriate sexualised behaviour

1. Initiated sexual behaviour that is inappropriate for a child's age and development.

and/or

2. Initiated sexual behaviour that is inappropriate in its context. For example behaviour that is considered acceptable in private, occurring in non-private circumstances.

and/or

 3. An initiated sexual act committed:

  (a) against a person's will

  (b) without informed consent

  (c) in an aggressive, exploitative or threatening manner.

Child sexual abuse

 1. Forced or coerced sexual behaviour that is imposed on a child (person under 18 years old).

and/or

 2. Sexual behaviour between a child and a much older person (five years or more age discrepancy), or a person in a care-taking role, or a sibling.

and/or

 3. Sexual behaviour where the recipient is defined as being unable to give informed consent by virtue of age, understanding or ability.

Contact and non-contact behaviours

Contact behaviours may involve: touching; rubbing; disrobing; sucking; and/or penetrating. They may include rape. Penetration may be oral, anal or vaginal and digital, penile or objectile.

Non-contact behaviours may involve: exhibitionism; peeping or voyeurism; fetishism (such as stealing underwear or masturbating into another's clothes), and obscene communication (such as obscene phone calls, and verbal and written sexual harassment or defamation).

Related circumstances

In collating information about the circumstances and background of the children and young people included in the sample, information was collected relating to: physical abuse; emotional abuse; neglect; parental or other loss; family problems; school problems; social isolation; 'looked after' physical disability; learning disability and delinquency. Each of these was defined as follows:

Physical abuse

This may involve hitting, shaking, throwing, poisoning, burning, scalding, drowning, suffocating or otherwise causing physical harm to a child. 'Munchausen Syndrome by Proxy' may also constitute physical abuse, whereby a parent or carer feigns the symptoms of, or deliberately causes ill-health in, a child (Department of Health 1999b).

Emotional abuse

This is the persistent emotional ill-treatment of a child in ways that cause severe and persistent adverse effects on the child's emotional development. It may involve conveying to children that they are worthless or unloved, inadequate or valued only in so far as they meet the needs of another person. It may involve causing children frequently to feel frightened or in danger, or the exploitation or corruption of children. Some level of emotional abuse is involved in all types of ill-treatment of a child, though it may occur in isolation (Department of Health 1999b).

Neglect

This is the persistent failure to meet a child's basic physical and psychological needs, likely to result in the serious impairment of the child's health or development. It may involve a parent or carer failing to provide adequate food, shelter and clothing, failing to protect a child from physical harm or danger, or the failure to ensure access to appropriate medical care or treatment. It may also include neglect of a child's basic emotional needs (Department of Health 1999b).

Parental and or other loss

This refers to any significant experience of loss suffered by the child or young person. It may refer to the death of a parent, close relative or close friend. It may also refer to a family disruption, involving a separation from parents, or it could refer to a foster home disruption, involving a separation from existing carers.

Family problems

This refers to any significant difficulties experienced by the child or young person within their family, either directly related to their own actions and behaviours, or relating to the impact of actions and behaviours of other family members. These are specifically problems that occur in addition to the reported acts of inappropriate sexualised behaviours committed by the child or young person.

School problems

This refers to any significant problem experienced by the young person at school. This may be related to relationships with teachers, or difficulties relating to schoolwork, or social and emotional problems within the child or young person's peer group, such as bullying, racism, name-calling, etc.

Social isolation

This specifically refers to the reported difficulties a child or young person may have in making and maintaining friendships and peer relationships. Often this is when there are reports of the child or young person spending large amounts of time alone, at home or elsewhere, or specific reports of being ostracised from a peer group.

'Looked after'

This refers to any situation where the child or young person is being 'looked after' by the local authority, under the requirements of the Children Act (1989).

Physical disability

This refers to any physical or sensory difficulties experienced by the child or young person in relation to their physical abilities.

Learning disability

This refers to any impairment of intellectual ability experienced by the child or young person, or reported in respect of the child or young person.

Delinquency

This refers to any conviction or caution (reprimand or final warning) the young person has, or other reports of anti-social behaviours, other than for sexual offences.

Findings

Tables A2.1 to A2.3 and Figures A2.1 and A2.2 present details of the background and circumstances of 248 children and young people who were referred to SIBS during the period 1997 to 2001, as having initiated inappropriate sexual behaviours.

Table A2.1 Total referrals

Year	SIBs	CSA or At risk of CSA
1997	50	17
1998	57	5
1999	50	20
2000	41	27
2001	50	27

Table A2.2 Ethnic minority referrals

Year	Ethnic minority N/Total	Per cent
1997	0/50	0
1998	2/57	3.5
1999	1/50	2.0
2000	2/41	4.9
2001	1/50	2.0

Average 6/248 (2.4%)

Table A2.3 Age and gender of SIBs referrals

Age	Number	Per cent
4–6	15	6.0
7–9	38	15.3
10–12	50	20.2
13–15	106	42.7
16–19	39	15.7
Gender		
Male	224	90.3
Female	24	9.7

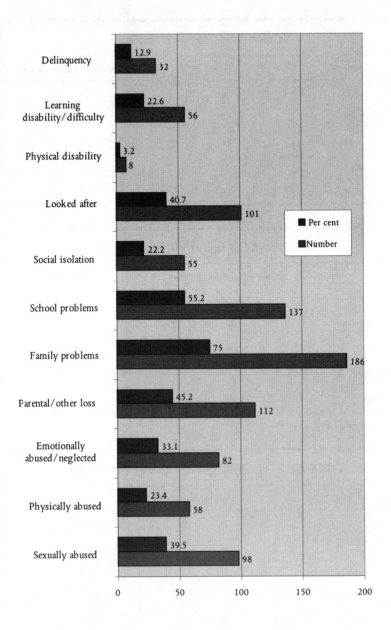

Figure A2.1 Child history details of a sample of 248 referrals to Warwickshire SIBS of children and young people reported during the five-year period 1997 to 2001 as having initiated inappropriate sexual behaviours

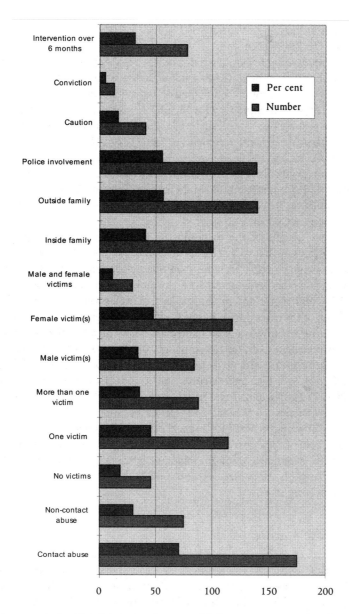

Figure A2.2 Details of inappropriate sexual behaviour in a sample of 248 referrals to Warwickshire SIBS of children and young people during the five-year period 1997 to 2001

Discussion

Table A2.3 shows that the majority of the sample was male (90.3%, 224/248). This is consistent with a large number of research studies which indicate approximately 90% of sexual abuse being committed by males (Bagley and Thurston

1996). There was a clustering of age at 13–15 (42.7%, 106/248) and to a lesser extent at 10–12 (20.2%, 50/248).

Figure A2.1 shows that fewer than half (39.5%, 98/248) of the sample were sexually abused, but it must be noted that not all abuse is reported and research suggests the likelihood of a significant degree of under-reporting, particularly for males (Durham 2003; Etherington 1995; Mendel 1995; Watkins and Bentovim 1992). The findings indicate a significant level of other forms of abuse or problems in the histories, particularly family problems at 75% (186/248) and parental loss 45.2% (112/248); 40.7% (101/248) were being 'looked after' by the local authority. There were only 3.2% (8/248) children with physical disability referred and only 2.4% (6/248) minority ethnic children referred. Approximately 6% of the school-aged population in Warwickshire are from minority ethnic backgrounds (Warwickshire County Council 2003).

Looking at the details of the inappropriate sexualised behaviours (Figure A2.2), the majority of which involve contact behaviour (70.6%, 175/248), 35.5% (88/248) of the sample victimised more than one person and 31.5% (78/248) engaged in behaviours that lasted in excess of six months. This indicates a pattern of sustained behaviour, requiring a substantial level of professional intervention. In 40.7% (101/248) of the cases the victims of the behaviour were immediate family members. Where the victim was not an immediate family member, the behaviour was often opportunistic, usually in circumstances of close contact with cousins, family friends, baby-sitting arrangements, or through school contacts. Of the sample, 33.9% (84/248) had male victims and 47.6% (118/248) had female victims; 11.7% (29/248) had male and female victims. For 18.5% (46/248) there was no identifiable victim; 16.5% (41/248) received cautions (or final warnings) and 5.2% (13/248) were convicted for a sexual offence. The police were involved with 56% (139/248) of the cases. This indicates that a large minority of the interventions had been negotiated through voluntary agreement, without statutory mandates for the work. It also indicates that it is likely that interventions had been taking place at an early stage.

Composite case studies

These case studies are composites based on details from actual cases referred to SIBS over the past few years. As composites, they are written in a manner that bears no identifiable resemblance to any person and all names are pseudonyms. All explicit details of sexual behaviours are excluded. These case studies have been used during the SIBS practice workshops and give an indication of the complexity of some of the circumstances of the young people who have been referred to SIBS. Each young person's circumstances of abusing are unique and have received a unique intervention. The interventions have been devised from an intervention and assessment schedule, based on the practice framework discussed in Chapter Five, and other materials and resources developed by SIBS. The case studies illustrate that quite often children and young people with sexual behaviour difficulties have very difficult lives, with multiple problems, at home and school. They underscore the need for sensitive holistic approaches to the therapeutic work undertaken and the need to address many complex issues in children's and young people's lives. It is likely that the young person's wider problems and difficulties will have significantly contributed to their decisions to engage in sexually abusive behaviours. The case studies also illustrate the contextual significance of peer and family experiences and how negative role modelling and social oppression, particularly that based on gender and sexuality, can have a marked impact on the young person, and again, contribute to his or her decision to sexually abuse.

Alan

Alan is 14 years old. Six months ago he received a caution for sexually abusing the two sons, Paul (aged 5) and Stuart (aged 7), of his father's partner Jill. This abuse came to light when Alan was caught attempting to abuse his female cousin Louise (aged 4), during a family visit. The abuse of the boys took place 15 months previously and for nine months remained undetected. The last time it took place was during a family holiday, when the three boys shared a room. Alan, his father (John) and Louise are white. Jill is a Black African and Paul and Stuart are mixed ethnicity; their father was white.

It is believed that the boys were abused on a regular basis over a three-month period. Alan then stopped abusing. There was a six-month gap before he abused Louise. Both boys are really fond of Alan and cannot fully understand why he is not allowed to come and visit any more. It does not appear that any of the abuse involved an overt use of force.

Alan had lived with different family relatives over the past five years, with aunts and uncles, paternal grandmother and sometimes with one of his two adult brothers. Alan's mother has a long-term addiction to heroin and is now critically ill. When Alan visits her, he finds this very difficult to accept and tries to force her to stop taking the drug. His contact with his mother is now infrequent. Alan's parents divorced four years ago. His father is now in a long-term relationship with Jill. Alan's father used to own several amusement arcades and a casino and for several years was wealthy. For various reasons, his businesses collapsed and he now runs a travel agency, which takes up a great deal of his time.

Since the abuse came to light, Alan has lived with his father's sister Alice, who is single and up to this point was living alone. She has always been fond of Alan, but in recent months has found him very difficult to live with. She often states that Alan 'can't be told anything' and always believes he is right. Added to this, Alan has had significant problems at school, and has received a series of short-term exclusions. He has often been the victim of homophobic name-calling; he is often called 'gay', 'bender' and 'pervert'. Alan gets depressed about this name-calling and often loses his temper when it happens. Alan is above average intelligence and performs well at sports. Until recently, he was in the top grade for all his major subjects. He has now been moved down to the second grade for maths and science.

Mark

Mark is 9 years old and has above average learning abilities, although it is reported that academically he significantly under-achieves at school. His teachers have reported that Mark finds it hard to concentrate and often leads classroom distractions, which involve other pupils. There have been occasions when Mark has been found bullying other pupils.

Mark has had a disrupted life. His parents separated when he was 4; at this time he lived for 15 months with his father in a one-bedroom flat, sleeping on a sofa-bed. For the past three years, Mark's father has been settled in a new family. He has re-married and has two step-children, Stephen (aged 6) and Jill (aged 4). Mark has considerable conflict with his step-mother, the outcome of which is that he can only stay with the family for limited periods of time. During this period, Mark has lived partly with his mother and partly with his paternal grandmother.

Mark's mother has bouts of severe depression and has an alcohol problem. Since separating from Mark's father, she has had several unhappy relationships with men. For 18 months she lived with a man who was physically and sexually violent towards her. On three occasions she has spent time in a woman's refuge; on two of these occasions she took Mark with her. On many occasions this man was physically violent towards Mark, often blaming him as the cause of the adults' problems. Mark also witnessed a great deal of violence. During this period, he spent long weekends with his father and step-mother and spent some of the school holidays with his paternal grandmother. Mark has always stated that he would like to live with his father.

Mark now lives on a permanent basis with his paternal grandmother, spending occasional and sporadic nights with his father's family. Mark's mother lives alone in temporary accommodation and has severe alcohol problems. Mark sees her occasionally, but rarely stays overnight with her.

It was reported to social services that at school, Mark had put his hand down another boy's trousers. Prior to this there had been other on-going concerns at school about Mark sexually touching other boys and girls during a playground game.

Two weeks later, there was a police and social services investigation which established that Mark had sexually abused his 6-year-old step-brother. It was also reported that Mark forced Stephen and Jill to sexually touch each other.

Penny

Penny is 14 and lives with her birth mother and adoptive father. She has an older brother Graham, who is 16, and a younger sister Sheila, who is 12, both living at home. Last spring, Penny was charged for indecent assaults on John and Ian, the 8-year-old twin sons of close friends of her mother and father. The twins made clear statements to the police about Penny sexually abusing them. Penny admitted these acts. When the police asked her if she had experienced any unwanted sexual contact herself, she said that she hadn't, but the interviewers noted a level of avoidance and discomfort in response to this question.

Penny is a friendly young woman and has engaged well in undertaking work to look at her behaviour. Penny has admitted to sexually abusing the boys over a nine-month period. She says that she likes them, gets on well with them and feels bad about what she has done. She maintains that she 'couldn't help herself' and that on several occasions she tried to stop herself from committing the abuse.

She says that at the time she did it, she did not think of it as being abuse, that when it started it was more like a game, that she did not think they minded taking their clothes off and that they seemed to be excited and happy. She admits that she did not think they were always happy and that Ian was less happy about the whole thing than John.

She has admitted to having sexual fantasies about having sexual contact with the boys several weeks before the incidents took place. Penny has said that she is very worried about what will happen to her in the future when she has sexual relationships. She lives in fear of her school friends finding out about what she has done. She says that sometimes when she sees boys who look like the twins, it reminds her of the abuse and that sometimes this makes her feel she could abuse again. She imagines thinking of a reason to go and talk to them.

Neil

Neil is 15 years old and lives with his mother Jan, his younger brother Ricky, who is 11, and his sister Becky, who is 6. Until recently, Jan's partner Ian, who is 25 and the father of Becky, also lived with the family. Following concerns raised by a GP about the origin of a medical complaint, Neil was jointly interviewed by the police and social services, whereupon he disclosed that he had been sexually abused by Ian. The sexual abuse was extensive and was sustained over a two-year period. Ian admitted abusing Neil and received a six-year prison sentence.

During the investigation it was reported that Neil was very reluctant to talk about the abuse and that he was very close to Ian, sharing many hobbies and common interests. Since Ian has left the family, Neil has become increasingly beyond his mother's control and has on three occasions been accommodated by the local authority. Jan has expressed increasing concerns about Neil leaving the house and not returning until either very late, or sometimes the next day.

Jan has expressed concerns about Neil gravitating towards his younger brother, when he uses the bathroom, and said that on some occasions Neil has exposed himself to Ricky and has led him into inappropriate conversations about sexual matters.

There was also a report from Neil's school about a series of incidents during a geography field trip, which although unspecified, led to rumours amongst the peer group that Neil and his friend Barry had been having some undefined form of sexual contact. As a result of these rumours, Barry has broken off his friendship with Neil, who is becoming increasingly isolated at school and is often absent.

Neil's mother Jan has often found Neil crying, and says that he has never really spoken to anybody about Ian, and often becomes distraught when his name is mentioned. Neil has said that he feels responsible for Ian being sent to prison and that he feels that he should not have told anybody about the abuse.

The Aims and Objectives of Stratford Children's Services Development Groups

Robin Hill

This appendix supplements Chapter Six. These Aims and Objectives were originally produced in 1995, and revised in 1997 and 2003.

1. The groups should each meet on a quarterly basis. They should be seen as the coordinating fora for the identification of areas of unmet children's services provision, and for the stimulation of new initiatives to fill these gaps. The fora should be convened and chaired by social services, but their structures and programmes should be planned in conjunction with the other statutory and voluntary agencies involved.

2. The groups should be responsible for the establishment of working sub-groups, involving participation from representatives of other agencies which may chair or play the leading role in some of these groups, depending on the topic under consideration.

3. The groups should act as a vehicle for promoting the collection and dissemination of statistical data in relation to areas of unmet need, both within geographical localities and across them. Such statistical data would relate to referral rates to the agencies concerned, youth crime rates and child protection referral trends, indicators of poverty and deprivation, health and education profiles, etc. From time to time it may be appropriate to commission directly the collection of data in relation to a specific topic.

4. The groups should act as reference points in relation to possible sources of funding for new projects which aim to address deficiencies in services to children and families. This would be secured by giving information about money available through collective bids, government schemes, trust funds and charitable sources, and by means of helping the relevant agencies to work together to enable their own resources to be targeted appropriately.

5. The groups should encourage its member agencies to ensure that equality issues are integrated within their functions, that gaps in services are identified, and that any issues regarding gender, culture, disability, race, religion, sexuality and language are considered within the context of legislation in force at that time.

6. The groups should review their activities and membership on a regular basis, including through an annual evaluation of their work programmes, which would examine their progress to date and set future agendas.

7. The groups should report on a regular basis to the strategic fora responsible for policy and decision-making within the authority, to ensure that appropriate accountability takes place, and that relevant items are placed on the agenda of the respective groups.

Outcome of Survey Assessing what Constituent Members of Local Partnership Teams Felt about Development Groups

Robin Hill

This survey, referred to in Chapter Six, was carried out by the local Partnership Officer in August 2002, with 13 responses.

1. *Do you feel that the aims and objectives of the Children's Services Development Groups are being met? If not, what is not being met?*
   Most respondents answered 'yes', with two members commenting that it would be ideal if all agencies involved could attend regularly, whilst a couple of replies wondered whether all areas of provision were represented.

2. *Is the frequency of meetings about right?*
   All but one respondent thought it was, with one professional commenting that there needed to be enough time allowed for sub-groups to work between meetings.

3. *What are the positive aspects of the meetings?*
   Many positive comments were recorded, including a number of references to networking, sharing information, meeting with key decision-makers in other agencies, and 'all agencies contributing to a rounded view of issues and sharing in…implementation', the development of partnership working on special projects, and the provision of a history of inter-agency cooperation in Stratford to develop new children's services.

4. *Is there anything about the meetings which you would like to see changed? If so, what?*
   One respondent wanted young people to join the meetings (this is being considered at the moment.) Another suggested more representation from the voluntary sector. Almost all respondents wanted the groups to continue meeting in the same way as before.

References

Adams, J. and Gifford, V. (1991) *'Taking Care' with Toby and the Puppet Gang.* North East Warwickshire and West Birmingham Health Authorities.

Adcock, M. (2000) 'The Core Assessment process – How to synthesise information and make judgements work.' In J. Horwath (ed.) *The Child's World: Assessing Children in Need.* Department of Health, NSPCC and the University of Sheffield.

Alaggia, R., Michalski, J.H. and Vine, C. (1999) 'The use of peer support for parents and youth living with the trauma of child sexual abuse: an innovative approach.' *Journal of Child Sexual Abuse 8*, 2, 57–73.

Aldgate, J. (1993) 'Respite care for children: an old remedy in a new package.' In P. Marsh and J. Triseliotis (eds) *Prevention and Reunification in Child Care.* London: Batsford.

Aldgate, J. (2002) 'Evolution not revolution: family support services and the Children Act 1989.' In H. Ward and W. Rose (eds) *Approaches to Needs Assessment in Children's Services.* London: Jessica Kingsley Publishers.

Aldgate, J. and Bradley, M. (eds) (1999) *Supporting Families through Short-term Fostering.* London: Stationery Office.

Aldgate, J. and Tunstill, J. (1995) *Section 17: The First 18 Months of Implementation.* London: HMSO.

Aldridge, M. (1994) *Making Social Work News.* London: Routledge.

Alford, J. (2001) 'The implications of "publicness" for strategic management theory'. In G. Johnson and K. Scholes (eds) *Exploring Public Sector Strategy.* London: Prentice Hall.

Araji, S.K. (1997) *Sexually Aggressive Children: Coming to Understand Them.* Thousand Oaks, California: Sage.

Archard, D. (1993) *Children: Rights and Childhood.* London: Routledge.

Association of Directors of Social Services (2002) *Tomorrow's Children.* London: Association of Directors of Social Services.

Audit Commission (1994) *Seen but not Heard: Co-ordinating Community Child Health and Social Services for Children in Need.* London: HMSO.

Audit Commission, Social Services Inspectorate and National Assembly for Wales (2002) *Guiding You Through: A Guide for Preparing for a Joint Review of Social Services.* London: Stationery Office.

Bagley, C. and Thurston, W. (1996) *Understanding and Preventing Child Sexual Abuse. Volumes 1 and 2.* Aldershot: Arena.

Baldwin, N. and Spencer, N. (1993) 'Deprivation and child abuse: implications for strategic planning in children's services.' *Children and Society 7*, 4, 357–375.

Barclay, P.M. (1982) *Social Workers: Their Roles and Tasks.* London: Bedford Square Press.

Barn, R. (1993) 'Black and white care careers: a different reality.' In P. Marsh and J. Triseliotis (eds) *Prevention and Reunification in Child Care.* London: Batsford.

Barrett, M. and Phillips, A. (1992) *Destabilizing Theory.* Cambridge: Polity Press.

Barter, K. (2001) 'Building community: a conceptual framework for child protection.' *Child Abuse Review 10*, 4, 262–278.

Beaumont, G. (1996) Review of 100 NVQs and SVQs. London: Department for Education and Employment.

Bebbington, A. and Miles, J. (1989) 'The background of children who enter local authority care.' *British Journal of Social Work 19*, 5, 349–368.

Bentovim, A. (1991) 'Significant harm in context.' In M. Adcock, R. White and A. Hollows (eds) *Significant Harm: Its Management and Outcome.* Croydon: Significant Publications.

Berridge, D. (2001) 'Foster families.' In P. Foley, J. Roche and S. Tucker *Children in Society: Contemporary Theory, Policy and Practice.* Basingstoke: Palgrave/Open University.

Bluner, J. (1990) *Acts of Meaning*. Cambridge, Massachusetts: Harvard University Press.

Boushel, M., Quinton, D., Bulley, L. and Daly, G. (eds) (2002) *Developing Needs-led Services in One Local Authority: Key Findings. A Report to Gloucestershire Social Services and the Centre for Evidence-based Social Services, University of Exeter. Executive Summary*. Exeter: University of Exeter.

Bremner, J. and Hillin, A. (1993) *Sexuality, Young People and Care*. London: CCETSW.

Briggs, F. and Hawkins, R.M.F. (1994) 'Choosing between child protection programmes.' *Child Abuse Review 3*, 272–284.

Butler, I. and Shaw, I. (1996) *A Case of Neglect?* Aldershot: Avebury.

Butler, I. and Williamson, H. (1994) *Children Speak*. Harlow: Longman.

Butt, J. and Box, L. (1998) *Family Centred: A Study of the Use of Family Centres by Black Families*. London: National Institute for Social Work, Race Equality Unit.

Calder, M.C. (ed.) (1999) *Working with Young People who Sexually Abuse: New Pieces of the Jigsaw Puzzle*. Lyme Regis: Russell House Publishing.

Calder, M.C. (ed.) (2002) *Young People who Sexually Abuse – Building the Evidence Base for Your Practice*. Lyme Regis: Russell House Publishing.

Calder, M.C. (2003) 'A Generic Framework for Conducting Risk Assessments'. Address to a Conference on Risk Assessment – Improving and Enhancing Evidence-based Practice. London: Congress Centre.

Campbell, B. (1988) *Unofficial Secrets*. London: Virago.

Care Standards Commission (2002) *National Minimum Standards – Fostering Services*. London. Department of Health.

Carrigan, T., Connell, B. and Lee, J. (1987) 'Hard and heavy: toward a new sociology of masculinity.' In M. Kaufman (ed.) *Beyond Patriarchy*. Buckingham: Open University Press.

Chief Secretary to the Treasury (2003) *Every Child Matters*. Cm. 5860. London: Stationery Office.

Cleaver, H., Unell, I. and Aldgate, J. (1999) *Children's Needs – Parenting Capacity: The Impact of Parental Mental Illness, Problem Alcohol and Drug Use, and Domestic Violence on Children's Development*. London: Stationery Office.

Collier, N., Fishwick, F. and Johnson, G. (2001) 'The processes of strategy development in the public sector.' In G. Johnson and K. Scholes (eds) *Exploring Public Sector Strategy*. London: Prentice Hall.

Commission for Health Improvement (2003) *An Audit of Child Protection Arrangements for Primary Care Trusts*. London: Commission for Health Improvement.

Connell, R.W. (1987) 'Theorising gender.' *Sociology 19*, 2, 260–272.

Connell, R.W. (1989) *Gender and Power: Society, the Person and Sexual Politics*. Cambridge: Polity Press.

Cooper, D. (1995) *Power in Struggle*. Buckingham: Open University Press.

Corby, B. (2002) 'Child abuse and child protection.' In B. Goldson, M. Lavalette and J. McKechnie (eds) *Children, Welfare and the State*. London: Sage.

Corby, B., Doig, A. and Roberts, V. (1998) 'Inquiries into child abuse.' *Journal of Social Welfare and Family Law 20*, 377–395.

Cornwall, A. and Lindisfarne, N. (eds) (1994) *Dislocating Masculinity*. London: Routledge.

Coulshed, V. and Mullender, A. (2001) *Management in Social Work* (2nd edn). Basingstoke: Palgrave.

Cunningham, C. and MacFarlane, K. (1996) *When Children Abuse*. Brandon, Vermont: Safer Society Press.

Dale, P., Green, R. and Fellows, R. (2002) 'Serious and fatal injuries to infants with discrepant parental explanations: some assessment and case management issues.' *Child Abuse Review 11*, 296–312.

Dartington Social Research Unit (1999) *Matching Needs and Services* (2nd edn). Dartington: Dartington Social Research Unit.

Dartington Social Research Unit (2003) *Matching Needs and Services: Cases Held on the Social Services Waiting Lists. Report of a Development Exercise between East Coast Area Health Board and Dartington Social Research Unit*. www.dartington.org.uk/documents/ECAHB%20Report.pdf. Dartington: Dartington Social Research Unit: accessed March 2003.

Darvill, G. (1998) *Organisation, People and Standards. Use of Formal Standards in Social Services: Report of a Survey (ADSS and NISW)*. London: National Institute for Social Work.

Deakin, N. (1994) *The Politics of Welfare: Continuities and Change* (2nd edn). Hemel Hempstead: Harvester Wheatsheaf.

De Waal, M. (1999) *Due Consideration.* Warwick: Warwickshire Social Services Department.

De Waal, M. and Foster, S. (2001) *Children First.* Warwick: Warwickshire Social Services Department.

Department of the Environment, Transport and the Regions (1998) *Modernising Local Government: Improving Local Services through Best Value.* London: Stationery Office.

Department of Health (1988a) *Protecting Children: A Guide for Social Workers Undertaking a Comprehensive Assessment.* London: HMSO.

Department of Health (1988b) *Report of the Inquiry into Child Abuse in Cleveland, 1987.* London: HMSO.

Department of Health (1988c) *Protecting Children: A Guide for Social Workers Conducting a Comprehensive Assessment.* London: Department of Health.

Department of Health (1991a) *Child Abuse: A Study of Inquiry Reports 1980–1989.* London: HMSO.

Department of Health (1991b) *Working Together under the Children Act 1989: A Guide to Arrangements for Inter-agency Cooperation for the Protection of Children from Abuse.* London: HMSO.

Department of Health (1994) *Children Act Report, 1993.* London: HMSO.

Department of Health (1995) *Child Protection: Messages from Research.* London: HMSO.

Department of Health (1998a) *The Quality Protects Programme: Transforming Children's Services.* London: Department of Health.

Department of Health (1998b) *Modernising Social Services: Promoting Independence, Raising Standards.* London: HMSO.

Department of Health (1998c) *Partners in Planning: Approaches to Planning Services for Children and their Families.* London: Department of Health.

Department of Health (1998d) *Local Authority Circular LAC(98)1: Social Services Training Support Programme, 1998/99.* London: Department of Health.

Department of Health (1999a) *The Government's Objectives for Children's Social Services.* London: HMSO.

Department of Health (1999b) *Working Together to Safeguard Children: A Guide to Interagency Working to Safeguard and Promote the Welfare of Children.* London: Stationery Office.

Department of Health (2000a) *The Children Act Report, 1995–1999.* London: Department of Health.

Department of Health (2000b) *Working Together to Safeguard Children: A Guide to Inter-agency Working to Safeguard and Promote the Welfare of Children.* London: Department of Health.

Department of Health (2000c) *Protecting Children, Supporting Parents.* London: HMSO.

Department of Health (2000d) *Studies Informing the Development of the Framework for the Assessment of Children in Need and their Families.* London: Stationery Office.

Department of Health (2001a) *Coordinated Service Planning for Vulnerable Children and Young People in England.* London: Department of Health.

Department of Health (2001b) *National Service Framework for Children, Young People and Maternity Services.* London: HMSO.

Department of Health (2001c) *Planning and Providing Good Quality Placements for Children in Care.* London: Department of Health.

Department of Health (2002) *A Joint Chief Inspectors' Report on Arrangements to Safeguard Children.* London: Department of Health Publications.

Department of Health (2003a) *The Victoria Climbié Inquiry: Report of an Inquiry by Lord Laming.* London: Stationery Office.

Department of Health (2003b) *What to Do if You're Worried a Child is Being Abused: Children Services Guidance.* London: Stationery Office.

Department of Health (2003c) *Children Looked After by Local Authorities. Year Ending 31 March 2002. England. Volume 2: Local Authorities Tables.* London: Department of Health.

Department of Health and Department for Education and Employment (1996) *Children's Services Planning: Guidance for Inter-agency Working.* London: Department of Health and Department for Education and Employment.

Department of Health, Department for Education and Employment and Home Office (2000) *Framework for the Assessment of Children in Need and their Families.* London: Stationery Office.

Department of Health and Social Security (1974) *Report of the Committee of Inquiry into the Care and Supervision Provided in Relation to Maria Colwell.* London: HMSO.

Department of Health and Social Security (1987) *The Law on Child Care and Family Services.* London: HMSO.

Department of Health and Social Services Inspectorate (1995) *The Challenge of Partnership in Child Protection: Practice Guide.* London: HMSO.

Department of Health and Social Services Inspectorate (2003) *Modern Social Services: A Commitment to Reform. The 11th Annual Report of the Chief Inspector of Social Services 2001–2002.* London: Stationery Office.

Department of Health, Social Services Inspectorate and Audit Commission (1998) *Getting the Best from Social Services: Learning the Lessons from Joint Reviews.* London: Audit Commission.

Donzelot, J. (1979) *The Policing of Families.* London: Hutchinson.

Durham, A.W. (1999) *Young Men Living Through and with Child Sexual Abuse: A Practitioner Research Study.* PhD Thesis. Coventry, University of Warwick.

Durham, A.W. (2003) *Young Men Surviving Child Sexual Abuse – Research, Stories and Lessons for Therapeutic Practice.* Chichester: Wiley.

Elliot, M. (ed.) (1993) *Female Sexual Abuse of Children.* Harlow: Longman.

Eppink, J. and de Waal, S. (2001) 'Global influences on the public sector.' In G. Johnson, and K. Scholes (eds) *Exploring Public Sector Strategy.* London: Prentice Hall.

Erooga, M. and Masson, J. (eds) (1999) *Children and Young People who Sexually Abuse Others: Challenges and Responses.* London: Routledge.

Etherington, K. (1995) *Adult Male Survivors of Childhood Sexual Abuse.* London: Pitman.

Fimister, G. (ed.) (2001) *An End in Sight? Tackling Child Poverty in the UK.* London: Child Poverty Action Group.

Finkelhor, D. (1986) 'Prevention: a review of programs and research.' In D. Finkelhor, S. Araji, L. Baron, A. Browne, S.D. Peters and G.E. Wyatt (eds) *A Sourcebook on Child Sexual Abuse.* Palo Alto, California: Sage.

Finkelhor, D., Araji, S., Baron, L., Browne, A., Peters, S.D. and Wyatt G.E. (1986) *A Sourcebook on Child Sexual Abuse.* Palo Alto, California: Sage.

Finkelhor, D. and Strapko, N. (1992) 'Sexual abuse prevention education: a review of evaluation studies.' In D. J. Willis, E.W. Holden and M. Rosenberg (eds) *Prevention of Child Maltreatment: Developmental and Ecological Perspectives.* New York: Wiley.

Fostering Network (1999) *UK National Standards for Foster Care and Code of Practice.* London: Fostering Network.

Fox Harding, L. (1991) *Perspectives in Child Care Policy and Practice.* Harlow: Longman.

Franklin, B. and Parton, N. (1991) *Social Work, the Media and Public Relations.* London: Routledge.

Frederickson, H.G. (1997) *The Spirit of Public Administration.* San Francisco: Jossey-Bass.

Friend, J. and Hickling, A. (1997) *Planning Under Pressure: The Strategic Choice Approach* (2nd edn). Oxford: Butterworth Heinemann.

Frosh, S. (1993) 'The seeds of masculine sexuality.' In J.M. Ussher and C.D. Baker (eds) *Psychological Perspectives on Sexual Problems.* London: Routledge.

Garbarino, J. (1981) 'An ecological approach to child maltreatment.' In L. Pelton (ed.) *The Social Context of Child Abuse and Neglect.* New York: Human Sciences Press.

Garrett, P.M. (2003) *Remaking Social Work with Children and Families: A Critical Discussion on the 'Modernisation' of Social Care.* London: Routledge.

Gergen, K.J (1982) *Towards Transformation in Social Knowledge.* New York: Springer-Verlag.

Gergen, K.J. (1985) 'The social constructionist movement in modern psychology.' *American Psychologist 40*, 3, 266–275.

Gibbons, J., Conroy, S. and Bell, C. (1995) *Operating the Child Protection System: A Study of Child Protection Practices in English Local Authorities.* London: HMSO.

Gil, D. (1970) *Violence Against Children.* Boston: Harvard University Press.

Gil, E. (1996) *Treating Abused Adolescents.* New York: Guildford Press.

Gil, E. and Johnson, T.C. (1993) *Sexualised Children.* Rockville, Maryland: Launch Press.

Gilchrist, A. (2003) 'Community development in the UK: possibilities and paradoxes.' *Community Development Journal 38*, 1, 16–25.

Gramsci, A. (1971) *Selections from the Prison Notebooks of Antonio Gramsci.* London: Lawrence and Wishart.

Griffiths Report (1988) *Community Care: Agenda for Action.* London: HMSO.

Grove, W. and Meehl, P. (1996) 'Comparative efficiency of informal (subjective, impressionistic) and formal (mechanical, algorithmic) prediction procedures.' *Psychology, Public Policy and Law 2*, 293–323.

Grubin, D. (1998) *Sex Offending Against Children: Understanding the Risk.* Police Research Series, Paper 99. London: HMSO.

Hague, G., Kelly, L. and Mullender, A. (2001) *Challenging Violence Against Women: The Canadian Experience.* Bristol: The Policy Press.

Hallett, C. (1991) 'The Children Act 1989 and community care: comparisons and contrasts.' *Policy and Politics 19*, 4, 283–292.

Hallett, C. (1995) *Inter-agency Coordination in Child Protection.* London: HMSO.

Hallett, C. (2001) 'Developing good practice: prospects and possibilities.' In V. White and J. Harris (eds) *Developing Good Practice in Community Care: Partnership and Participation.* London: Jessica Kingsley Publishers.

Hardiker, P. (1996) 'The legal and social construction of significant harm.' In M. Hill and J. Aldgate (eds) *Child Welfare Services: Developments in Law, Policy, Research and Practice.* London: Jessica Kingsley Publishers.

Harding, L. (1999) 'Children's rights.' In O. Stevenson (ed.) *Child Welfare in the UK.* Oxford: Blackwell.

Harris, J. (1998) 'Scientific management, bureau-professionalism and new managerialism. The labour process of state social work.' *British Journal of Social Work 28*, 839–862.

Harris, J. (2002) 'Caring for citizenship.' *British Journal of Social Work 32*, 267–281.

Harris, J. (2003) *The Social Work Business.* London: Routledge.

Haydon, D. (2002) 'Children's rights to sex and sexuality education.' In B. Franklin (ed.) *The New Handbook of Children's Rights. Comparative Policy and Practice.* London: Routledge.

Haydon, D. and Scraton, P. (2002) 'Sex education as regulation.' In B. Goldson, M. Lavalette and J. McKechnie (eds) *Children, Welfare and the State.* London: Sage.

Hearn, J. (1996) 'Is masculinity dead? A critique of the concept of masculinity/masculinities.' In M. Mac-an-Ghaill (ed.) *Understanding Masculinities.* Philadelphia: Open University Press.

Herman, J.L. (1990) 'Sex offenders: a feminist perspective.' In W.L. Marshall, D.R. Laws and H.E. Barbaree (eds) *Handbook of Sexual Assault.* New York: Plenum.

Hill, M. and Aldgate, J. (1996) 'The Children Act 1989 and recent developments in research in England and Wales.' In M. Hill and J. Aldgate (eds) *Child Welfare Services: Developments in Law, Policy, Research and Practice.* London: Jessica Kingsley Publishers.

Hill, M. and Tisdall, M. (1997) *Children and Society.* London: Longman.

HMSO (1986) *Working Together: Education and Training.* London: HMSO.

Hollows, A. (2003) 'Knowledge and Judgement in Risk Assessment.' Address to a Conference on Risk Assessment – Improving and Enhancing Evidence-based Practice. London: Congress Centre.

Holman, B. (1996) 'Fifty years ago: the Curtis and Clyde reports.' *Children and Society 10*, 3, 197–209.

Home Office (1997) *Criminal Statistics for England and Wales 1996.* London: Government Statistical Service.

Hood, C. (1991) 'A public management for all seasons?' *Public Administration 69*, 3–19.

Horwath, J. (2000) 'Assessing the world of the child in need: background and context.' In J. Horwath (ed.) *The Child's World: Assessing Children in Need.* London: NSPCC, Sheffield University and the Department of Health.

Horwath, J. and Morrison, T. (2000) 'Assessment of parental motivation to change.' In J. Horwath (ed.) *The Child's World: Assessing Children in Need.* London: NSPCC, Sheffield University and the Department of Health.

Howe, D. (1995) *Attachment Theory for Social Work Practice.* Basingstoke: Palgrave.

Humphreys, C., Hester, M., Hague, G., Mullender, A., Abrahams, H. and Lowe, P. (2000) *From Good Intentions to Good Practice.* Bristol: The Policy Press.

Hussey, D. (2000) *Strategy and Planning: A Manager's Guide.* Chichester: Wiley.

Jack, G. (2000) 'Ecological perspectives in assessing children and families.' In M. Adcock, R. White and A. Hollows (eds) *Significant Harm: Its Management and Outcome.* Croydon: Significant Publications.

Jackson, S. (1992) 'The amazing deconstructing woman.' *Trouble and Strife 25*, 25–31.

Jenkins, A. (1990) *Invitations to Responsibility.* Adelaide: Dulwich Centre Publications.

Johnson, G. and Scholes, K. (eds) (1999) *Exploring Corporate Strategy: Text and Cases* (5th edn). Harlow: Prentice Hall.

Johnson, T.C. (1999) *Understanding Your Child's Sexual Behaviour – What's Natural and Healthy.* Oakland, California: New Harbinger Publishers.

Joint Initiative for Community Care (1998) *Caring with Competence.* Cambridge: Joint Initiative for Community Care.

Joll, J. (1977) *Gramsci.* Glasgow: Fontana.

Jones, A. (2003) *An Analysis of Risk Within the Education Setting.* Unpublished. Warwick: submitted to Warwickshire Local Education Authority.

Jones, C. (2002) 'Children, class and the threatening state.' In B. Goldson, M. Lavalette and J. McKechnie (eds) *Children, Welfare and the State.* London: Sage.

Jones, C. and Novak, T. (1999) *Poverty, Welfare and the Disciplinary State.* London: Routledge.

Jones, K. (2000) *The Making of Social Policy in Britain from the Poor Law to New Labour.* London: Athlone Press.

Jubber, K. (1991) 'The socialization of human sexuality.' *SA Sociological Review 4*, 1, 27–49.

Kahn, T.J. (1990) *Pathways.* Brandon, Vermont: Safer Society Press.

Kaplan, C. (1999) 'The real risks children face: the role and perspectives of the child psychiatrist.' In A. Stevens and G.J. Rafferty (eds) *Health Care Needs Assessment.* London: Free Association Books.

Katz, I. (1997) *Current Issues in Comprehensive Assessment.* London: NSPCC.

Kaufman, M. (1987a) 'The construction of masculinity and the triad of men's violence.' In M. Kaufman (ed.) *Beyond Patriarchy.* Toronto: Open University Press.

Kaufman, M. (ed.) (1987b) *Beyond Patriarchy.* Toronto: Open University Press.

Kaufman, R. (2000) *Mega Planning: Practical Tools for Organisational Success.* London: Sage.

Keady, C. (1998) 'Measuring up to expectations.' *Municipal Journal* 18 September, pp.37–44.

Kelly, L. (1988) *Surviving Sexual Violence.* Cambridge: Polity Press.

Kelly, L., Regan, L. and Burton, S. (1991) *An Exploratory Study of the Prevalence of Sexual Abuse in a Sample of 16–21-year-olds.* London: Child Abuse Studies Unit, Polytechnic of North London.

Kitzinger, J. (1990) 'Sexual abuse and the violation of childhood.' In A. James and A. Prout (eds) *The Social Construction of Childhood.* Oxford: Oxford University Press.

Krivacska, J.S. (1990) *Designing Child Sexual Abuse Prevention Programmes: Current Approaches and a Proposal for the Prevention, Reduction and Identification of Sexual Misuse.* Springfield, Illinois: Charles C. Thomas.

Lansdown, G. (1996) 'Implementation of the UN Convention on the Rights of the Child in the UK.' In M. John (ed.) *Children in our Charge: The Child's Right to Resources.* London: Jessica Kingsley Publishers.

Little, M., Bullock, R., Madge, J. and Arruabarrana, I. (2002) 'How to develop needs-led evidence-based services.' *Building Knowledge for Integrated Care 10*, 3, 28–32.

Loney, M. (1980) 'Community action and anti-poverty strategies.' *Community Development Journal 15*, 2, 91–103.

Luthera, M. (1997) *Britain's Black Population: Social Change, Public Policy and Agenda.* Aldershot: Arena.

Lyndon, P. and Payne, M. (2003) *Warwickshire's Integrated Children's System.* Warwick: Warwickshire Social Services Department.

MacIntyre, D., Carr, A., Lawlor, M. and Flattery, M. (2000) 'Development of the Stay Safe Programme.' *Child Abuse Review 9*, 200–216.

Macleod, M. and Saraga, E. (1991) 'Clearing a path through the undergrowth: a feminist reading of recent literature on child sexual abuse.' In P. Carter, T. Jeffs and M. Smith (eds) *Social Work and Social Welfare Yearbook 3.* Buckingham: Open University Press.

MacPherson, W. (1999) *The Stephen Lawrence Inquiry.* Report of an Inquiry. London: The Stationery Office.

Maddocks, P. (2002) *Fostering for the Future: Inspection of Foster Care Services.* London: Department of Health and Social Services Inspectorate.

Masson, H. and Morrison, T. (1999) 'Young sexual abusers: conceptual frameworks, issues and imperatives.' *Children and Society 13*, 203–215.

McKechnie, J. (2002) 'Children's voices and researching childhood.' In B. Goldson, M. Lavalette and J. McKechnie (eds) *Children, Welfare and the State.* London: Sage.

Melamid, E. (2002) *What Works? Integrating Multiple Data Sources and Policy Research Methods in Assessing Need and Evaluating Outcomes in Community-based Child and Family Service Systems.* Santa Monica, California: Rand.

Melton, G.B. (1992) 'The improbability of prevention of sexual abuse.' In D.J. Willis, E.W. Holden and M. Rosenberg (eds) *Prevention of Child Maltreatment.* New York: Wiley.

Mendel, M.P. (1995) *The Male Survivor.* Thousand Oaks, California: Sage.

Meredith, S. (1997) *Growing Up – Adolescence, Body Changes and Sex.* London: Usborne.

Miller, W. and Rollnick, S. (1991) *Motivational Interviewing: Preparing People to Change Addictive Behaviour.* New York: Guildford Press.

Milner, J. and O'Byrne, P. (2002) *Assessment in Social Work* (2nd edn). Basingstoke: Palgrave.

Moore, B. (1996) *Risk Assessment: A Practitioner's Guide to Predicting Harmful Behaviour.* London: Whiting and Birch.

Moore, S. and Rosenthal, D. (1994) *Sexuality in Adolescence.* London: Routledge.

Morris, J. (1995) *Gone Missing? A Research and Policy Review of Disabled Children Living Away from their Families.* London: The Who Cares Trust.

Morris, J. (1998) *Accessing Human Rights: Disabled Children and the Children Act.* London: Barnardos.

Morris, J. (1999) 'Disabled Children, Child Protection Systems and the Children Act 1989.' *Child Abuse Review 8,* 91–108

Morris, J. (2000) *Having Someone Who Cares.* London: National Children's Bureau and Joseph Rowntree Foundation.

Morrison, T. (1991) 'Change, control and the legal framework.' In M. Adcock, R. White and A. Hollows (eds) *Significant Harm: Its Management and Outcome.* Croydon: Significant Publications.

Morrison, T., Erooga, M. and Beckett, C. (eds) (1994) *Sexual Offending Against Children.* London: Routledge.

Morrison, T. and Print, B. (1995) *Adolescent Sexual Abusers: An Overview.* Hull: NOTA.

Munroe, E. (2002) *Effective Child Protection.* London: Sage Publications.

National Commission of Inquiry into the Prevention of Child Abuse (NCIPC) (1996) *Childhood Matters. Report of the National Commission of Inquiry into the Prevention of Child Abuse.* London: HMSO.

National Foster Care Association (1997) *NVQs and SVQs: National Qualifications for Foster Carers.* London: National Foster Care Association.

Nayak, A. and Kehily, M.J. (1997) 'Masculinities and schooling: why are young men so homophobic?' In L. Steinberg, D. Epstein and R. Johnson (eds) *Border Patrols.* London: Cassell.

NCH Action for Children (2002) *The NCH Factfile 2002–03: Key Facts and Statistics about Children in the UK.* London: NCH Action for Children.

NCVQ (1997) *The NVQ Awarding Bodies' Common Accord.* London: QCA Publications.

NCVQ (2002) *The NVQ Code of Practice.* London: QCA Publications.

Novak, T. (2002) 'Rich children, poor children.' In B. Goldson, M. Lavalette and J. McKechnie (eds) *Children, Welfare and the State.* London: Sage.

Office of Public Management and Department of Health (London Region Research and Development Directorate) (eds) (2003) *E2A: Understanding the Transition from Evidence to Action in Health and Social Care.* London: Office of Public Management.

O'Hagan, K. and Dillenburger, K. *Abuse of Women in Childcare Work.* Berkshire: Open University Press.

Packman, J. and Hall, C. (1998) *From Care to Accommodation: Support, Protection and Control on Child Care Services.* London: Stationery Office.

Packman, J., Randall, J. and Jacques, N. (eds) (1986) *Who Needs Care? Social Work Decisions about Children.* Oxford: Blackwell.

Parton, N. (1999) 'Ideology, politics and policy.' In O. Stevenson (ed.) *Child Welfare in the UK.* Oxford: Blackwell.

Plummer, K. (1983) *Documents of Life: An Introduction to the Problems and Literature of a Humanistic Method.* London: Unwin Hyman.

Pollitt, C. (1990) *Managerialism and the Public Services: The Anglo-American Experience.* Oxford: Basil Blackwell.

Postlethwaite, J. (1998) 'A critical approach to working with young abusers.' *Nota News 28,* 30–38.

Powell, F. (2001) *The Politics of Social Work.* London: Sage Publications.

Pringle, K. (1995) *Men, Masculinities and Social Welfare.* London: UCL Press.

Prochaska, J. and DiClementi, C. (1982) 'Transtheoretical therapy: towards a more integrative model of change.' *Psychotherapy Theory Research and Practice 19,* 3, 276–288.

Protchaska, J. and DiClemente, C. (1986) 'Towards a comprehensive model of change in treating addictive behaviours.' In R. Miller and N. Heather (eds) *Processes of Change.* New York: Plenum Press.

Quade, E.S. (Revised by Carter, G.M.) (1989) *Analysis for Public Decision* (3rd edn). New Jersey: Prentice Hall.

Reder, P. and Duncan, S. (1995) 'The meaning of the child.' In P. Reder and C. Lucey (eds) *Assessment of Parenting: Psychiatric and Psychological Contributions.* London: Routledge.

Reder, P., Duncan, S. and Gray, M (1993) *Beyond Blame: Child Abuse Tragedies Revisited.* London: Routledge.

Reder, P. and Lucey, C. (1995) 'Significant issues in the assessment of parenting.' In P. Reder and C. Lucey (eds) *Assessment of Parenting: Psychiatric and Psychological Contributions.* London: Routledge.Robson, C. (1993) *Real World Research: A Resource for Social Scientists and Practitioner-researchers.* Oxford: Blackwell.

Rose, W. (1994) 'Protecting Children through Family Support.' Keynote Address by Chief Inspector of the Social Services Inspectorate (Department of Health) to the Michael Sieff Conference. Cumberland Lodge.

Rowlingson, K. and Mckay, S. (eds) (2002) *Lone Parent Families: Gender, Class and State.* Harlow: Prentice Hall.

Rutter, M. (1981) 'Stress, coping and developing: some issues and some perspectives.' *Journal of Child Psychology and Psychiatry 22,* 322–356.

Rutter, M. (1985) 'Resilience in the face of adversity: protective factors and resistance to psychiatric disorder.' *British Journal of Psychiatry 147,* 598–611.

Rutter, M. (1988) 'Introduction.' In M. Rutter (ed.) *Studies of Psychosocial Risk: The Power of Longitudinal Data.* Cambridge: Cambridge University Press.

Ryan, G.D. and Lane, S.L. (1991) *Juvenile Sexual Offending.* Lexington, Massachusetts: Lexington Press.

Salter, A.C. (1988) *Treating Child Sex Offenders and Victims.* Newbury Park, California: Sage.

Saradjian, J. (1998) *Women Who Sexually Abuse.* Chichester: Wiley.

Sargeant, A.V. (2000) 'An exploratory study of the effects of progression towards National Vocational Qualifications on the occupational knowledge and care practice of social care workers.' *Social Work Education 19,* 6, p.639–661

Seden, J. (2001) 'Assessment of children in need and their families: a literature review.' In J. Seden, R. Sinclair, D. Robbins and C. Pont (eds) *Studies Informing the Framework for Assessment of Children in Need and their Families.* London: Stationery Office.

Sedgwick, E.K. (1990) *Epistemology of the Closet.* Berkeley and Los Angeles: Columbia University Press.

Seebohm Report (1968) *Report on the Personal and Allied Social Services,* Cmnd. 3703. London: HMSO.

Sellick, C. (1996) 'Short-term foster care.' In M. Hill and J. Aldgate (eds) *Child Welfare Services: Developments in Law, Policy, Research and Practice.* London: Jessica Kingsley Publishers.

Shaw, M. and Hipgrave, T. (1989) 'Young people and their carers in specialist fostering.' *Adoption and Fostering 13,* 4, 11–17.

Sinclair, R. (1996) 'Children's and young people's participation in decision-making: the legal framework in social services and education.' In M. Hill and J. Aldgate (eds) *Child Welfare Services: Developments in Law, Policy, Research and Practice.* London: Jessica Kingsley Publishers.

Sinclair, R. and Bullock, R. (2002) *Learning from Past Experience – A Review of Serious Case Reviews.* London: Department of Health.

Sinclair, R. and Carr-Hill, R. (eds) (1996) *The Categorisation of Children in Need: A Report to the Department of Health.* London: National Children's Bureau.

Sinclair, R. and Little, M. (eds) (2001) *Developing a Taxonomy of Children in Need.* London: National Children's Bureau/Dartington Social Research Unit.

Smale, G. and Tuson, G. with Brahal, N. and Marsh, P. (1993) *Empowerment, Assessment, Case Management and the Skilled Worker.* London: National Institute for Social Work.

Social Services Inspectorate (2003) *Audit Tool for the Audit of Services to Children in Need in Response to the Practical Recommendations of the Victoria Climbié Inquiry.* London: Department of Health.

Space and Polity (2003) Special Issue on Children and Young People. *Space and Polity 7,* 2.

Steinberg, L., Epstein, D. and Johnson, R. (1997) *Border Patrols*. London: Cassell.

Stevenson, O. (1999) 'Social work with children and families.' In O. Stevenson (ed.) *Child Welfare in the UK*. Oxford: Blackwell.

Thomas, N. (2001) 'Listening to children.' In P. Foley, J. Roche and S. Tucker (eds) *Children in Society: Contemporary Theory, Policy and Practice*. Basingstoke: Palgrave/Open University.

TOPSS (Training Organisation for the Personal Social Services) (2000a) *Developing Strategic Uses of National Occupational Standards*. Leeds: TOPSS England.

TOPSS (Training Organisation for the Personal Social Services) (2000b) *Modernising the Social Care Workforce – The First National Training Strategy for the Social Care Workforce in England*. London: Department of Health. www.topss.org.uk/summaries.childpq2.htm

TOPSS (Training Organisation for the Personal Social Services) (2001) *Guide to Links between National Occupational Standards and Service Standards in Foster Care*. Leeds: TOPSS.

Towl, G. and Crighton, D. (1996) *The Handbook for Forensic Practitioners*. London: Routledge.

Triseliotis, J., Borland, M. and Hill, M. (eds) (2000) *Delivering Foster Care*. London: British Association of Adoption and Fostering.

Trotter, C. (2002) 'Worker skill and client outcome in child protection.' *Child Abuse Review 11*, 38–50.

Tuck, V. (1995) *Links Between Social Deprivation and Harm to Children: A Study of Parenting in Social Disadvantage*. Unpublished PhD thesis. Milton Keynes: The Open University.

Tuck, V. (2000a) 'Links between social deprivation and harm to children.' In N. Baldwin (ed.) *Protecting Children: Promoting Their Rights*. London: Whiting and Birch.

Tuck, V. (2000b) 'Socio-economic factors: a neglected dimension in harm to children.' In J. Batsleer and B. Humphries (eds) *Welfare, Exclusion and Political Agency*. London: Routledge.

Tucker, S. (2001) 'Community development: a strategy for empowerment.' In P. Foley, J. Roche and S. Tucker (eds) *Children in Society: Contemporary Theory, Policy and Practice*. Basingstoke: Palgrave/Open University.

Twelvetrees, A. (1991) *Community Work* (2nd edn). Basingstoke: BASW/Macmillan.

UK Joint Working Party on Foster Care (1999) *UK National Standards for Foster Care*. London: National Foster Care Association.

United Nations (1989) *Conventions on the Rights of the Child*. New York: United Nations. www.unicef.org/crc/crc.htm

Utting, D. (ed.) (1998) *Children's Services Now and in the Future*. London: National Children's Bureau.

Wadsworth, M.E.J. (1988) 'Intergenerational longitudinal research: conceptual and methodological considerations.' In M. Rutter (ed.) *Studies of Psychosocial Risk: The Power of Longitudinal Data*. Cambridge: Cambridge University Press.

Ward, H. and Skuse, T. (eds) (2002) *Looking after Children: Transforming Data into Management Information. Report from First Year of Data Collection*. Loughborough University and Dartington Social Research Unit.

Warner, M. (1993) *Fear of a Queer Planet*. Minneapolis: University of Minnesota Press.

Watkins, B. and Bentovim, A. (1992) 'The sexual abuse of male children and adolescents: a review of current research.' *Journal of Child Psychology and Psychiatry 33*, 1, 197–248.

Webb, A. and Wistow, G. (1987) *Social Work, Social Care and Social Planning: The Personal Social Services since Seebohm*. Harlow: Longman.

White, V. and Harris, J. (1999) 'Social Europe, social citizenship and social work.' *European Journal of Social Work 2*, 3–14.

White, V. and Harris, J. (2001) 'Changing community care.' In V. White and J. Harris (eds) *Developing Good Practice in Community Care: Partnership and Participation*. London: Jessica Kingsley Publishers.

Wigan Social Services Department (November 2002) *Joint Review Position Statement*. Wigan: Wigan Social Services Department.

Willis, D. (1992) *Prevention of Child Maltreatment: Developmental and Ecological Perspectives*. New York: Wiley.

Wisniewski, M. (2001) 'Measuring up to the best: a manager's guide to benchmarking.' In G. Johnson and K. Scholes (eds) *Exploring Public Sector Strategy*. London: Prentice Hall.

Wolfe, D.A., Wekerle, C. and Scott, K. (1997) *Alternatives to Violence*. Thousand Oaks, California: Sage.

The Contributors

Andrew Durham is a specialist in post-abuse counselling and interventions for children and young people with sexual behavioural difficulties. He is currently the Consultant Practitioner for the Sexualised Inappropriate Behaviours Service in Warwickshire. He is a visiting lecturer in the School of Health and Social Studies, University of Warwick. He also works as an Independent Child Care Consultant, and has been an advisor to the BBC.

Chris Hallett is Assistant Head of Children's Services in Warwickshire Social Services Department, with responsibility for quality, planning and development. He held a variety of social work posts before moving into managerial positions. He has also been a quality assurance officer and a staff development manager. He is an Associate Fellow in the School of Health and Social Studies, University of Warwick.

John Harris is a professor in the School of Health and Social Studies, University of Warwick. Before entering posts in higher education, he worked as a generic social worker, training officer and district manager in a social services department.

Robin Hill is Assistant Head of Assessment and Care Planning in Derby Social Services Department. Formerly he was employed as a front-line children's services manager in Warwickshire Social Services for 14 years, having previously worked in Northamptonshire and Leeds.

Rebecca Johnson undertook a number of research projects within the health and social care sectors before commencing her role as a Children's Planning Officer with Warwickshire Social Services Department. Within this role she has taken responsibility for projects centred on data analysis, research, user involvement, strategic planning and policy making.

Simon Lord is seconded from his post as Head of Children's Services in Warwickshire Social Services Department to the post of Assistant Chief Education Officer in the Education Department. He has previously worked in the Probation Service, in the social services field and residential posts and in management posts in Warwickshire Social Services Department, covering all service user groups, operations and support services.

Jude Quiggin worked with girls' and women's groups in a community setting in Coventry following qualification as a social worker. She then moved to statutory social work in a preventive role at a Family Centre in Warwickshire Social Services Department for 12 years, first as a social worker and then as Senior Social Worker. In 1997 she moved to manage another Family Centre with a focus on a therapeutic approach to assessment work. More recently, she became a Children's Guardian with the Children and Family Court Advisory and Support Service.

Phil Sawbridge is the Head of Children's Planning for Warwickshire Social Services Department. He has worked in a range of settings in children's services, including fieldwork and residential care. Since moving to Warwickshire in 1994, he has worked as a manager in a number of front-line teams, moving to children's planning to oversee the implementation of 'Quality Protects', before being promoted to his current post.

Ann Seal moved to health visiting after training as a general nurse, gaining paediatric experience and completing obstetrics training. She has worked as a health visitor for 15 years and taught for five years at a Further Education College. She has been running the 'Taking Care' project since 1999 on a part-time basis, alongside practising as a health visitor and teaching.

Satwant Shergill worked for 10 years in Warwickshire in a race equality development role, promoting, developing and integrating race equality principles across all services and later specialised in work with older people. She now lives in Calgary, Canada.

Vic Tuck is Development Officer for Warwickshire Area Child Protection Committee, which involves delivering multi-agency training, undertaking research and audit activities and promoting a media relations strategy for child protection. Prior to this, he was Programme Director for an accredited local authority post-qualifying training programme in child protection. He has worked with all groups of service users, and has managed a Family Placement Unit.

Sylvia Vickers has worked in Children's Services in Warwickshire Social Services Department for over 15 years. She is the Marketing and Training Manager for Fostering Services and is responsible for the recruitment and training of foster carers in Warwickshire. She manages the Warwickshire (Foster Care) NVQ Assessment Centre, which is approved for a number of awards including 'Caring for Children and Young People – Level 3' and the Assessor, Internal Verifier and Mentoring awards.

Mandy de Waal moved into the voluntary sector, after practising criminal and family law, to run a research and support project for the parents and carers of mixed parentage children. She has worked for Warwickshire Social Services Department on a number of projects over the last few years, whilst running a small training and research consultancy and sitting as a lay magistrate.

Vicky White is a lecturer in the School of Health and Social Studies, University of Warwick. Previously she worked as a generic social worker, a hospital social worker, a residential social worker and in a family placement unit.

Subject Index

Author Index

Page numbers followed by n refer to notes